D0874222

European
Witch Trials

European Witch Trials

Their Foundations in
Popular and Learned
Culture, 1300–1500

Richard Kieckhefer

University of California Press
Berkeley and Los Angeles 1976

First published in U.S.A. 1976
by University of California Press
Berkeley and Los Angeles
California
Copyright © 1976 by Richard Kieckhefer
No part of this book may be reproduced in
any form without permission from the
publisher, except for the quotation of brief
passages in criticism

ISBN 0–520–02967–4
Library of Congress Catalog Card Number 74–29807

Printed in Great Britain
by Western Printing Services Ltd, Bristol

Contents

Preface

The topic of witchcraft has enjoyed popularity for some time, both among scholars and with the broader reading public. It has aroused numerous controversies, and the positions taken in these debates have been diverse. One might pardonably ask whether there is reason for still further work on such well-tilled soil. Clearly my answer would be affirmative. I have profited greatly from the research of many scholars, and made use of their material and analyses; I can hardly presume to supersede their treatment of the subject entirely. If there is any justification for my turning to late medieval witch trials anew, it is the need for methodologically rigorous study of the evidence. The methods used in this work, though neither technical nor revolutionary, are in some measure distinctive. The application of these methods results in a picture of the topic which is revisionist both in general outline and in many details. If the revisions gain acceptance, or even if they provoke discussion, I shall be gratified to have contributed toward knowledge of this important subject.

The scope of this work, as sketched in the Introduction, is admittedly broad: I have endeavored to cover most of western Europe, for a period of two centuries. A study of some specific locality might have better claim to being complete and definitive. Yet the purpose of this work is to ascertain what effects the proposed methodology will have on the total picture of late medieval witchcraft; the patterns produced by a local study would in this regard be of little consequence, since there are so few extant documents from any given region. I have made every effort to take into account all relevant trials cited in modern literature on witchcraft, plus some cases that have been missed in this literature. I have undoubtedly overlooked some records, and there are surely further manuscripts that await systematic investigation in European (and especially English) libraries and archives. One may reasonably conjecture, however, that the broad patterns revealed in presently known materials will not be seriously disrupted by later discoveries. It is theoretically conceivable that unexpected masses of documents will come to light, but given the generally fragmentary character of records from the fourteenth and fifteenth centuries it is unlikely that future discoveries will greatly outweigh materials now at hand.

Even if it could claim to be definitive, a work of this breadth suffers a further handicap: when one draws upon records of widely distant regions, the commonalities in the witch beliefs stand out more clearly than the local variations. I have tried to point out regional particularities when they are clearly significant; for example, the reader will encounter contrasts between Swiss and Italian ideas of witchcraft. For various reasons, however, there would be little purpose in making these discrepancies the object of sustained inquiry. In the first place, information from many regions is so meagre that it would be impossible to discuss the topography of witch beliefs with confidence. Second, even if one could isolate distinctive features of regional tradition, any explanation for these variations would in most cases be merely hypothetical, because the social context has been studied unevenly and for many regions insufficiently. It appears, for example, that Swiss traditions were distinctive in many ways. Yet Switzerland is precisely one of the areas for which least social history has been written in recent years, and until the nature of Swiss society has been studied more carefully it would be futile to speculate about the reasons for specifically Swiss popular beliefs.

If this work is general in its geographical and chronological scope, the thematic focus is quite specific. As the title indicates, this is not a comprehensive investigation of late medieval witchcraft, but specifically an examination of the witch trials. Witchcraft literature and legislation are of only peripheral relevance. For these topics Joseph Hansen's *Zauberwahn, Inquisition und Hexenprozess* is still worth consulting, as is Jeffrey Russell's *Witchcraft in the Middle Ages*. I have nothing new to add on these subjects; prolonged discussion of them would merely be a distraction. The subtitle further circumscribes the topic of this work: Certain aspects of the witch trials, such as judicial procedures and political context, receive only tangential consideration here. Emphasis lies on the one central problem, the distinction between popular and learned notions of witchcraft, as these are revealed in the trials. I have treated the content of popular witch beliefs in detail. Because the substance of learned tradition has already been discussed at length in analyses of the witch treatises, and because the learned notions found in the trials are fundamentally the same as those in this literature, I have given them less attention.

Among the scholars who have benefited me most are those whose bibliographic spadework has unearthed many of the late medieval trials. The early work of Joseph Hansen brought hundreds of cases to the attention of scholars generally, and in recent years the bulk of known material has been swelled greatly by the exhaustive work of Jeffrey Russell. My approach to the sources, on the other hand, has been influenced to no small degree by the studies of Keith Thomas and Alan Macfarlane, though they deal mostly with centuries later than those that concern me, and work with problems different from those I have encountered.

Norman Cohn's book, *Europe's Inner Demons*, appeared after I had completed the present study, but I have been able to take his suggestions into account in eleventh-hour revision of my work. Cohn's discussion overlaps mine in some areas. Most significantly, we independently recognized that the materials given by Étienne-Léon de Lamothe-Langon are forgeries (though I had not realized until reading Cohn that the legal opinion of Bartolo of Sassoferrato, for the case of *c.* 1340 at Novara, is also a fabrication). On the whole our studies are mutually collaborative and complementary. In some cases I have taken issue with his interpretations, and have expressed my disagreement usually in my notes. If I can claim to have advanced beyond Cohn it is in my systematic investigation of the judicial sources, and in my effort to make that distinction between popular and learned beliefs that Cohn explicitly poses as an area for further research.

I am greatly indebted to many teachers, colleagues, students, and friends for their assistance. Indeed, it is a source of wonderment to me how heavily indebted I have become in writing such a short book. Robert E. Lerner read the book with painstaking care, and provided a wealth of detailed and insightful suggestions. Likewise, Charles Bowlus, Ilse Bulhof, and Clarke Garrett each read the manuscript at some stage of its preparation and made valuable comments. In March 1974 I delivered a preliminary study for this work at the South-Central Renaissance Conference; I am grateful to the program committee of this conference, especially Marcus Orr, for allowing me a forum for expression of my thoughts.

Many libraries and archives have furnished materials necessary for my work. I have relied heavily on the excellent resources and services of the Bayerische Staatsbibliothek in Munich. In addition I have received help from the Universitätsbibliothek Erlangen-Nürnberg, the British Museum, the Österreichische Nationalbibliothek at Vienna, the Archives de l'État at Neuchâtel, the Archives Cantonales Vaudoises at Lausanne, and the Archives Départementales de l'Isère at Grenoble. Mrs Jo Anne Hawkins and other personnel in the Interlibrary Service at the University of Texas have borne with interminable requests for materials.

I would also like to express my gratitude to the Deutscher Akademischer Austauschdienst for a grant for research in Munich during the year 1971-2. Though I was in Munich for research on a dissertation, dealing with a wholly distinct subject, I was able to begin collecting materials for the present study during the few spare moments that I had abroad.

My greatest debts of gratitude are personal ones. In addition to helping with correction of the manuscript, my wife Margaret bore patiently, as usual, with all the inconvenience of having a husband immersed in such a project. And the Department of History at the University of Texas, in particular the chairman, Professor Clarence Lasby, helped me with numerous kindnesses during the time I was working on this book.

Chapter I Introduction

Certain recent historians of witchcraft have adopted their mode of inquiry from anthropology.[1] Recognizing the close correspondence between European witchcraft and witchcraft in non-Western societies, they have made use of anthropological comparisons in analyzing the development of witch beliefs and the motives for witch persecutions. Most importantly, they have followed anthropologists in attending to the social context that gave rise to accusations of witchcraft. Studies of this kind lend themselves to an important criticism: European society at the time of the witch trials was already distinct in many ways from primitive societies. Its political systems, family-structure, and educational development were significantly different from those of non-Western societies, and it is misleading to suggest that the social mechanisms in early Europe are directly comparable to those of African or American Indian cultures.[2] Still, the fact remains that the phenomena of witchcraft, witch accusation, and witch hunting in early Europe are indeed closely analogous to such phenomena in primitive societies, whether one thinks they should be or not. One can only conclude that the mechanisms that underlie these activities are independent of the distinctive features of Western and non-Western societies. In early European society, as in primitive cultures, one finds a lack of rigidity in notions of causality: magical explanations persist alongside natural and religious ones, with no suggestion of any incompatibility. And more importantly, the situations that call for magical explanation seem to be closely comparable in the two settings.

There are other problems, however, that arise in carrying out anthropological analysis of European witch trials. The methodological difficulties are especially great in treatment of Continental cases. Because torture and other judicial coercion played an important role in Continental proceedings, the records that survive can scarcely be taken as accurate reflections of popular tradition. The mentality of the accusers is thus obscured, and the social setting of the witch trials becomes only dimly perceptible. The problem may be illustrated with the trial of Pierre Chavaz in the diocese of Lausanne.[3] Pierre supposedly belonged to a sect of devil-worshippers, who renounced the Catholic faith, raised storms, and killed infants. Because the devil was hidden in his hair, he was unable to confess his deeds until he had been shaved all over his body. He had been accused by other witches, and according to the inquisitorial protocol public infamy further branded him as a witch. The document narrating his case is extensive, but it tells little that is interesting from an anthropological viewpoint. There is no accurate information about the circumstances that gave rise to accusation; there is no way of determining, from the information given in this particular document, whether Pierre's fellow-townsmen raised the specific charges against him or whether these allegations came from court officials. And the same difficulties arise in countless analogous cases.

The general problem that confronts the historian of witchcraft is a familiar one: it is notoriously difficult to glean the beliefs of the illiterate masses when the only sources are texts drawn up by the literate élite. Essentially the same problem confronts scholars dealing with mythology, legends of the saints, rural festivals, and other subjects.[4]

Despite the enormous body of scholarship on European witchcraft, the problem remains unsolved. To be sure, various historians have intuited distinctions between learned and popular levels of witch belief. Rossell Hope Robbins, for example, has argued that witchcraft proper, which he defines as 'a form of religion, a Christian heresy,' involving allegiance with the devil, was never 'of the people.' The practice of witchcraft, in Robbins's interpretation, was a fiction, devised wholly by theologians and inquisitors.[5] Joseph Hansen reached much the same conclusion: that notions such as diabolical assemblies, transformation into animal-shapes, flight through the air, and so forth, were taken by medieval theologians from Christian and Graeco-Roman tradition, and woven into a 'cumulative concept' of witchcraft that had no foundations in popular belief or practice.[6] A contrary view was stated in the nineteenth century by Jacob Grimm, who suggested that the concepts associated with witchcraft arose from Germanic folklore, and thus by implication derived from popular tradition, and not exclusively from learned belief.[7] More radical still are those scholars who think of witchcraft as rooted not merely in popular tradition but in actual practice; numerous scholars have argued that the people accused of witchcraft did in fact engage in some kind of illicit rites. The most extreme advocate of this view was Montague Summers, whose faith in the real existence of demons and in the genuine alliance between witches and Satan remained unshakable.[8] For some time the anthropological interpretation of Margaret Murray and her followers was considered more respectable than the extreme credulity of Summers. Miss Murray suggested that witchcraft was the pre-Christian fertility religion that survived as an underground cult after the nominal adoption of Christianity in Europe.[9] One of Miss Murray's numerous critics, Elliot Rose, set forth the fascinating hypothesis that high medieval goliards may have organized pagan vestiges and fostered the parodies of Christianity that inquisitors labeled synagogues or Sabbaths.[10] And the notion has often been set forth that diabolism was a form of protest. Jules Michelet viewed it as a protest against medieval society;[11] Pennethorne Hughes thought of it as largely a female reaction against male domination;[12] Jeffrey Russell has explained it as an outgrowth of heresy, and a manifestation of dissent against the established Church.[13]

Views on the foundations of witch beliefs thus fall into three main classes, emphasizing respectively the role of learned tradition, popular tradition, and actual practice. None of these divergent views is either manifestly absurd or self-evidently correct. And the questions they raise are clearly fundamental. Before one can begin to analyze the social mechanism that underlay persecution, one must know what the actual grounds were for accusation of witchcraft, and one must determine the social levels from which specific accusations arose. Yet historians have failed to devise a way of answering these questions. Perhaps in despair of ever formulating the required methodology, they have typically proceeded on the basis of *a priori* intuitions of one form or another. Thus, Elliot Rose openly admits that in judging whether witch beliefs were based on real practice 'we must ultimately rely on taste or intuition, the *feel* of the language employed.'[14] And H. C. Erik Midelfort, citing Rose with qualified approval, agrees that 'so long as the bulk of our information is tracts on the threat of witchcraft and records of trials for witchcraft, his statement is substantially true.'[15] The present work will suggest that this counsel of despair is not necessary. Following chapters will propose a methodology for sorting out fact and fiction, popular and learned tradition, with some confidence and in some detail.

One might ask whether it is valid to distinguish between popular and learned beliefs, or whether it might not be reasonable to assume that the learned and unlearned classes in early European society held witch beliefs that were substantially identical. Indeed, it is likely that popular culture had many features in common with learned tradition, and was subject to constant influence from it. There were numerous possibilities for contact and exchange between the literate and illiterate classes. Parish priests, and perhaps merchants and other groups, might stand midway between the two extremes; they were frequently from the lower or middle classes, and remained constantly in touch with these classes, yet at the same time they were exposed to the beliefs of cultured individuals. Sermons and plays could readily serve as media for popular dissemination of originally learned notions. Hansen suggested that the theatrical devils of the medieval stage influenced popular notions of how devils act.[16] Even woodcuts could fulfill a similar function so long as there was someone on hand to interpret their representations in the intended sense.[17] The scandal aroused by trials for witchcraft might in itself spread learned notions about witches among the populace, whose presence at the executions would be a matter of common occurrence. In one instance the number of spectators at an execution was estimated between six and eight thousand;[18] even allowing for exaggeration, there must have been many people present, and many of them must have known the specific crimes to which the subject had confessed. During the sixteenth century, when extended series of witch trials occurred in many communities, it would be odd indeed if these notions failed to permeate the people at large.

Yet when all of this is admitted, there remains a substantial difference between the educated élite—people who could resurrect through their reading ideas that had lain dormant for centuries in unread manuscripts, who could easily maintain contact with centers of intellectual activity remote from their own countries, and who were trained in the arts of speculation and deduction—and the illiterate masses. Though there was no impenetrable barrier between them, the gap was wide enough that the preoccupations of one class can scarcely be assumed to have been shared by the other. One may presume that there were general forms of culture, particularly religious culture, that were shared by people of all classes. And one may further take for granted that most people were exposed to some variety of learned notions expounded from the pulpit. Yet one cannot assume that any *specific* idea took hold on the popular imagination, unless specific evidence bears out this conclusion. One must operate on the working hypothesis that there were differences between popular and learned culture, and then proceed to discern how substantial those differences were.

The present work, then, will attempt to trace the origins, popular or learned, of various types of witch belief. Before doing this, one must recognize the various types of concept that are to be distinguished. The notions to be analyzed fall into three general classes: sorcery, invocation, and diabolism. The nature of each will become clarified in the course of this study, but for present purposes it may be useful to give brief descriptions.

The first of these phenomena, sorcery, might be defined as maleficent magic, such as rendering a person lame by making an image of the victim and breaking the leg of the image, or inducing love or hatred through administration of magical potions. Though in many ways the concept eludes rigid definition, sorcery is characterized by three general features. First of all, an act carried out through sorcery is in some way extraordinary: it occurs in extraordinary circumstances, or through use of extraordinary substances, or through the power of extraordinary individuals. Granted, it is not always possible to determine how contemporaries distinguished between ordinary and exceptional events or processes. This is a problem that will arise later, in discussion of magical potions and powders; contemporaries did not distinguish clearly between these and sheerly natural poisons.[19] Yet in most instances the charge of sorcery implied that the misdeed was in some way distinct from those normally performed, even if the accusers could not pinpoint the exact difference. Second, sorcery works by processes that are in principle not subject to empirical observation. Again, the distinction is not absolute. A person who injures his enemy by mutilating an image may not be able to explain the mechanism of his act, but for that matter a specialist in folk medicine might be just as unable to explain how a particular herb takes effect. The folk remedy may in principle be explicable through empirical observation, but when technology for such inquiry is lacking this theoretical possibility is not a significant feature of the process. In general, however, a relative distinction does hold. For most processes that they employ, people have some vague (and perhaps incorrect) notion of the mechanism involved, or else they assume that they could ascertain this mechanism if they so endeavored, or they take it on faith that someone understands the link between cause and effect. But the man who mutilates his enemy's representation cannot make any of these claims. He may believe that the magical act works, but he cannot explain how. Third, sorcery is distinguished from beneficent magic by virtue of its harmful intent. It is designed to cause illness, death, poverty, or material damage. Even this feature is not wholly unambiguous. For instance, one might argue that love magic is not necessarily deleterious—that the person who drinks a love potion may profit from the relationship to which it leads. But a person who views it as beneficent will *eo ipso* not classify it as sorcery. The word thus implies a value judgment of the effects sought or attained—a judgment passed not by the historian, but by the contemporaries who are afflicted. In the following pages, magic will be referred to as maleficent, and thus as sorcery, only when it was viewed as harmful by the persons affected or by others who brought judicial accusation.

Although sorcery is not in all respects purely a natural phenomenon, it is not supernatural in the sense of involving the participation of spirits. Invocation, on the other hand, is supernatural in that sense: it consists in calling upon the devil to obtain instruction or execution of one's wishes. It may or may not involve a pact with the devil, after the manner of Faust. If a pact is involved, it is contractual rather than religious. The person engaging in invocation does not view the devil as worthy of veneration, but merely uses him as a necessary agent for some end.[20] In most instances, however, records of alleged invocation say nothing about a pact. In any event, invocation requires an explicit, deliberate act of calling upon the devil.

Closely akin to invocation, yet distinct from it, is diabolism: deliberate worship of the devil, or of demons. This worship involves a variety of ritual actions, usually occurring at the diabolical assembly, or 'synagogue', or 'Sabbath'. It entails a pact in which the devotee submits himself wholly before the devil, accepting him as lord; it further may involve sexual intercourse with the devil in the human form of an *incubus* or *succubus*, receipt of the devil's prick or 'mark' on one's body, flight through the air on an anointed stick, transformation into the shape of an animal, and so forth.

It may be argued that these distinctions are overly subtle, and not borne out in the sources. Their applicability to the historical evidence can only be shown in the course of following chapters. By way of general introduction, it should be admitted that in *learned* tradition the various notions did blend. For example, a man who began by invoking the devil would find himself persuaded to make a submissive pact with Satan, committing him to both diabolism and sorcery; he would receive his magical unguents and powders, along with instructions on how to use them, directly from the devil. Scholastic theologians held that in principle both invocation and sorcery were accomplished only through alliance with the devil. This bond might take the form of an explicit, deliberate pact, or it might be merely an implicit pact, entered upon through the simple consent of the devotee, without formalities. In either event, it would be through pre-established association with the devil that invocation and sorcery have their effect.[21] Yet there is no evidence that this interpretation was adopted by people at large. Thus, the historian cannot suppose that when a townsman accused someone of sorcery the accuser presupposed that the culprit engaged in invocation or diabolism as well. Contemporaries no doubt did not maintain a rigid, formal distinction between the various concepts, but on the other hand one cannot assume in any given case that they conflated the different notions. Simply to specify the nature of the charges as recorded, the historian needs a set of closely defined, specific terms. In a few cases the sources leave room for doubt about the categories being employed. For example, one finds sorceresses described as 'imbued with a malign spirit and inflamed with diabolical art,'[22] or as operating 'through the devil's art.'[23] These terms suggest the charge of invocation, but it is not clear from the context that such an accusation was intended. In many other trials the terms employed are so vague that it is impossible to state whether invocation, diabolism, or mere sorcery was alleged. Yet the most important documents are those that state the charges most clearly, and a necessary condition for accurate discussion of these records is a reasonably precise vocabulary.

Perhaps the most problematic word used in such contexts is the term 'witchcraft.' Neither historical nor modern works maintain any clear and consistent definition of the word. Some authors virtually equate it with diabolism, while others, with perfect etymological justification and historical precedent, use it also when speaking of sorcery. Anthropologists have suggested numerous ways of

distinguishing between witchcraft and sorcery. For example, E. E.
Evans-Pritchard speaks of sorcery as accomplished through external
means, such as rituals, verbal formulas, and material substances,
whereas witchcraft works by virtue of a special power resident
within the witch.[24] But none of these sets of definitions seems
greatly useful in treatment of European sources.[25] In the present
work, then, no endeavour will be made to endow the words 'witch'
and 'witchcraft' with any technical or specific meaning. 'Witchcraft'
will be used in an inclusive sense, applying to sorcery, *or* diabolism,
or invocation, *or* any combination of these. Likewise, 'witch' will be
used in a broad sense, for a practitioner of any or all such acts. The
latter term will thus correspond to the various words employed in
the documents—*sortilegus, maleficus, veneficus, striga,* and their
vernacular equivalents—which, whatever their original specific
meanings, quickly assumed general significance. Words of this sort
are required for those many contexts in which the sources afford no
clue to what the specific charge may have been. When a definite,
technical meaning is required, the words 'witch' and 'witchcraft'
will be avoided, and others used in their place.

This study will deal specifically with the period 1300–1500. These
limits are not totally arbitrary. Prior to this period the incidence of
witchcraft was so rare that it is impossible to detect patterns of
accusation, and reliable sources for genuinely popular belief are
virtually non-existent. To be sure, there were scattered trials for
both sorcery and diabolism centuries before 1300, and any general
study of European witchcraft would have to take them into account.
But the evidence for these cases does not lend itself to the kind of
analysis required in this specific investigation. In discussion of the
various types of sorcery there will be occasion to make comparison
with earlier material, but this will not be of primary interest. And
in study of witch trials from the period after 1500, the attempt to
distinguish popular from learned traditions becomes increasingly
problematic. The likelihood of intermixture of the two traditions
becomes greater, and the number of people with some kind of
formal education increases significantly if one goes much beyond the
specified time limit.

The geographical scope of this inquiry is indicated even more
clearly by the nature of the subject. So far as the extant records
indicate, witchcraft was practised or alleged between 1300 and 1500
predominantly in England, the Low Countries, France, Italy,

Switzerland, and Germany. Occasionally there were trials in neighboring countries, such as Spain, and these instances will be included in this work, though their importance is minimal.

The following chapter will furnish the essential diachronic context by sketching in rough overview the development of witch prosecution. Chapter III will then undertake the main task of this study, the differentiation of popular and learned beliefs. It will then be possible to analyze the component elements of popular and learned traditions, and to show how these beliefs related to the tensions and anxieties of late medieval society.

In comparison with the mass persecution of following centuries, the witch trials of the years 1300–1500 were few and sporadic. There was seldom a sustained effort in any one community to exterminate witches, as occurred frequently in the sixteenth and seventeenth centuries. Even in years when there were multiple trials, they generally occurred in widely separate towns. Yet historians have rightly viewed the fourteenth and fifteenth centuries as witnessing the initial stages of the European witch craze. It was during this period that prosecution of witches first gained real momentum— gradually and fitfully, as indicated on the graph. And the intensified hunts of the sixteenth and seventeenth centuries can be explained only as outgrowths of an earlier obsession.

Even during the period 1300–1500, though, one must distinguish various stages of prosecution. On the one hand, the rate of frequency changed sharply; on the other, the nature of the accusations altered significantly. Bearing in mind both the intensity and the form of witch hunting, one can perceive four broad periods during the fourteenth and fifteenth centuries, extending roughly from 1300 to 1330, from 1330 to 1375, from 1375 to 1435, and from 1435 to 1500.

During the first period, the rate of prosecution was low indeed. For all of Europe, the trials occurred on an average of roughly one each year. Slightly more than half of these come from France; among other countries, only England and Germany had significant numbers of witch hunts.[1]

Probably the most remarkable feature of the trials during this first phase is their political character. Almost two-thirds of them involved prominent ecclesiastical or secular figures, sometimes as suspects but most commonly as sorcerers' victims. The political climate was ideal for fostering the obsession that leaders everywhere were being attacked through the surreptitious weapons of sorcery. In France, the Capetian dynasty had lost the blessing of longevity

10

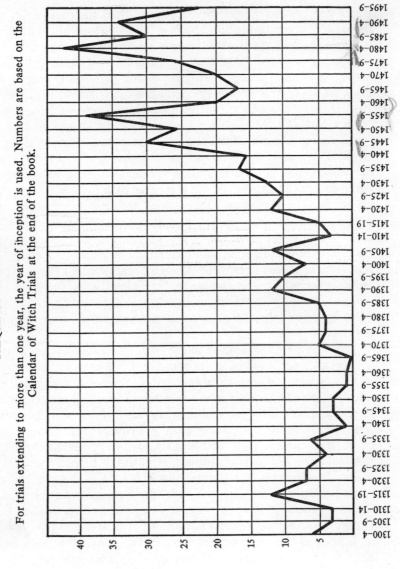

FREQUENCY OF WITCH TRIALS

For trials extending to more than one year, the year of inception is used. Numbers are based on the Calendar of Witch Trials at the end of the book.

which had favored its members for more than three centuries. In the early fourteenth century the last four Capetian kings died, all within a space of twelve years; it was easy to imagine that they had succumbed to bewitchment. Suspicions of this kind had arisen earlier, as when the nephew of the bishop of Bayeux went to his death in 1278 for allegedly attempting sorcery against Philip III.[2] In the early years of the fourteenth century, however, the charge became virtually habitual as an explanation for deaths within the royal family, or as a credible excuse for prosecution among political rivals. The trial of the Templars no doubt helped to heighten fear of witchcraft, though the Templars were accused of diabolism rather than sorcery.[3] It was during the course of their famous trial, in any event, that the bishop of Troyes stood trial for image magic and invocation of the devil—practices which had supposedly succeeded in bringing the demise of the queen, though they had failed in their further objective of killing other members of the French court.[4] A few years later Enguerrand de Marigny was executed along with a female associate for using image magic against Louis X and Charles of Valois.[5] And with the rapid succession of monarchs who fell ill and died young, the charge arose seven more times within the next few years.[6]

The papacy was not subject to the same difficulties. Pope Clement V was sickly for much of his pontificate, but he reigned from 1305 to 1314, which was a respectable length of time considering that he, like most popes, was elected at an advanced age. And many churchmen would have been gratified if his successor John XXII had lived less than his eighteen years after election to the papacy. Yet the papal court was ridden with factionalism, which generally followed national lines: the Italian cardinals, resentful of French domination in the Avignonese papacy, were openly hostile to the Frenchmen, while the latter group was divided by the formation of a specifically Gascon faction. It was the animosity of these groups that led to a two-year vacancy between the death of Clement V and the election of John XXII; no one faction was powerful enough to secure the election of its own candidate. Nor did hostilities between Italians and Frenchmen cease altogether when a French cardinal at last became John XXII. The atmosphere of contention fostered lasting suspicion. In addition, John appears to have been naturally superstitious, and given to such practices as keeping a magical snake-skin to detect poisoned food and drink.[7]

Through most of his pontificate John was active in prosecution of sorcerers and invokers of demons. The year after his election, Bishop Hugo Géraud of Cahors went to the stake for involvement in a conspiracy against the pope and certain cardinals. The bishop and his accomplices had allegedly employed wax images and other magical objects to bring about the pontiff's ruin; after the plot was detected, various clerics at the papal court confessed under torture that they had dabbled in sundry forms of witchcraft.[8] Two years later, the Franciscan Bernard Délicieux, earlier a harsh critic of inquisitorial procedures, was brought to trial on charges of witchcraft. He was acquitted of one charge, that of attempting to bewitch one of John XXII's predecessors through drinks and powders. But on the grounds of possession of magical books he was sentenced to life imprisonment.[9] On three occasions—in 1318, 1320, and 1326—Pope John took initiative in the investigation of those persons in southern France who were forming pacts with the devil, employing image magic, abusing the sacraments, and committing other such offenses.[10] In a trial with clear political implications, the archbishop of Milan and an inquisitor charged that Matteo and Galeazzo Visconti, two of John's main political adversaries, had entered a pact with the devil, had invoked the devil on numerous occasions, and had used sorcery against the pope.[11] Meanwhile the pope issued commands to the bishop of Ancona and an inquisitor, directing them to prosecute other political enemies on the charges of idolatry, heresy, and diabolism.[12] And on two occasions, the pope aided in investigation of sorcery directed against the French kings.[13]

Likewise, the English monarch Edward II, whose weak hold on the throne led to deposition in 1327, found witches among his opponents. Even in the early years of his reign, a rebel was found who had allegedly made a pact with the devil to obtain the crown.[14] Less directly affecting the throne was the trial of Edward I's treasurer and minister, Walter Langton, bishop of Coventry. Charged before the pope of having formed a pact with the devil and kissed him on the posterior, Langton received the king's support, and ultimately obtained acquittal.[15]

The best known political trials of the early fourteenth century are those of the Templars and of Dame Alice Kyteler. The Templars, tried on the urging of the French crown, were convicted of charges that were certainly exaggerated, if not wholly fabricated. In addition to sodomy, blasphemy, and other species of immorality, they are supposed to have venerated the devil in the guise of an animal named Baphomet.[16] Whereas the motives in many political trials are only vaguely ascertainable, the desire of Philip IV to confiscate the Templars' abundant wealth is notorious. Almost as apparent were the political motives in the trial of Alice Kyteler, an aristocratic lady of Ireland.[17] This woman had family relations with numerous political leaders, and the best accounts of her trial explain it as largely an outgrowth of feuds among these aristocratic families.[18] Her accusers charged that she had killed three husbands and reduced a fourth to debility through sorcery; she had furthermore maintained an imp named Robert Artisson, and engaged in diabolical rituals.

The prominence of the sorcerers and victims in these trials is of the utmost importance. Though in some instances the accusers may have raised the charges cynically as ways of undermining their opponents, in the majority of cases the charges were no doubt based on sincere belief in the reality of witchcraft. Yet the fact that these trials reflect concern with sorcery and invocation is less important in the long run than the likelihood that they intensified this concern throughout western Europe. The notoriety and suggestive force of these episodes may have been largely responsible for the gradual increase in witch prosecution through the following generations.[19]

Apart from the political character of prosecution during the first phase, its most significant feature is the mildness of the allegations. Sorcery was by far the most common charge; invocation was not so frequent, but was known; diabolism, though, was extremely rare, and even when alleged it was usually not described in great detail. Even in the trials of Walter Langton, the Templars, and Alice Kyteler, the depictions of devil-worship are less lurid than in later trials. Pope John XXII routinely spoke of pacts with the devil, yet did not specify whether these agreements led to diabolism or merely to invocation of the devil. One of the more elaborate cases was that of the Carmelite friar Peter Recordi, who was charged with a peculiar mixture of sorcery, invocation, and mild diabolism.[20] On various occasions, Recordi had made five wax images and performed conjurations and invocation of demons over them. He had poured over these images poisons and blood extracted 'in a terrible and horrible manner' from a toad. He had then placed the figures on a table, covered them with a cloth, and sprinkled them with blood from his own nostrils, mixed with saliva, as an immolation to the devil. After this, he placed the images under the thresholds of women he wished to seduce. Through these means he had succeeded in seducing three women, and had he not been transferred to a new residence by his order he would have ensnared two more. After the images had accomplished their purpose, he cast them into the water, completing the ritual by sacrificing a butterfly to the devil. He had believed that such figures had power not only to constrain women, but to bring afflictions upon them if they refused his advances. To test their magical properties, he had once stuck one of the figures in the stomach, and blood oozed out. Such, in any event, were the charges brought forth. Yet even here the classic elements of diabolism that later became important, the Sabbath and all its attendant ceremonies, are absent.

Long before it appeared independently or in connection with sorcery, the charge of diabolism had been used in trials against heretics. No matter how rigorous their moral codes might be, medieval heretics such as the Cathars and Waldensians were believed to reject moral law entirely—a position known as antinomianism. They allegedly held nocturnal orgies, and in some instances were thought of as paying homage to the devil.[21] In a few trials of the early fourteenth century charges of diabolism seem to have been made against heretics, in the specific form of Luciferanism. The basic premise of Luciferanism, if indeed anyone actually subscribed to the doctrine, seems to have been that Lucifer would eventually attain salvation, and would even rule over creation in place of the Christian God. Churchmen accused Luciferans of venerating the devil in underground assemblies. To be sure, in most instances the charge of Luciferanism is related only in chronicles, usually of questionable veracity. Thus it is not even fully certain that the accusation actually arose in the heresy trials, much less that it was accurate.[22] In any case, the allegation was set forth a few times in the years 1300–30,[23] though its importance was apparently minimal.

The second period, from around 1330 to about 1375, is like the first in that the accusations were still for the most part relatively tame, but unlike it in that trials connected with important public figures were virtually unknown. Changes in the political environment may have influenced the character of prosecution. Edward III and Philip VI brought stable government to England and France, and though there were two trials in 1331 for attempts to bewitch the French king the furor quickly subsided. John XXII died in

1334, and his successor Benedict XII turned his witch hunting zeal toward unimportant suspects. This shift occurred in part, perhaps, because the charge of witchcraft had been overworked during the first thirty years of the century. The political trials of those years had aroused widespread attention, and may have aggravated general concern about witchcraft, but may also have made people skeptical about accusations that arose specifically from political or personal motives. Possibly also there were would-be assassins who, having witnessed the prosecutions of the early fourteenth century, were less inclined to view sorcery as a safe method for murder with impunity. The fact that stands out is that, for whatever reason, known political trials cease abruptly shortly after the year 1330. Largely because of the decrease in political trials, the rate of prosecution in the second phase was slightly less than in the first. With a few exceptions, trials centered in France and Germany, with only a scattering of cases in England and Italy. Once again, apart from a few trials for Luciferanism, the charge of diabolism was rare and undeveloped.[24]

In short, until about 1375 the emphasis was mainly on sorcery, and to a lesser extent on invocation; diabolism seldom arose in the allegations, and when it came forth at all it took a vague or subdued form. One possible exception to this rule, however, is a series of trials at Toulouse and Carcassonne, in which diabolism is supposed to have figured prominently even in the mid-fourteenth century. The source for these trials is of some interest in itself. In 1829, Étienne-Léon de Lamothe-Langon published a three-volume history of the French Inquisition, including lengthy translations or paraphrases from inquisitorial records.[25] By the late 1800s these documents were nowhere to be found, but at the turn of the century Joseph Hansen reprinted the relevant excerpts from Lamothe-Langon's work.[26] Ever since then they have constituted perhaps the most important single body of sources for early European witch trials, and as such have received the detailed attention of historians. Indeed, some scholars have built critical arguments upon them.[27] The importance of these records lies partly in the sheer number of trials to which they refer: while giving the details of a few cases, Lamothe-Langon indicated that there were as many as 1,000 trials for witchcraft in Toulouse and Carcassonne between 1320 and 1350, and that 600 of these proceedings led to executions—at a time when other regions witnessed only a handful of such proceedings.[28] The records are also crucial for the nature of the charges: the earliest detailed accounts of diabolical rites in connection with sorcery are contained in these cases, and while other documents from the same period refer almost invariably to sorcery alone, diabolism appears to have been a prevailing obsession in these two cities of southern France.

What historians have failed to recognize, however,[29] is that there is serious reason to believe that Lamothe-Langon's texts are forgeries. The highly atypical nature of the allegations might reflect genuinely anomalous circumstances, and the mysterious disappearance of his documents would in itself prove nothing, though such losses were more common before and during the French Revolution.[30] But when one couples these facts with certain inaccuracies and anachronisms in the reports, credibility is strained. In particular, Lamothe-Langon uses the word 'Sabbath' in rendering documents for fourteenth-century diabolical assemblies, though this word did not begin to displace the term 'synagogue' or 'synagogue of Satan' until well into the fifteenth century.[31] Suspicion is heightened by his failure to specify where he found the documents, though he alluded vaguely to archives throughout southern France.[32] And a review of Lamothe-Langon's biography does little to reinforce one's confidence in the value of his account.[33] He devised other known forgeries; to persuade his contemporaries that he came from a long-established noble family he concocted several genealogies showing his illustrious ancestors. Much of his literary work consisted of memoirs ostensibly written by various figures of the late eighteenth and early nineteenth centuries; these volumes were no doubt based on a mixture of known fact and plausible fantasy. His reputation was based mainly on his prolific authorship of popular novels, particularly *romans noirs*, dealing with such subjects as vampires and demons. As a minor governmental official he was guided more by a desire to enhance his career than by principles of conventional ethics; to gain favor with the restored monarchy he betrayed his Bonapartist allegiance with an unflattering book on Napoleon. One might furthermore question how he could have produced as swiftly as he seems to have done a historical work which would have been laborious even if he had had background in paleography. His literary output was extraordinary, to be sure, but when faced with the requirements of archival research he would surely have found it difficult to maintain his accustomed rate of several volumes each year. In addition, his history of the Inquisition was one of a series of polemic works—all of them bitterly attacking agencies of repression—which had been sparked by the censorship he himself had encountered. Hence, he had motivation to embellish his account, and quite possibly to invent substantial portions of it. Lurid details of inquisitorial work against witches might indeed have stirred more widespread revulsion in nineteenth-century France than a less sensational recounting of antiheretical proceedings. One further consideration is relevant: there were in fact inquisitorial documents from Carcassonne that survived into modern times, but were lost possibly during the French Revolution, if not earlier. By the mid-nineteenth century, in any event, only a summary inventory of these documents survived or had been uncovered; it was published in 1855.[34] And there is no correspondence whatsoever between this inventory and the materials in Lamothe-Langon.

Perhaps each of these arguments can be explained away. One could point out that the inquisitors cited in Lamothe-Langon are known from other records—though this perhaps proves only that Lamothe-Langon was careful enough to establish his stories on a minimal basis of fact. One could also allude to the abundant independent evidence that there was prosecution of magicians at this time in southern France, largely at papal instigation—although these separate sources say little about sorcery, and nothing about diabolism.[35] Judgment on the matter can perhaps never be definitive, unless someone uncovers the documents Lamothe-Langon claims to have used. Even if there is an element of truth in his presentation, the main conclusions of the present study remain unaffected. But in delineating the general pattern of early witch prosecution it is of some importance to note that Lamothe-Langon's evidence for early concern with diabolism is at best highly questionable.

It was during the third period, then, roughly 1375 to 1435, that a twofold change took place. Throughout these years there was first of all a steady increase in the number of trials for witchcraft in general, and second an intensification of concern for diabolism. The rise of prosecution during this period may in part be an optical illusion caused by the general increase in extant judicial records from these years. But it is surely not coincidental that the later part of the fourteenth century was the period when in many places municipal courts began to adopt inquisitorial procedure.[36] Once such procedure was adopted, even if the judges were not yet familiar with theological notions of diabolism there would be machinery appropriate for handling sorcery charges that arose among the populace. Perhaps the most important feature of inquisitorial procedure, for present purposes, is that it did away with the earlier custom of judicial penalties for an accuser who failed to substantiate his charges.[37] In trials for sorcery it would be particularly difficult for the accuser to prove his case, because the alleged culprit was not connected with the victim in the usual ways; the sorcerer might carry out his deed several blocks away from the scene of the crime. Prior to the development of inquisitorial justice, it must therefore have been particularly dangerous to accuse someone of sorcery or of witchcraft generally. In one peculiar case from Strassburg in the mid-fifteenth century the provisions of earlier, accusatory procedure were revived: a man accused a woman of weather magic, and when he was unable to prove his claim he himself was drowned.[38] If these judicial rules had been maintained throughout Europe, no doubt very few people would have raised accusations of this kind, difficult as they were to prove. After the introduction of inquisitorial procedure, one might expect a surge of prosecution such as in fact occurred. And to some degree the concern with trials for sorcery would be self-perpetuating; under appropriate circumstances, the sensation aroused by one trial could generate a chain of further trials. Indirectly, the spurt of witch trials beginning around 1375 may also have been influenced by the plague. The long-term social effects of the plague, particularly in those areas where it brought migration from the countryside into the cities, may have stimulated social friction that could have aggravated the preoccupation with witchcraft.[39]

It has also been suggested that inquisitors began prosecuting witches—or began prosecuting people *as* witches—when they had succeeded in exterminating Cathars and Waldensians.[40] It is true that in circumstances in which papal inquisitors faced a shortage of legitimate subjects they frequently tended to focus their attention on religious eccentrics, marginally heretical communities, political subjects, and alleged witches. This was true most of the time in Germany, Spain, and other countries.[41] But the chronology of witch trials does not suggest that this was a major factor in their development. Catharism was uprooted from southern France, and Waldensianism driven safely underground, by the early fourteenth century. But unless one accepts Lamothe-Langon's evidence, prosecution for sorcery did not gain full momentum until late in the century, and trials for diabolism were not widespread until the following century. The lessened threat from heresies may have been important as a factor which *allowed* ecclesiastical judges to attend to witchcraft, but not as a positive cause of the rise in witch trials. Even apart from the chronological gap between the decline of heresies and the acceleration of witch trials, it should be borne in mind that the trials of this third phase were not led exclusively by inquisitors or other ecclesiastical judges. The connection between the fate of earlier heresy and the intensified obsession with witchcraft is thus tenuous.

The over-all acceleration can be traced most clearly for Switzerland, where conditions in modern times have favored the survival of documents that might have been lost elsewhere. Prior to 1383 there are no known instances of sorcery in Swiss territories. In the last decades of the fourteenth century there were four minor cases, each involving a single sorceress—though in one of these there seem to have been no judicial proceedings.[42] Around the turn of the century there was a famous outbreak in Simmenthal under the secular judge Peter of Greyerz, who related his discoveries to the Dominican John Nider.[43] The original records do not survive, but if one can believe the much later account that Nider wrote, the subjects in this case were accused of diabolism as well as sorcery. They were supposed to have made homage to their 'little master,' repudiated the Catholic religion, and devoured a total of thirteen infants. When the authorities sought to capture one member of the 'sect,' their hands began to tremble uncontrollably, and their noses were assaulted with a loathsome stench. Yet the judge was zealous, and despite severe opposition from the witches he managed to apprehend and burn numerous offenders.

Between the turn of the century and the year 1435 there were more than twenty trials in various towns of Switzerland, notably Lucerne, Basel, and Fribourg. In most, the charges were simple sorcery. In 1428 there was extensive persecution in Valais; whereas the fragmentary judicial documents speak only of sorcery, the chronicler John Fründ gives abundant details about a devil-worshipping cult in southern Switzerland.[44] According to Fründ, the devil seeks out men who are in a state of doubt or despair, and promises to make them rich, powerful, and successful, and to punish those who have done them harm. First, though, they must dedicate themselves to him, deny their former faith, and make some kind of sacrifice to him—a black sheep, one of their bodily limbs (to be claimed after death), or some other offering. Fründ tells of wild assemblies in which the devil appeared in bestial form and encouraged the witches to commit foul deeds; the witches are supposed to have flown to orgies or elsewhere on chairs that they anointed with an unguent. Though not typical of Swiss witch cases during this period, this chronicler's account shows the kind of extravagant detail that was beginning to be associated with maleficent activities.

Italy, like Switzerland, joined with France and Germany in the forefront of witch persecution during this third period. But there is another, more important respect in which Italy took the lead at this time: with the exception of the trials in Simmenthal and Valais, it is from Italy that the only definite instances of prosecution for diabolism come during this phase. Historians have long thought of southern France as the area in which diabolism and sorcery were joined to form a composite notion of witchcraft, chiefly because of the evidence proffered by Lamothe-Langon. Judging from the most reliable records, though, the honor of priority goes instead to Italy. This adjustment makes the development of witch beliefs more plausible: instead of finding a thousand trials all at once, with full-blown diabolism prominent in the charges, one finds gradual evolution and elaboration of witch prosecution. The trials from Italy during the late fourteenth and early fifteenth centuries were still for the most part restrained; the allegation of diabolism, though more common, was still often vague and peripheral. Thus, a Florentine subject named Niccolò Consigli was accused primarily of sorcery, necromancy, and unlicensed exorcism, but an additional charge was that, while imprisoned, he dedicated himself to demons named Lucifer, Satan, and Beelzebub. No further elements of diabolism are mentioned in the records of his proceedings.[45]

In a small minority of Italian trials, one finds admixture of charges that cannot be categorized as either sorcery or typical diabolism. For example, a Milanese woman who went before an inquisitor in 1384 confessed that each Thursday evening she went to an assembly led by a woman named Oriente. There was every kind of animal at this meeting except the ass, which was excluded because of its role in Christ's passion. Oriente gave instruction to her followers, foretold future events and revealed occult matters. After their deaths, the followers' souls were received by the *signora*.

Perhaps the most important statement by the accused woman is that she had never confessed her involvement in these activities, because it had never occurred to her that they were sinful.[46] The details of this case, which do not at all fit the stereotype of contemporary demonology, suggest that the woman was merely engaging in a popular festivity or ritual. The gatherings that she attended may have survived from before the conversion of the Italian countryside to Christianity; yet it would be misleading to speak of them as conscious and deliberate pagan survivals, since the participants seem to have viewed themselves as Christians, despite the reservations that churchmen evidently held.[47] In an age when notions of diabolism were becoming important, however, a sinister interpretation of these activities lay readily at hand. When this woman relapsed into her illicit activities she again fell prey to an inquisitor, and this time went to the stake for outright diabolism.[48]

Why did diabolism enter into witch trials during this period? The component elements of diabolism—veneration of Satan, nefarious assemblies, flight through the air, formation of a pact, and so forth—had been known for centuries. They had arisen in trials of heretics as early as the eleventh century. In the course of the thirteenth and fourteenth centuries, jurists and theologians tended increasingly to view witchcraft as a form of heresy—a development which was traced in detail by Joseph Hansen, and which Jeffrey Russell has recently examined anew.[49] The theological faculty of the University of Paris deliberated in 1398 whether *maleficia*, or acts of sorcery, entailed idolatry and apostasy if they were accomplished through a tacit or express pact with the devil. The conclusion reached was that such deeds did involve idolatry and apostasy, and were thus tantamount to heresy.[50] This decision —which was merely the culmination of a series of writings to the same basic effect—was intended to justify the prosecution of witchcraft by inquisitors, whose main task was supposed to be the extirpation of heresy.[51] A secondary result of this definition of witchcraft as heresy was that the stereotypes earlier found in heresy trials now increasingly transferred to witch trials.

The new obsession with diabolism was also related to developments in the theological literature of the late fourteenth and early fifteenth centuries, which set forth all the elements of diabolism in great, pornographic detail.[52] The first of these writings were brief treatises, or sections in judicial manuals; for the most part they were technical works, yet they evidently circulated widely among the people engaged in prosecution. They both symptomized and augmented the concern with witchcraft among the educated élite. Whether this literature in itself was enough to stimulate the increase in witch trials is a question for later chapters. For present purposes it is sufficient to note the correlation between the literary and judicial developments. The correlation may be extended one step further: it is not surprising that the first well authenticated series of trials for diabolism occurred in Italy; it was there that legal scholarship was most developed, and it was in the Italian courts that one might expect to find ideas of the literate élite reflected in judicial practice.[53]

The full force of the new composite notion of witchcraft came only in the fourth phase of witch prosecution, from around 1435 to 1500. This is the longest of the four stages, and in virtually every way the most important. Trials were particularly frequent during the years 1455–60 and 1480–5, while during the intervening years the rate of prosecution remained higher than it had been in any previous period. The intense witch hunting of this stage anticipated, if it did not equal, the witch craze of the sixteenth and seventeenth centuries. Once again there is correlation between judicial and literary developments. Around the year 1435, an extended and non-technical account of devil-worship was produced with the fifth book of John Nider's *Formicarius*.[54] Further writings followed; the publication of Jacob Sprenger and Henry Institoris's *Malleus maleficarum* in 1487 made available a fully developed manual for witch hunters.[55] Even if these writings were not solely responsible for the acceleration of trials, they surely must have contributed greatly towards that result.

By far the majority of cases during this final period occurred in France, Germany, and Switzerland. Only a few took place in England and Italy, and virtually none in further countries. Once again the majority of trials were for sorcery alone, or for vaguely specified 'witchcraft', with no specific allegation of diabolism. Yet in addition there were now many trials throughout Europe in which diabolism was charged, and when it came forth at all it was usually the prominent allegation. Thus, more than any previous period, this fourth phase was a time of sensational trials. Some of the earlier political trials—those of the early fourteenth century, and especially that of Joan of Arc in 1431—had aroused widespread attention. But

in the later fifteenth century the charge of diabolism or even sorcery
by itself, regardless of political implications, was enough to produce
a dramatic episode. In the mid-fifteenth century an epidemic that
struck a French town resulted in vigilante prosecution of sorceresses
thought to be culpable; the affair aroused such attention that the
king himself intervened, and punished the local officials for failure
to maintain order.[56] A famous trial that began a few years later at
Arras led to hearings before the Parlement of Paris.[57] By the end of
the century, secular and ecclesiastical dignitaries commonly recognized a duty to purge their lands of the menace: examples such as
Sigismund of Tirol or Innocent VIII are merely the best known.
Nor was the concern limited to ruling circles. The above-mentioned
case of vigilante justice, as well as other incidents, suggest that the
people at large were keenly aware of the supposed problem.

Three examples may suffice to epitomize the witch persecutions
of this period. In 1459, a woman named Catherine Simon went
before the secular authorities at Andermatt, and confessed that one
Jagli Jeger had taught her the art of witchcraft.[58] He had given her
a box with salve, with which she could turn herself into a fox, a cat,
or a wolf. She also received instruction from a certain woman of
Andermatt, and in turn she taught her own daughter Grete how to
repay offenses with evil deeds. Catherine went to an assembly at
Wallenboden, where she renounced God and the saints, and swore
to do the devil's will; her daughter did likewise at a later meeting.
After they had formed this allegiance with the devil, he accompanied them occasionally as they went about doing harm to their
neighbors. On one occasion Catherine turned herself into a fox,
and in the devil's company went out to create an avalanche that
killed a woman. Another time she transformed herself into a wolf,
while the devil rode along on another wolf, and together they
caused another avalanche. She confessed to numerous further misdeeds: infliction of illnesses, killing of livestock, and still more
avalanches. In some instances she was unable to carry out her
maleficent desires. She wanted to afflict a man named Heini Krieg
with a disease so severe that he would lie in bed for a month or two,
but she was unable to approach him to impose the malady. On
another occasion she wanted to poison her son-in-law (whether
naturally or magically), but failed for lack of the requisite poison.
More often than not, however, her sorcery took effect. On her conviction, the court declared that the local executioner 'shall take her

to the place of execution and with his sword divide her into two pieces, of which one shall be her head and the other her body, which shall be so completely severed that a cartwheel can be rolled between them.' Both sections of her remains were then to be burned, and the ashes cast into the Reuss River, 'so that no further harm may ensue therefrom.'

In 1477, in the Savoyard town of Villars-Chabod, a woman called Antonia stubbornly refused to confess what the inquisitor Stephan Hugonodi demanded that she admit.[59] After more than a month, the imprisonment and torture to which she was subjected broke her resistance, and at last she gave a lengthy confession. About eleven years earlier, one Massetus Garini found her in a state of sorrow and discontent, and ascertained that she had fallen into financial embarrassment. He told her that she could solve her problems by going with him to a certain friend. Reluctantly she left her home with him one evening and went to Giessbach, where a 'synagogue' was being held, with a large number of people feasting and dancing. Allaying her apprehensions, Massetus introduced her to a demon named Robinet, in the form of a black man, and said that he was the master of the group. He explained that to obtain her desires she would have to pay homage to this demon by denying God, the Catholic faith, and the Blessed Virgin, and taking Robinet as her lord and master. She hesitated. Robinet addressed her in a barely intelligible voice, promising her gold, silver, and other good things; others in attendance likewise encouraged her. Then she consented, kissed the demon's foot, received a 'sign' on her left little finger (which was deadened ever afterward), and trampled and broke a wooden crucifix. The demon gave her a purse full of gold and silver, a container full of unguent, and a stick. When she rubbed the stick with the unguent and recited an appropriate incantation, the stick would transport her through the air to the synagogue. After further feasting and dancing, the members of the sect paid homage to the demon—who by now had changed into the form of a black dog—by kissing him on the posterior. Then the demon cried out 'Meclet! Meclet!' and the fire was put out, whereupon the participants in the festivity gave themselves over to each other sexually, 'in the manner of beasts.' When the meeting was over Antonia went home, only to find that the purse she thought was filled with gold and silver was in fact empty. In further confessions she told of the activities she engaged in as a member of the sect:

further synagogues, consumption of human infants, manufacture of maleficent powders from the bones and intestines of these babies, use of such powders to inflict illness and death on men and animals, and desecration of the eucharist.

The last example is a less involved episode, which occurred in Constance at the end of the century.[60] The wife of a cobbler was apprehended for witchcraft, and at first the devil kept her from confessing her guilt. The only item of information that the judges could extract from her was that the demon to whom she had dedicated herself was named Haintzle. After obtaining this lead, the judges dismissed the woman until the next day, detaining her in a tower prison for the interim. During the night, the devil went to her in the tower, and confronted her so violently that the watchman thought twenty or thirty horses were loose in the building. At last, the fiend strangled her, and when the authorities entered the next morning they found her lying dead, crumpled over, with her head awry. They placed her body in a cask and floated it down the Rhine. In any event, these were the details furnished by a local chronicler.

As already indicated, even during the years 1435–1500 cases of this kind were less common than trials for mere sorcery, yet the incidence of diabolism was far greater than in any previous period. Such trials raise numerous questions. We must now turn to the one most fundamental problem that these incidents pose: which of the notions set forth arose from popular tradition, and which came from learned belief.

Chapter III

Distinction of Popular and Learned Traditions

The first step towards ascertainment of popular tradition is to determine which documents are most faithful repositories of that tradition. For obvious reasons literary texts—treatises on witchcraft, judicial manuals, chronicles, sermons, and so forth—cannot qualify as faithful sources for the beliefs of the illiterate masses. They no doubt incorporate material that derived from popular belief, but the historian has no assurance that they present folk tradition in a pure form, unmixed with distinctively learned notions. Even when an author claims to be representing popular belief one cannot accept his testimony as ideal evidence. Elliot Rose has correctly emphasized that litterateurs such as Jean de Meung frequently claimed to be relating contemporary folklore when they were in fact merely paraphrasing texts from canon law.[1] Some of the literature of the high and late Middle Ages was 'popular' in the sense that its content was intended for widespread dissemination. This is true of anecdotal collections and of many chronicles, which were written in large part to furnish material for preachers.[2] Yet there is no assurance that the stories narrated in such literature had popular origins, or that they did in fact take hold on the popular imagination.

Nor are most of the judicial records a great deal more helpful to the student seeking authentic folklore. In most instances the only extant records of trials are the documents drawn up at the end of judicial interrogation, stating in summary fashion the charges 'proven' against the subject. In some cases there are records of questions posed to the accused, with the answers that were in some way extracted from them. Yet even when these documents claim that the confessions were made 'voluntarily,' or 'spontaneously,' the historian can seldom be sure that the admissions were not elicited through judicial coercion. In many cases there is evidence for confession under torture; in other instances, reference to voluntary

27

confession indicates only that the subject's admissions were confirmed after torture had ceased, but under threat of resumed torture.
One might argue that for present purposes torture did not prejudice
the evidence. The confessions elicited from witch suspects may not
have been true, but it might be argued that the subjects knew in
advance what witches were commonly believed to do, and that when
they confessed to these deeds they were merely applying popular
tradition falsely to themselves. Yet not even this can be assumed.
As will be seen in a later chapter, the information that judges wished
to educe could easily be suggested to the subjects through use of
interrogatories, or lists of leading questions.[3] And even if the suspects did know what their judges expected to hear, they may have
learned the proper details not from popular tradition but from
inquisitors' sermons and from reports of earlier trials. Both in
general themes and in specific details, judicial records are thus likely
to reflect influences other than pure folk tradition.

On the other hand, one should not give up in despair on the
assumption that all judicial documents are uniformly subject to
corruption by learned influence. In a small number of cases, the
ipsissima verba of the accusers are recorded, or at least close paraphrases: the testimony given by the original witnesses, made at the
beginning of proceedings, before the formal interrogation of the
subjects, and before the application of coercive measures. In a few
cases, to be sure, the original accusations were made by members
of the educated élite; in a few others, they came from persons already
convicted of witchcraft, who were exposed to the judges' notions of
the crime during their own interrogations, and were later asked to
incriminate their supposed accomplices. But in most instances the
original depositions represent the sentiments of the witch's neighbours, who sought to secure her conviction. Out of about 500 witch
trials between 1300 and 1500, these depositions survive in only
twenty-one cases. Fifteen come from Switzerland,[4] three from
Germany,[5] and three from France.[6] The preponderance of Swiss
trials is not surprising; in general, the judicial records from Switzerland are more abundant than for most other regions, frequently with
fuller information for individual trials. And there is enough evidence
of various types from other regions that it is reasonably easy to
discern those respects in which Swiss cases are or are not distinctive.[7] Apart from these twenty-three cases there are fourteen further
trials in which the proceedings were initiated by the persons who

had been accused of witchcraft. Desiring to clear their reputations, they brought charges of defamation against their accusers. Seven of these are from Swiss towns,[8] six from England,[9] and one from Germany.[10] In this case the high number of records from England is interesting, and can probably be explained as a result of the relatively lenient views of English judges, who were frequently more inclined to try those persons who had defamed others than to punish the witch suspects themselves. In these trials for defamation there was no reason for either the judge or the plaintiff to introduce extraneous, distinctively learned concepts of witchcraft, and the notions recorded may once again be taken as faithful reflections of popular tradition. One might hypothesize various reasons why one or another of these thirty-five trials (including both groups) could have been influenced by originally learned notions, but they are the most reliable texts available, and the likelihood of their contamination is so slight that one may confidently use them as touchstones for analysis of further documents.

Apart from these thirty-five trials, there are certain categories of trial which taken as classes are superior to others, even though individual trials within these groups may be unreliable. Thus, trials from England, where there was less judicial coercion than on the Continent, are less likely to reflect learned notions, though in certain specific English cases one may suspect the heavy hand of an educated judge in the statement of charges. Likewise, secular courts were in general less prone to transmission of learned concepts than were ecclesiastical courts. Lay tribunals were not wholly immune to ideas that developed in theological and judicial scholarship. There are many cases in which secular authorities maintained close contact with inquisitors, and could easily assimilate ideas that originated in clerical circles.[11] Furthermore, some lay judges could read Latin treatises on demonology; and many of these men were certainly familiar with vernacular works which eventually translated late medieval demonology into an attenuated but still vivid idiom.[12] Thus, the records of secular courts have no absolute claim to reliability as repositories of popular tradition, but as a class they may be judged more trustworthy than ecclesiastical records. Even within secular tribunals, one must differentiate between records written in Latin and those drawn up in the vernacular. It is seldom possible to ascertain definitely whether there was anyone in the court who had personally read the current demonological literature, or whether there was a written formulary at hand for use in interrogations, but these influences were more likely in trials for which the records were composed in Latin. Hence, the documents in the vernacular form a third class of relatively reliable texts, alongside English records and those of lay courts generally.

It might seem useful to distinguish further between trials initiated 'from above' and those begun 'from below.' When inquisitorial procedure was introduced into European courts it was no longer necessary for the authorities to wait for accusation from the aggrieved parties before instigating prosecution. One of the main points of inquisitorial procedure was that it permitted judicial officials to act on their own initiative.[13] Virtually all the witch trials of the fourteenth and fifteenth centuries seem to have employed inquisitorial procedure, in that there was no formal accuser who took upon himself responsibility for proving the charges. Yet this does not mean that these trials all began 'from above' in any absolute sense. Even when the procedure was inquisitorial, prosecution typically began in response to popular complaint. At times the records state explicitly that proceedings began both *ex mero officio* and *fama publica referente*.[14] Even in those relatively rare cases in which inquisitors made use of a 'general inquisition' to uproot witchcraft from an entire community, their own concern was supplemented by that of the witnesses (usually laymen) on whom they relied for names and specific charges.[15] It was always possible for inquisitors themselves to furnish the specific data for initiating trials, but evidently this seldom happened, and even when they did act on their own suspicions they no doubt typically solicited and obtained corroboration from the populace. In short, most witch trials appear to have been products of cooperation, in some form or other, between the people and the authorities. (And there is no reason whatsoever to think that the general populace was uncooperative; local authorities resisted proceedings on rare occasions, but even in the celebrated trial at Innsbruck in 1485 the witches' neighbors brought forth accusations enthusiastically.) In the majority of cases witnesses from the population were heard, whether they came forth spontaneously to state their grievances or whether judges sought them out. Unfortunately, the records seldom indicate how the witnesses got to court. For present purposes, however, the question is of little significance, since the initiative for prosecution did not necessarily have bearing on the content of the charges. So long as the populace played a role, popular beliefs were likely to enter into the accusations; and in any type of trial there was the possibility that popular notions would be overlaid with distinctively learned opinions. It was perhaps more likely that learned tradition would take precedence when authorities manifested their own spontaneous concern with witchcraft, either by holding general inquisitions or by acting on their own suspicions about specific defendants. But such cases were apparently rare, and are generally impossible to isolate on the basis of surviving documents.

Turning, then, to the records which are individually of high reliability, one finds fundamental commonalities. When witnesses' depositions or charges of defamation survive, the overwhelming emphasis is upon sorcery. Occasionally there were further charges: in a few Swiss trials the defendants were supposed to have ridden on wolves, and in a minority of trials the defendants had allegedly invoked demons for the fulfillment of their wishes.[16] But the charge of diabolism—with veneration of the devil, formation of a pact, reception of the devil's mark, attendance at the Sabbath, flight through the air on route to the Sabbath, ritual repudiation of Christian faith, intercourse with *incubi* or *succubi*, and so forth—is altogether absent from these records. If these trials are typical—and further evidence will suggest that they are—diabolism played little or no role in popular belief.

To elucidate the nature of these trials, it may be useful to examine some of the ones for which relatively extensive records have survived. The trial of Dorothea Hindremstein from Lucerne, in the mid-fifteenth century, is in many ways typical.[17] After a minor quarrel, Dorothea had allegedly inflicted a sickness of three weeks' duration on a neighbor's child; the sorceress had made some kind of vague threat to the child, and the illness that ensued was taken as the result of this curse. Other townsmen tried as best they could to avoid dealings with the woman, for fear that they might antagonize her and suffer bewitchment by her. Yet willy-nilly they came into contact with her, and the resultant conflicts terminated with sundry diseases, cows that gave blood instead of milk, and doubtless many other complaints. Witnesses furthermore swore that Dorothea had used a magical rite to multiply a quantity of cereal, so as to provide enough to feed ten people. The subject herself was not accused of diabolism, but oddly a possessed woman had accused her once of being a witch, claiming to know this on the authority of Beelzebub.

In this case, then, even one of the accusers had closer contact with Satan than did the sorceress herself.

When another woman went before the town court several years later, the accusations were more diverse, yet they still did not encompass diabolism.[18] The records of this trial are replete with cows that yield nothing but blood, storms produced by maleficent magic, shriveled onions, geese that have gone mad, and so forth, but the devil makes no appearance. The subject is supposed to have caused pain in another woman's bosom by approaching her one day, grasping her on the breast, and asking why she was so wanton with her breasts. On another occasion, the subject's children were discussing their respective pets with certain playmates, and divulged the information that their mother kept pet foxes and wolves, which she fed when their father was away from home. Other witnesses told that they had seen the woman riding on a wolf—though neither to nor from a Sabbath. Anyone familiar with the demonological literature of the century would have had ample occasion to suggest the charge of diabolism, but so far as the record shows no one made this transition.

Two trials from the diocese of Lausanne are especially instructive, since they include both the witnesses' depositions and the later records of interrogation, and they make abundantly clear that popular tradition emphasized sorcery, while the learned tradition of the judges focused on diabolism. In the first instance, in 1464, the accused was a woman named Perrussone Gapit.[19] The first two witnesses told of bewitchments they had suffered: one had eaten some pears that Perrussone had cooked, and predictably he had become so ill that he could scarcely arise from bed. The mother of a newborn baby alleged that Perrussone had tried to kidnap the infant. After one thwarted attempt, as Perrussone ran away from the house, the mother tried to call out, 'Wicked woman, you shall not have him!' but was mysteriously unable to utter the words. At length, Perrussone succeeded in killing the infant. More than that, one day she placed her hand on another child's head, causing paralysis in the child's right side. The judge asked one witness whether he had heard Perrusonne recite the creed, and the man said he had, but only in an unintelligible mutter, 'in the manner of old people.' The first interrogation of the subject herself was conducted by a notary and his assistants, and dealt exclusively with the witnesses' charges. Perrusonne either denied the allegations or gave different interpretations of the events. For example, she admitted having gone to the bedroom of the mother with the newborn baby, yet claimed that her motive was not kidnapping, but merely solicitude for the mother. Soon afterwards, however, an inquisitorial vicar entered the case. Within two days, he had the subject confessing that she had attended diabolical assemblies, had intercourse with the devil (who, true to form, was unbearably cold and ugly), and paid homage to the devil both in human form and in the shape of a bear. On one occasion she had kissed the bear as a sign of homage, and soon afterward the beast had scratched her so roughly on the finger that she feared it had come off; indeed, even at the time of the interrogation it was still sore. In the company of devil-worshippers she had been induced to kill children and raise storms. In these last-mentioned details the inquisitor shared with the original accusers an interest in sorcery. But he was above all concerned with diabolism, and with a modicum of inducement—at least some of the confessions were extracted under torture—he succeeded in eliciting the expected information.

A trial in the same diocese at the end of the century was analogous.[20] The witnesses focused upon the powers of the accused, a man named François, to raise storms and bewitch cattle. Several persons related a curious episode in which the accused appeared to have fallen to the ground from out of a storm-cloud. But once again, the inquisitor set aside these relatively mild offenses and proceeded to more extravagant charges. François was made to confess that he had gone to diabolical assemblies, eaten the flesh of decapitated babies, made magical powder from the bones of these infants, and so forth. Pressed further by the inquisitor, he named his accomplices in these activities. Before making these confessions, though, François attempted an unusual argument in his own defense: he denied that he was a witch, and as evidence cited the fact that demons communicate with witches, but that no demon had ever spoken with him. Thus the accused was familiar with the idea of invocation, even though it did not arise in the depositions of his accusers.

Once again for a trial at Boucoiran in 1491 both the original deposition of witnesses and later testimony of the accused survive, and the pattern is the same as in the trials already discussed.[21] The trial in this case was sparked by a rash of sudden deaths among infants and animals. Witnesses testified that the subject and her mother had both been known as sorceresses; they furthermore told of the promiscuous life that the subject had led. After their depositions there is a lacuna in the manuscript. When the record resumes the interrogation is underway: the accused is telling how a demon appeared to her one night in the form of a tall man with a raucous voice, in which he proclaimed to his terrified devotee, 'I am the devil, and you shall call me Robin.' The further revelations are largely elaborations on her allegiance to this demon.

Most of the remaining documents merely confirm the impressions already obtained. Some of them are extremely brief, and contain little information on the allegations. The charges vary slightly, as in one trial in which the accusers insisted that the accused had carried out divination.[22] In no case did the witnesses charge the defendants with diabolism. There are three extended reports though, that deserve special attention because of their exceptional character. In all of these the witnesses did charge that the accused had in some way invoked demons, but not that they had paid homage to them.

In a trial at Basel in 1407 various women were charged with use of spells and potions.[23] They had brought certain of their victims to their graves, had inflicted illness on others, and stirred others to infatuation. In some cases, the spells called upon the saints, the wounds and nails of Christ, and so forth. Other formulas, however, had explicitly enjoined devils and werewolves to tear the victims asunder, suck the blood out of their hearts, and accomplish other morbid tasks. One book of magic included the pictures of numerous devils, painted red, black, and blue. Yet one receives the impression that these sorceresses probably relied on purely natural substances at least as much as on supernatural agencies: the records speak explicitly of poison.

The next case is in Provence, in 1439.[24] A woman named Catherine David had gone to a sorcerer to request a potion that she could give to her father, so as to induce him to disinherit his three other daughters and leave his entire estate to her. One of the witnesses, though, gave a vital item of information: it was not the sorcerer himself who had concocted the magical potion; he had obtained it from a demon named Barrabas. So far as the witnesses' depositions go, this is all that was involved; there was no diabolism of any sort. In the later interrogations the sorcerer admitted that Barrabas had appeared to him several times in prison in the shape of a black cat, but even then the cat did not require the obscene homage that his counterparts demanded at the Sabbath, or any other sign of veneration.

Likewise, the charge of contact with devils arose briefly and peripherally in the trials at Innsbruck in 1485.[25] Significantly, the inquisitor here was a man unquestionably qualified to introduce notions of diabolism into the trial: Henry Institoris, principal author of the *Malleus maleficarum*. His witnesses claimed that their assailants had bewitched them by use of numerous magical substances: powders, hairs of men or animals, bones of unbaptized babies, and even excrement procured from the town's Jewish quarter. Buried within about forty pages of such testimony, though, are a few passing references to the devil. One set of witnesses told that sorcery was accomplished by invocation of the devil, and that a certain maid had practiced sorcery by using shavings of red colour from pictures of St Christopher and of the devil.[26] Another witness told how one of her neighbours would sometimes call upon the devil's aid in bringing her husband home.[27] Yet another related a guaranteed way to force a sorceress to reveal herself when she had been stealing milk from a cow: one only needed to hang a milk-pail over a fire and beat on it 'in the devil's name.'[28] And one sorceress had, according to a witness, instructed young girls and other persons how to bring about love or illness through invoking the devil.[29] In about forty pages of testimony this is all the witnesses had to say about matters diabolical. In contrast with confessions that both ecclesiastical and secular courts had been eliciting for decades, this sort of accusation is mild indeed.

It is interesting to note that in this case there is proportionally more about the devil in the inquisitor's comments on the testimony than in the testimony itself. The trial was not allowed to complete its normal course. Zealous as the inquisitor was, he encountered determined resistance from episcopal authorities, and was forced to end his prosecution. In hopes that someone else would resume where he left off, he furnished instructions for further proceedings, making it clear that the charge of diabolism would have come far more to the fore if the trial had gone on. In one instance he suggested that a sorceress's pact with the devil should be investigated;[30] in another, he stated that the devil always forces a witch to reveal herself through words or actions;[31] he was especially eager to find information about unguents prepared by diabolical art from the bodies of unbaptized children.[32] None of these notions had occurred in the witnesses' depositions, but one may be sure that if the inquisitor had had his way they would have found their place in the suspects' eventual confessions.

The trials for defamation frequently give less information than those with witnesses' depositions; they sometimes convey only the meagre information that one person had called another a witch. When the type of witchcraft receives elaboration, though, it is clear that it consisted of sorcery alone, and not diabolism. For example, in one trial three men were admonished for having accused two women of using a stake 'to bind virile members so that they are incapable of coition.'[33] In another case the defendants were fined for accusing two women of love magic.[34] In these trials, as in the deposition of witnesses, there is no mention of diabolism.

In short, the thirty-five most reliable trials point to a clear conclusion: in the majority of cases, the townsmen or villagers who took their neighbors to court did so for essentially practical reasons. They felt that these individuals were noxious creatures, who were undermining their health and welfare. Though in a few cases the accusers suggested that bewitchment was accomplished through invocation of the devil, there is no indication of popular belief in veneration of the devil. No ritual contact with him was alleged, and even the nature of the connection was generally left unspecified. The devil appears in these documents more as a legendary figure of folklore than as the master of a demonic cult. Historians have traditionally contrasted English and Continental diabolism, portraying the former as less extravagant than the latter. But the most reliable texts show no major difference at the popular level between English witch beliefs and those of the Continent. The idea of diabolism, developed and elaborated on the Continent, was evidently the product of speculation by theologians and jurists, who could make no sense of sorcery except by postulating a diabolical link between the witch and her victim.

The conclusion that these superior documents suggest, then, is not merely that the accused were innocent of diabolism, and that their confessions were extracted through the techniques of inquisitorial justice. The position here is a far more radical one: that so far as reliable evidence reveals the charge of diabolism was not even grounded in contemporary popular belief. To be sure, this conclusion is by no means self-evident: anthropological work among non-Western peoples has shown amply that notions closely akin to those

of Christian demonology can and do arise among the unsophisticated, at least in some types of society.[35] But to determine whether
ideas of this sort developed or were common among people at large
in early Europe one must restrict oneself to documents from the
period and region in question; this type of commonality between
early European and non-Western cultures cannot merely be
assumed.

Apart from the documents which are of optimal reliability as
individual texts, there are the classes of document which taken
together are relatively reliable. These confirm the conclusions
already proposed. The notion of diabolism occurred only with
extreme rarity in English trials, and when it arose it was clearly the
result of learned influence.[36] Whereas it arose in fully 54 per cent
of the ecclesiastical trials, it appeared in only about 11 per cent of
the cases in secular courts. And while secular records in Latin
contain reference to diabolism about 27 per cent of the time, those
in the vernacular make such reference in only 6 per cent of the
cases.[37] The correlation is unmistakable: in those courts which
were most likely to transmit learned notions, the charge of diabolism
was most likely to occur. Thus, even if analysis of these superior
documents is not absolutely compelling, its suggestions are un-
equivocal; the basis that they furnish for the proposed conclusions
is firmer than any evidence yet adduced for contrary hypotheses.

It should be pointed out, incidentally, that even if one accepts
Lamothe-Langon's evidence as authentic the present conclusions
are unaffected. Lamothe-Langon speaks of one trial in which the
inquisitor told the accused women that witnesses had seen them
at a Sabbath. Presumably the accusers in this instance are supposed
to have been persons already convicted of witchcraft.[38] But Lamothe-
Langon does not present any cases in which the original deposition
of witnesses or charges of defamation survive. Because his cases are
Continental trials before ecclesiastical tribunals, inclusion of them
in the above-cited statistics would if anything provide a stronger
case for present arguments.

Further evidence for the distinction between popular and learned
notions can be furnished by analysis of the patterns of prosecution.
Briefly stated, the charges of sorcery and diabolism increased in
frequency in different times and under different circumstances. Thus,
the concern with these two offenses can best be explained as arising
from distinct causes. As already suggested, the heightened concern

with sorcery (during the third phase of prosecution) was apparently the result of numerous factors, including the introduction of inquisitorial procedure into secular courts, the social effects of the Black Death, and no doubt many other considerations. None of these factors, however, can explain the later spread throughout Europe of trials specifically for diabolism (in the fourth phase); the chronological lag cannot be explained away. The later development can best be accounted for as a reaction of the intellectual élite to the rise in trials for sorcery. Theologians and jurists in the late fourteenth and early fifteenth centuries evidently recognized that there were important developments occurring in the lawcourts, with widespread trials for sorcery, and sometimes also for diabolism. For reasons that can most conveniently be discussed in a later chapter, these members of the intellectual élite could not make sense of sorcery except by assuming that the devil had a role in it. This conclusion is clearly reflected in the demonological and judicial literature of the period, and the dissemination of this literature made the stress on diabolism all the more pronounced in the courts. As suggested in the last chapter, the leading role of the educated élite in the development of diabolism and in its passage from the schools to the courtroom readily explains why Italy—the country where both ecclesiastical and secular judges were exposed at an early date to learned traditions —was the first land to witness a dramatic increase in trials for diabolism. These patterns of prosecution would not by themselves prove that sorcery and diabolism derived from distinct traditions, but analysis of these patterns tends to reinforce the conclusions reached on other grounds.

One type of text, however, remains to be discussed. The canonical collections of the high Middle Ages included a number of canons proscribing not witchcraft, but belief in phenomena that later became associated with witchcraft. The most influential text was the canon *Episcopi*, issued around the turn of the tenth century, and later incorporated in the collections of Burchard of Worms, Ivo of Chartres, and Gratian.[39] This canon condemned women who believed that they rode about at night in the company of a pagan goddess, known to the author of the text as Diana. At the end of the canon there is an extraneous sentence condemning belief in the transformation of men into animal shape. Traditionally, scholars have viewed this and similar canons as manifestations of early medieval rationalism: instead of condemning and burning witches, the authors of these texts condemned the superstitious belief that such occurrences are real. Recently, however, Jeffrey Russell and Erik Midelfort have independently pointed out, with full justification, that the attitude of the author of the canon *Episcopi* is not rationalist; this author condemned the specified beliefs not as mere errors that needed correction, but as diabolically inspired illusions, whose adherents were subject to severe penalties.[40] In any event, one might argue that legal texts of this sort were directed against popular belief in diabolism—belief whose survival is indicated by the repeated issuance of the canons. Two observations, though, are apposite. First, there are important differences between the beliefs condemned in these canons and the ideas regarding diabolism that were elaborated and blended together in later demonology. The canon *Episcopi*, composed not long after the Christianization of northern Europe, is part of a long series of texts designed to combat pagan survivals.[41] In accordance with the standard *interpretatio Christiana*, the translation of pagan notions into Christian terms,[42] the author equated pagan deities with demons, and attributed the popular belief in nightly rides to the suggestion of malign spirits. But the *intepretatio Christiana* did not suggest that pagans recognized the true identity of their gods and persisted in venerating them despite this knowledge, as in diabolism. Nor did this interpretation imply that there was any sort of reciprocal pact between the devil and his adherents. Although the notion of a nightly ride was later incorporated into the complex of witch beliefs, it is incorrect to state that the canon *Episcopi* condemned either witchcraft or belief in witchcraft, unless one defines witchcraft in an uncommonly broad sense.[43] Second, the continued issuance of this canon in judicial collections does not show its continued applicability. Persistent need for a law is only one reason for its repeated issuance; throughout the Middle Ages, many laws were repeated and borrowed simply because they were incorporated in established, authoritative, and conveniently accessible bodies of prior legislation.[44]

It is likely that beliefs more or less similar to those condemned in the canon *Episcopi* persisted on a popular level, though the evidence is almost exclusively literary, and it would be futile to estimate the extent or distribution of such survivals.[45] In any event, this speculation says very little about the status that such beliefs held in folk tradition. There are, after all, different types of folklore. Some folk beliefs are practical and immediate, in the sense that they are of potential relevance to one's day-to-day affairs; others are remote, and pertain to distant or undefined spatio-temporal realms, which the believers do not expect to be relevant to their own lives. The boundary may be fluid, and what one member of a culture takes as a mere fairy-tale may be the occasion of anxiety for another member who perceives the dangers related as threatening him personally. The essential point remains firm: the occurrence of a folklore motif within a culture is no evidence that this motif had practical consequences for those who related it. People in the late Middle Ages may have told stories about women who went on mysterious nightly rides, and they may have believed that these things actually occurred in some unspecified time and place. That does not necessarily mean that they expected these women to come flying through their own windows, or that they were prepared to accuse their neighbors of such activities. And there is absolutely no evidence that these beliefs mingled on a popular level with notions of sorcery. A late medieval villager might take his neighbor to court for bewitching his wife, and he might also believe in the remote possibility of women who went on nocturnal rides with some mysterious goddess. But if any such villager took the sorceress to court on both charges the case has apparently escaped reliable historical record. Even on a learned level it would be difficult to pinpoint elements of witch beliefs that must have been taken from this body of folklore.

It might be objected that, while the arguments thus far advanced show that witch beliefs were not rooted in popular tradition, they may still have had foundation in actual fact. In other words, even if people at large did not think of their neighbors as venerating the devil, the neighbors may in fact have been doing so anyway. It must be admitted that in some instances charges of witchcraft clearly were based on *misinterpreted* rituals of one sort or another. The secret assemblies of heretics lent themselves to misrepresentation, and inquisitors seem to have taken advantage of the opportunity. In some cases, communities prosecuted for witchcraft were probably groups of Waldensian heretics pure and simple.[46] The charges of witchcraft were sometimes grafted on to standard doctrinal charges made against Waldensians.[47] In other cases the supposed witches were described as simulating orthodox piety to evade detection—a common feature of Waldensians throughout Europe.[48] It is also likely that isolated remnants of the pagan past were interpreted during the witch prosecutions as forms of diabolism. It is especially likely that some of the Italian trials centered about cultic vestiges of paganism, though (as shown in the last chapter) the rituals involved do not indicate the existence of an organized cult, and the practitioners do not generally seem to have perceived any disharmony between their rites and Christianity.[49] There were all sorts of popular festivals, some traditional and some probably spontaneous, that inquisitors and secular judges may have found suspect, even if they actually had no inherent religious character. Thus, the bailli of Briançonnais made inquiry in 1395 into the popular celebration of the *ludus Stelle*, in which men of Valpute gathered periodically for festivity under a leader known as the *rex Ribaldorum*. As Jean Marx has observed, affairs of this kind may have given rise to charges of diabolism.[50]

It is furthermore conceivable that occasional eccentrics may actually have venerated the devil. Heretics, dualist or otherwise, may have gone to extremes at times in their unorthodox rites, and may have venerated a person or animal representing Satan. Perhaps more importantly, it is possible that people who heard inquisitors' sermons may eventually have taken their cues from the preachers' diatribes, carrying out in action what was originally sheer fantasy. The colonial police in Rhodesia, who investigated witch accusations to prove them false, routinely had women confess that they had performed patently impossible acts, such as riding on hyenas and pouring poison down the throats of sleeping men. But in one case subjects claimed to have killed a child, cut his body in half, and then eaten it, and when the police searched for the corpse they indeed found only half of it. In this instance the subjects evidently acted out fantasies which their society suggested to them.[51] It is possible that similar occurrences happened in late medieval Europe. To be sure, some historians have been unduly accommodating in their effort to interpret the phenomena of the witches' Sabbath as plausible and real occurrences. For example, some scholars cite recipes for hallucinogenic ointments that are supposed to have given witches the sensation of flying through the air.[52] These recipes can be traced back no further than Johannes Weyer, a sixteenth-century physician whose intent was to explain witch beliefs away in rationalist terms. Furthermore, according to both court records and demonological literature, at least from the period 1300–1500, the witches' supposed ointment was usually applied not to their bodies but to the sticks or other implements on which they rode.[53] The amount that would rub into their bodies would thus be minimal. Still, even if one dismissed many of the details of the Sabbath as imaginative embellishments, it is conceivable that anti-authoritarian, devil-worshipping assemblies may have taken place. Their occurrence is not demonstrable, but it is conceivable.

Hypothetical atypicalities, however, are of little historical interest. And the evidence at hand suggests that actual diabolism, if engaged in at all, can scarcely have been of frequent occurrence. If it had been common, it would surely have attracted more attention, and would have come forth in the original accusations. The best available evidence does not even suggest that misunderstood festivals or rites served frequently as a basis for witch trials. Where the mechanism of prosecution is at all perceptible, charges seem most commonly to have originated in three types of circumstance: first, persons who in fact engaged in sorcery were taken to court, where they might furthermore be charged with diabolism; second, beneficent magicians or practitioners of folk medicine, distrusted by the authorities and perhaps also by their clients, were taken to court for sorcery and convicted of witchcraft in one or more of its species; third, persons who practiced neither sorcery nor beneficent magic nor folk medicine might become embroiled in quarrels with their neighbors, find themselves accused of sorcery, and be left at the mercy of a court. Trials of these kinds are far more numerous than those in which the surviving evidence suggests the genuine occurrence of ritual gatherings, whether properly or improperly understood. The number of cases of the latter sort can be multiplied only by further manuscript discoveries—which are not likely to outbalance currently known evidence—or by sheer conjecture.

It might be argued that even if diabolical rites were in fact being practiced they would be secret and unknown to the witnesses. Thus, they would be revealed only in the course of judicial interrogation. It is known that heretics such as Waldensians avoided prosecution for decades through systematic dissimulation. Devil-worshippers might have done much the same thing. If their ceremonies even approximated the descriptions given in the judicial and demonological texts, they must have been more difficult to conceal than the discreet assemblies of the Waldensians, but in principle it is possible that they would have been veiled in secrecy. Yet this line of argument is ineffective for two reasons. First of all, it is wholly speculative; even if the possibility of genuine diabolism remains, the only solid evidence at hand is that which suggests that sorcery was the routine basis for prosecution. Second, if diabolism was well concealed, why would the authorities be the ones to detect it? They were if anything in less contact with the offenders than were people from the general community (whose cooperation in ordinary heresy trials must always have been essential); they had less opportunity to observe people's comings and goings, and to develop suspicions about their behavior. Hence, even if the rites were secret one would expect them to be uncovered, if at all, in popular testimony. The proposed argument could only be salvaged by postulating that the offenders were taken to court on some charge other than diabolism (whether sorcery or some wholly unrelated accusation), and that in the course of proceedings it was discovered that they were in fact guilty of devil-worship. But a thesis that needs to be defended this circuitously scarcely deserves defense.

Recognizing the lack of specific evidence for the period in question, historians have frequently adduced historical parallels as grounds for believing in the actuality of diabolism, as also of antinomianism. The argument is that there are known cases of groups that have practiced antinomianism, or diabolism, or both, particularly in modern and contemporary society. Thus it is viewed as likely that such allegations in early Europe were based on a kernel of fact.[54] Yet there are also contrary cases in which accusations of antinomianism have been false.[55] Thus, reference to historical parallels is methodologically unsound. Without specific evidence for the cases in question, one cannot determine which parallels are applicable; the best one can do is speculate one way or the other. Because there is no reliable specific evidence to demonstrate or refute the reality of diabolism in the fourteenth and fifteenth centuries, the only facts that one can take as at all established are those pertaining to popular beliefs about witchcraft. Rather than making assumptions on the basis of mere intuition, it is better to make use of whatever evidence is at hand. This means taking the judicial texts of optimal reliability and using them first as touchstones for popular belief, but second as grounds for decision regarding actual practice. And given the information that is available, diabolism seems to have played little or no role in either belief or practice on a popular level.

There are two classes of document, then, that do not raise great methodological difficulty. Those containing original depositions or charges of defamation may be accepted as having optimal value. Those containing reference to diabolism, on the other hand, may safely be dismissed as contaminated by the influence of learned tradition. In between these two extremes, however, lies the largest class of records. In the majority of cases there are neither original depositions nor charges of diabolism; thus, while there is no positive evidence that these records contain learned tradition, neither is there any assurance that they relate popular belief. In this middle class, any act of sorcery that is reported may have been suggested to the accused by the judge, and the confession may have been extorted through the same means of judicial coercion that were used in trials for diabolism. What evidential value, then, does this mass of documents have? The problem is solved by an examination of the charges in these texts. In all essential respects, they are identical with the accusations in the texts of optimal reliability. Not only is sorcery the primary offence specified in them, but the kinds of sorcery, and even the fundamental conception of the nature of sorcery, are the same, whereas investigation in a later chapter will show that learned tradition brought above pervasive changes in all these areas.[56] The clear implication is that judges did not use judicial coercion merely to force the accused to confess more acts of bewitchment, or to place in the mouth of the defendant admissions of sorcery that arose from a distinctively learned tradition. When the courts used judicial coercion, they sought a much more radical transformation of the charges. With all due caution, one may thus conclude that the majority of trials, lacking as they are in any reference to diabolism, convey an understanding of witchcraft which is not in any important way modified by distinctively learned tradition.

A further problem arises in trials in which, while there is no mention of diabolism, either the witnesses or the suspects belonged to the literate élite. In certain fourteenth-century political trials, for example, both the accusers and the accused were clerics. In other political trials members of the clergy may well have taken part in the formulation of charges. It would obviously be hazardous to use cases of this sort as evidence for popular notions. Yet on the other hand the content of the accusations is frequently the same as in superior texts. After all, the fact that a man was literate and cultured did not make him impervious to popular notions. Many of these ideas would remain prominent in his intellectual outlook, along with the learned beliefs that he adopted. The documents in this class may thus serve as supporting evidence for popular tradition, though their use in any given context must be accompanied by an explicit warning that the source of evidence is not ideal.

There are, then, four classes of document; in descending order of reliability, they are: first, original depositions of witnesses or charges of defamation; second, texts consistent with those in the first class in their content, with no apparent potential source of learned influence; third, texts consistent with those in the first class in their content, with information deriving (or probably deriving) from a member of the intellectual élite; and, fourth, texts containing charges of diabolism. In most cases a document can be assigned clearly to one of these four classes. In a few exceptional instances the first portion of a judicial text will fit into the first or second category, while the remainder (usually testimony given under the influence of judicial coercion) will belong to the fourth; in cases of this kind, the separate sections must be dealt with independently. The first three classes of document, which may collectively be designated 'superior' texts, will be analyzed in the following chapter. The fourth, or 'inferior' texts, will be discussed separately in Chapter V.

If this ranking were based on an *a priori* methodological postulate, it would of course be circular. It would proceed from the assumption that diabolism occurs only in corrupt texts, and would then establish reference to diabolism as a criterion of corruptness. The method used here, though, is quite different. Inherently superior records are isolated on formal grounds, and on investigation are found to share material commonalities (especially preoccupation with sorcery rather than diabolism). These material features are then taken as a criterion for further grading of texts. The matter is one of basic empirical procedure. If investigation shows that all ravens are black, then a red bird is unlikely to be a raven. If inquiry shows that all available demonstrably superior documents allege sorcery and invocation alone—and especially if there is further evidence that broad classes of relatively reliable documents tend strongly to give only these charges—then sources that speak of diabolism are in all likelihood not superior. In empirical inquiry one deals, of course, with probabilities, and the chance of counterexamples can never be dismissed. In the present case one is hampered by paucity of data, and the findings may not be as definitive as one might hope; witch trials are unfortunately more difficult to survey than ravens. Yet the lack of absolute certainty does not vitiate the conclusions.

One further methodological problem remains. As already suggested, witch trials appear to have arisen most commonly from three types of circumstance: use of sorcery, use of beneficent magic or folk medicine, and mere quarrels. Thus, while the popular notions of witchcraft revealed in the court records are in some instances based on fact, in other cases they are not. The folklore revealed in the documents is therefore of two sorts. There is a folklore of practice, consisting of what people actually did if they wanted to bewitch their fellow townspeople. And there is a folklore of belief, consisting of what the accusers thought was being done to them (or their relatives, or property, or animals). Unfortunately, it is in most cases impossible to determine which category a particular charge falls into. The difficulty is, however, not crucial. The important questions for present purposes are whether a particular form of sorcery was believed effective and whether it aroused concern. And to answer questions of this order one does not need to know whether the charges in any particular case were true or false. Furthermore, one may probably assume a high degree of fluidity between popular belief and popular practice. If a form of magic was widely believed effective it would occasionally be attempted, and if a type of magic was in fact commonly tried it would eventually arouse considerable concern. The primary object of study, then, is the context of belief which on some occasions gave rise to actual employment of maleficent magic.

Chapter IV
The Content of Popular Tradition

Intellectual and cultural historians have traditionally referred to the intellectual assumptions of the educated élite as constituting the early European world-view. The beliefs of the uneducated populace regarding the spiritual and material worlds have meanwhile remained in large part *terra incognita*. Only certain salient features of the popular mind, and particularly of popular religion, are genuinely well known. It would lead too far astray to attempt a general survey of popular religious and cosmological notions, but one should at least bear in mind that the widespread preoccupation with sorcery was part of a general framework that encouraged belief in superstition.[1] While literate members of the upper and middle classes were attracted by devotional and mystical movements, and a minority of extremists rejected the paraphernalia of Catholicism altogether, the bulk of the populace relied heavily on external observances, relics, pilgrimages, and rituals, in ever-increasing abundance. Churchmen endeavored (though with less than total consistency) to discourage overtly superstitious beliefs and practices, which seemed to compel magical results without affecting the spiritual life of the practitioner. But the distinction between superstition and legitimate devotion was largely one of intention, which was impossible to legislate or regulate. Even some of the Church's favored practices lent themselves readily to magical employment: examples such as the 'agnus dei,' a wax medallion made originally from paschal candles, come easily to mind. While some of these customs (veneration of wells, recitation of charms, etc.) can be traced directly to the paganism of western Europe, others (such as magical employment of saints' relics) were introduced by Christian missionaries. The general mentality that underlay these practices was in any case neither specifically pagan nor distinctively Christian; it was a natural result of circumstances in which religious leaders

47

exercized only loose control over the populace, and to a large degree shared the religious conceptions of the laity. The present chapter, then, will examine the superior documents from the witch trials in the attempt to shed further light on one aspect of this popular frame of mind.

As was stressed in the last chapter, the most frequent allegation in the superior texts is sorcery. It is not always possible to determine in detail what form of sorcery a witch is supposed to have perpetrated. Indeed, one general problem with the superior sources is that they tend to be shorter and less informative than the inferior ones, perhaps because scribes found Sabbaths and *incubi* more titillating than maleficent magic, and more worthy of detailed exposition. Whatever the reason, one commonly finds less information in the superior documents than one would like. In extreme cases they tell nothing more than that a particular person was tried 'for witchcraft,' or 'for sorcery.' Still, the mass of superior evidence, considered as a whole, does permit some estimation of the patterns of witchcraft in late medieval Europe.

The kinds of sorcery can be classified either according to the means or procedures that sorcerers employed (potions and powders, image magic, incantations, etc.) or according to the ends that they sought to accomplish. In the following exposition the main categories will be based upon the ends of sorcery, while within each main class there will be sub-classes based on means employed. The main kinds of sorcery—bodily harm, love magic, weather magic, and theft—will receive separate treatment. After this there will be a section dealing specifically with the means of sorcery. Finally, the charges other than sorcery will be discussed.

BODILY HARM

Trials for bodily harm (bringing sickness or death to men or animals) rank among the most abundant witch trials in the period 1300–1500. In addition, they fall more evenly throughout western Europe than do trials for other kinds of sorcery. In virtually every country for which there are known witch trials, this type of bewitchment was common.

The means used to bring physical harm were various. In some cases they involved direct and overt physical contact with the victim: pressing his chest, smearing him with an unguent, or beating him with a stick. These procedures, however, are found almost exclusively in the inferior texts, molded by learned tradition. The superior documents speak instead of subtler methods for inflicting harm: image magic, placement of magical substances in proximity to the person afflicted, and recitation of incantations. Administration of magical (or 'poisonous') food or drink lies midway between the extremes, since it entails direct contact with the person to whom the food is served, but the actual harm is not performed through the physical contact itself. Thus, bewitchment through such means is the only form that occurs commonly in both superior and inferior records. These differences are fairly easy to explain. If a sorcerer genuinely was attempting to bewitch his neighbor he would in all likelihood do so through indirect means, which might arouse some suspicion but would not make his responsibility altogether obvious. A sorceress would particularly be inclined to choose such means if she lacked both physical power and social influence, and was resorting to sorcery as her only possible way to attain some desired end— as seems frequently to have been the case. Likewise, if an alleged victim was seeking to explain some sudden illness as caused by sorcery it would in most cases be easier to postulate indirect means than to recall a plausible instance of physical assault by a likely suspect. When the defendant appeared in court, however, it would not be difficult for the judges to convict him or her of using direct means of bewitchment, for reasons to be discussed in the next chapter.[2]

Administering lethal potions and powders was one of the most common ways of killing someone or rendering him ill.[3] Perhaps it is not extravagant to see in this fact the mentality of a society ridden with plague. The popular attribution of this disease to poisoned water supply would, one might think, radically increase people's anxieties about the substances they were ingesting. Another reason for the popularity of this means—assuming now that sorcerers actually were using it—is that it worked more consistently than other means, particularly when natural poisons were used.

It must often have been difficult for contemporaries to decide whether the deleterious effect of a given food or drink was natural or magical. In proceedings at Innsbruck, Henry Institoris was uncertain whether an alleged sorceress had accomplished her victim's demise by poison or by bewitchment, though he inclined toward the latter suspicion on the peculiar grounds that the suspect had a history of sexual laxity, and was thus no doubt prone to such base activities as witchcraft.[4] If the active ingredient of the substance could be isolated and identified, experiments could be performed to determine whether it had the same effect in all circumstances, in which case its power would presumably be natural. But even if technology for such investigation had been available, the ingested substance would in most cases have been lost to inquirers in the mere act of digestion. (It is presumably for this reason that most of the relevant sources speak of the harmful substances only in vague terms, affording the historian no clue what materials were used in these crimes.) Not surprisingly, the Latin term *veneficium*, or 'poisoning', was applicable even in antiquity to both natural and magical species of harm. Likewise, lawcodes of the early and high Middle Ages tended to cite poisoning and this form of sorcery as closely analogous, if not equivalent, offenses.[5] The ambiguity prevails in the later judicial records, in which a given deed might be referred to indifferently as sorcery or as poisoning.[6] A woman beheaded at Appenzell had bewitched cattle, and had killed a neighbor by means of a 'poisoned' apple; it would be futile to speculate about the nature of the poison.[7] No doubt there were many instances in which a person with evil intentions would attempt both natural and magical poisons, with little concern for their metaphysical differences.

In some cases, to be sure, at least the external trappings were clearly magical. Thus, a priest in the diocese of Soissons in the mid-fifteenth century set out to wreak vengeance on his enemies.[8] He consulted a sorceress, who advised that he baptize a toad, giving it the name John, and administer a consecrated host to the creature. The priest did this, and then took the toad to the sorceress, who tore it to pieces. From the animal's remains she made poisons that were so potent that the priest's enemies perished miserably. Even if a genuinely poisonous substance was extracted from the toad,[9] the animal's baptism and viaticum cannot have contributed materially towards this result. Ultimately the sorceress also perished, though through the perfectly natural process of combustion.

Perhaps equally common as a means for inflicting bodily harm was image magic.[10] This is the best known species of what James Frazer called homeopathic magic, in which the harm done to a person's representation (made of wood, cloth, wax, lead, or some other material) is thought of as happening to the person himself.[11]

The antiquity of image magic is well documented, particularly for England. It was forbidden in the early medieval penitential of Ecgbert: 'If anyone drives stakes into [the image of] a man, let him fast for three years. . . .' The same penitential further recognizes the possible efficacy of this sorcery, and specifies that if the victim dies the perpetrator should fast for seven years.[12] The testimony of this text is supported by an example from the mid-tenth century. An English woman and her son attempted to kill a man named Aelsie by driving iron stakes into a representation of him. The 'deadly image' was discovered in their closet and removed. The woman was drowned, and the son, who escaped, was outlawed.[13] The same practice was forbidden a century and a half later, under the designation *invultuatio*, in the laws of Henry I.[14] It remained popular in the late Middle Ages. The practitioners sometimes claimed that their motive was to obtain the subjects' friendship—an excuse that seems to have met with skepticism from the judges.[15] The obvious end in most cases was illness or death of some enemy.

In some cultures such magic is sometimes accomplished by hostile action toward a person's shadow, or by desecration of a tablet on which his name is written.[16] In one trial in late fifteenth-century London a sorceress endeavored to commit murder by melting a wax candle, on the theory that 'as the candle consumes, the man [represented by the candle] must waste away.'[17] In most instances, though, late medieval sorcerers appear to have used more or less realistic figures, usually made of wax, in their image magic.

Around the turn of the century the bishop of St David's provoked a sorceress named Tanglost to use image magic against him.[18] She had been living adulterously with one Thomas Wyriott, until the bishop placed her in captivity for her marital offense. Her lover broke into the episcopal castle with the aid of twenty-four men, thus releasing the woman. When his lawful wife died soon afterwards rumour attributed the death to Tanglost's witchcraft. The bishop, upon hearing of this 'riotous dealing,' first imprisoned Tanglost anew and then banished her from his diocese. She then allegedly tried to retaliate by hiring two other women to assist her in making a series of wax representations of the bishop himself, so as to destroy him. If the charge was true—and Tanglost denied it—the women were apparently unsuccessful in their attempt.

Usually the wax image was first pricked with pins and then left by the victim's house, or in some other place where he would come into contact with it, though either step was apparently considered sufficient. A sorcerer in Florence pricked a wax image with pins, and then tried to suffocate it with incense and myrrh; he also wrote an inscription on another wax image, and buried it in a street over which his intended victim would walk.[19] The notion of piercing a wax image occurred again at Péronne in 1465,[20] while twenty years later a sorceress at Innsbruck was found to have deposited a strangely formed piece of wax in a victim's house.[21] In the same case at Innsbruck, a woman who suffered pains throughout her body solicited the aid of a certain potter, whose familiarity with magical arts enabled him to uncover a wax image under the woman's threshold. This figure, about the size of a person's hand, had been pierced with holes all over, while two needles that were still implanted in the wax lay in areas where the woman suffered most acutely: from her breast to her left shoulder, and from her breast to her back.[22] At roughly the same time a sorceress in Southwark was accused of burying images and other substances near a certain house, presumably for a similar purpose.[23] A Tyrolean sorceress attempted to kill a provost by using a variety of magical ploys, among them placement of a wax image under his choir seat.[24] More elaborate still were the preparations of learned sorcerers such as those at Milan who essayed the killing of Pope John XXII: their silver image, complete with genitalia, had symbols and names of demons inscribed on it, and was equipped so that substances could be placed in a cranial hole and then burned over a fire; before using this image for their maleficent purposes, the sorcerers incensed it for nine nights and exposed it to the elements for seventy-two nights. Though more refined than the procedures of the unlearned, these efforts were similar to those of popular magic in their basic conception.[25]

One remarkable feature of image magic is the frequency with which it occurs in political trials, or cases involving prominent personages. In the political cases during the first period of prosecution (1300–30) it was the most important single means of sorcery. To take one example for which there is relatively full information, image magic was central in the case at Coventry in 1324.[26] Twenty-seven discontented residents of this town are supposed to have solicited the aid of a sorcerer and his assistant in the undoing of their political lords: the king of England, the prior of Coventry, and others. Using seven pounds of wax and two ells of canvas, the sorcerer and his assistant made seven representations, one of which showed the king wearing his crown. The assistant then stuck a lead pin two inches into the forehead of one of the images, and the real victim at once suffered debilitating frenzy; the same image was pierced in the heart, and three days later death ensued. Before the rest of the victims could be given the same treatment, the assistant revealed the plot to the authorities, and the twenty-seven clients evidently destroyed the images to prevent their own incrimination. Similarly, the charge of image magic was routine in the French trials of this period, though information is seldom so full as in the Coventry affair.[27] When a plot against John XXII was uncovered in 1317, it was discovered that the conspirators had already killed the pope's favourite nephew through image magic. After this initial success they procured three wax figures from a Jew, baptized them (presumably to effect a mystical connection between the images and the persons with whose names they were baptized), and wrapped them in strips of parchment inscribed with ominous curses. The next step was to conceal the figures inside loaves of bread and smuggle them into the papal palace, but it was in this last step that the conspiracy became disclosed.[28] Later in the century, however, and even in the following century, image magic was still repeatedly employed or alleged in trials involving prominent figures.[29]

As already mentioned, wax images were sometimes placed in proximity to the person afflicted. With this exception, bewitchment through contact with magical substances occurred rarely; the only trial in which it was prominent was that of 1485 in Innsbruck.[30] Numerous different materials figured in this trial as maleficent charms: powders, wax, chalk, hair of men or animals, bones of unbaptized babies, nuts, fragments of wood from a gallows, threads from altar cloths, dead mice, and human excrement. One sorceress had allegedly rendered another woman delirious for more than half a year by sending her a bundle containing various such items.[31] Another sorceress placed charms of this kind under a woman's bed, causing a lingering illness and then death; to test the cause of this demise another woman tried lying in the bed, and found that she felt pain only when she lay in it, so that eventually she discovered the cause of the bewitchment.[32] A further case is important because it served as a model for a story in the *Malleus maleficarum*: a sorceress was performing a magical cure for a client's headache, and when her maid became irritated at the superstitious ceremonies the sorceress threatened her with a similar disease in three days. After the specified time the maid began suffering maddening pain in her head, and black, purulent boils covered her whole body. The sorceress's husband then grew angry, because the ill maid was unable to attend to the cattle as she was supposed to do. One day he discovered a linen bundle that someone, presumably his wife, had placed in the cow-stall. Taking it down and cutting it open, he found that it contained a yellowish powder (which according to the report looked like dried feces or gore), human hairs, and grains. When he cast these substances into a fire the maid was healed. He later warned his wife not to dabble in such activities any further, for fear that she would eventually get into serious trouble.[33] When another sorceress likewise used a bundle of eighteen different substances to inflict various maladies on an adversary, the latter consulted a seeress, who recommended throwing all the materials into a fire. When the recommendation was carried out the woman recovered her health.[34] On another occasion a sorceress cast bewitchment by rubbing a salve on a piece of cloth that was to be used in making a tunic.[35]

There are two similar episodes from a trial in fifteenth-century Todi.[36] In one, a man was bewitched by a feather that had been placed in his pillow; in the other, a sorcerer or sorceress had placed three black animals, described as looking like mice, under the threshold of a house, thus afflicting one—and, oddly, only one—of the residents.

The documents that survive for all these modes of sorcery seldom indicate the specific disease inflicted. Some of the sources refer to the illnesses as protracted,[37] but only a handful of records give details of the symptoms. When such information is forthcoming the diseases appear to be common ailments, which could be induced psychosomatically but could also occur naturally: lameness,[38] headache,[39] blindness,[40] boils,[41] and mental disturbance or delirium.[42] Approximately half the time the illness is recorded to have been fatal. Frequently, especially in trials involving important public figures, the alleged sorcery was unsuccessful.

In two known instances epidemics were popularly attributed to sorcery. In 1491 an epidemic at Boucoiran was killing babies and animals, according to the judicial record.[43] Eventually a likely suspect was found: a woman whose mother had earlier been thought of as a sorceress, and whose own immoral life was notorious. She was subjected to lengthy interrogation, and presumably sentenced to death. A similar occurrence at Marmande in 1453 led to an even more tragic outcome.[44] A serious epidemic of some unspecified disease had caused numerous deaths in the community, and the municipal authorities interrogated a certain woman who had been accused of causing the blight. When townsmen ascertained what was transpiring they said that they knew of many more sorceresses in the community who should likewise be arrested. The authorities did not act on this recommendation, so the assembled mob of two hundred or more people divided into two groups, each under a leader, and captured ten or eleven further suspects that very night, delivering them over to jail. Against the will of the authorities, two or three hundred people assembled the next day to determine what action they should take next. They decided to torture the suspects, and to capture one further woman. Within a few days the torture ensued, despite the legal irregularity of proceeding to torture without obtaining prior information or issuing an interlocutory sentence. Some of the women confessed under torture that they were sorceresses, and had killed numerous children through their arts. Those who made these admissions were burned, while two others died from the torture itself.

The subjects of bodily harm were by far most commonly human. But in eleven trials (mostly from Switzerland) there is reference to bewitchment of animals, either along with men or else alone.[45] When specific animals are mentioned, cattle are cited most frequently as suffering bewitchment, though occasionally other farm animals, such as pigs and horses, were afflicted. The reasons for affliction of farm animals seem clear enough: if a sorceress actually wished to injure a man she could jeopardize his very livelihood by bewitching these creatures. Furthermore, because farm animals typically lived in close proximity to their owners, some of them would perhaps command some measure of affection, so that they might have sentimental as well as financial value. Thus, even if there was no genuine attempt at bewitchment, illness or sudden death of these animals might naturally arouse suspicion of witchcraft. In one instance a farmer trapped a sorceress as she was entering his barn to carry out her maleficent work.[46] Presumably this woman intended to give the farmer's cattle a noxious powder or potion—a means of bewitchment that seems to have been favored for afflicting animals.

Although magical cures do not actually belong in a discussion of specifically maleficent magic, it is worth noting that in certain cases the same persons were supposed to heal diseases as well as inflict them. Thus, in the trial at Innsbruck in 1485 one sorceress was charged with inflicting a disease on her maid when the latter objected to her magical cure of a client's illness.[47] It seems probable that many of the women prosecuted as sorceresses had curing as their main occupation: they were beneficent magicians, practitioners of folk medicine, or perhaps midwives. Not uncommonly, persons tried for witchcraft are designated in the judicial records as *medicus* or *medica*, or a vernacular equivalent.[48] Healers of this kind would be especially susceptible to prosecution because their remedies frequently combined herbal lore with religious practices, and the latter could easily be construed as superstitious or even as mockeries of Christian devotion. Thus, a woman called 'Maria medica' who was tried at Brescia was accused of teaching her patients to 'abuse' holy oil by applying it for medicinal purposes. Likewise, she recommended that people recite perfectly orthodox prayers, such as the Pater Noster and the Ave Maria, three times, 'in the name of the Trinity, but for the reverence and honor of the devil' (as the court concluded).[49] Another woman, tried in Velay, used charms in conjunction with pilgrimages.[50]

In one instance the border between beneficent and maleficent magic was obliterated, when a sorceress cured a patient's disease by transferring it to someone else. A lame man came to her requesting a cure. First she boiled thirty herbs in a pot of water; then she cast this water out on to the street, so that the next person who walked by would assume the illness and relieve the man presently afflicted with it.[51] A business of this sort might be lucrative; in the case at hand the record specifies that the magical deed was performed for a fee. But it could also be dangerous. After this woman had confessed a number of crimes she was condemned to be led out of town on an ass, with a mitre on her head and her hands bound behind her. She was to be taken to a place of execution, and burned 'in such a way that she dies utterly, and her soul is separated from her body.' The fear of physical harm through bewitchment was clearly acute.

LOVE MAGIC

Magical attempts to spark love or arouse revulsion were roughly as common in the fourteenth and fifteenth centuries as were efforts to bring physical harm. The geographical distribution of love magic, though, is not so even. In particular there is a high proportion of cases from Italy, and a low percentage from Switzerland. One might seek to explain the discrepancy with reference to the social complexions, and particularly the position of women, in the respective countries. Robert Redfield found in Yucatan that the prevalence of unmarried women, and the ease with which married men formed secondary unions, led frequently to jealousy among women that resulted in accusations of witchcraft.[52] The large number of unmarried women in Italian towns may have had a similar result, and if so it would be natural, if not inevitable, for love magic to figure prominently in the accusations. The tendency of men in these towns to marry late in life, and the inevitable mortality among these procrastinating males, resulted in a substantial number of women who would never have the chance to marry. It is this latter class of woman whose quest of marital security might most readily lead to love magic, or suspicion of such magic.[53] Still, it is difficult to establish this kind of connection with confidence, especially because a great deal of work remains to be done on the social history of Italy and other areas.

Usually the trials in this class involved women who attempted to win the affections of recalcitrant men. Or, from a different viewpoint, they involved men who sought to excuse their love affairs by attributing them to the bewitchment of their seducers. The magical means for manipulating affections were exactly the same as those employed to inflict bodily harm. To be sure, in many trials the procedures used are stated vaguely or not at all.[54] Yet all of the means that served to bring illness and death could just as well arouse love or hatred.

The most common form of love magic appears to have been love potions. A prohibition of this practice in the penitential of the Pseudo-Ecgbert indicates that it was known in Germanic antiquity, though the extent of its continuous survival can only be conjectured.[55] Substances employed to induce love in the period 1300–1500 include powders of various sorts,[56] pulverized bird-bones,[57] ashes from burned reeds,[58] water with which one's feet had been washed,[59] herbs and herbal extracts,[60] hair,[61] menstrual blood,[62] and human excrement.[63] In some instances the specific substance is not recorded.[64] A sorcerer in Lorraine confessed in the early fifteenth century that he had abused eighteen women in a single day through use of love philtres, though one might well wonder whether it was the women or the sorcerer himself who consumed these potent concoctions.[65] In some instances the receptacle for the potion was as important as the ingredients, as when a Florentine sorceress gave a man a mixture of water and wine in a skull to arouse his passions.[66] When a sorceress was brought to justice at Todi, it was found that she had given a client an egg and a certain herb, and instructed her to cook them and feed them to her husband so that he would stop mistreating her. When the husband devoured these foods he was 'infatuated as if in frenzy' for a space of three days.[67] A sorceress at Reggio employed more exotic remedies.[68] On one occasion she was approached by a woman named Francischina, whose husband had taken another woman as concubine. Francischina wanted some means to make her husband love her once again. The sorceress told her to take some hairs from her thighs (meaning presumably pubic hairs) and some fingernails from her husband, and place them inside the heart of a black hen. Then she was supposed to place this heart in her own privy parts, and take nine steps with a blessed candle in her hand. After this she was to take the heart, along with the contents and certain pulverized plants, and feed the concoction to her husband, whereupon he would love her with all his heart. The same sorceress gave a substantially identical prescription to another woman in similar circumstances, telling her that after removing the hen's heart from her own *vituperosa natura* she should feed this 'dainty dish' (*epulum delicatum*) to her spouse. Seven years after receiving this advice the client returned to the sorceress and complained that her husband still mistreated her, and that the remedy had done little or nothing to alleviate the condition. The sorceress then gave her another prescription, which was less interesting than the first, though perhaps more effective.

In some cases sorceresses do not seem to have distinguished carefully enough between love potions and drugs intended for bodily harm. Matilda of Artois was accused of killing Louis X with a love potion made with powders of toads and snakes.[69] A woman who engaged in folk medicine was executed in Velay in 1390 because she had administered a fatal love potion to a man in the endeavor to restore his relations with his wife.[70] When a sorceress at Putten gave a prospective lover a magical food or drink to win his affections, he lost his senses for a period of time.[71] And a sorceress at Lucerne was punished for administering a love potion that had lethal effect.[72]

Superior texts contain a few references to image magic for arousing love. A prominent merchant of Florence denounced a woman named Catarina for bewitchment of his brother. By placing a wax image of him in his own bed she had won his affections, caused him to neglect his business and his family, and enticed him into giving her a large amount of money.[73] When a concubine of a priest in Todi went to a sorceress she complained that the priest had ceased loving her, and in fact had taken to beating her; she asked how she could revive his affections. The sorceress had her bring a wax image, which they placed over a fire while reciting an incantation. This remedy seems to have worked; at least the client later told the sorceress that the priest again loved her and did whatever she wanted him to do.[74] A woman named Catarina went to the same sorceress with a similar complaint about her husband. The sorceress told her to produce an image, presumably representing the husband, and when Catarina brought the desired figure the sorceress wrapped it with the girdle of a virgin. She then instructed Catarina to place the figure at the head of their bed, reciting three times a specified incantation, where-upon her husband would once again love her.[75] Similarly elaborate were the rituals of a priest of Tournai, who attempted to seduce a girl by drawing her image with charcoal on a piece of tile, then baptizing the image and sprinkling it with holy water. He then made a second image of wax, and baptized it also. Invoking demons in accordance with the prescriptions of a book on magic, he carried out repeated conjurations with both figures—though the effect remains unrecorded.[76] Although the specific details in this case were surely affected by the priest's literacy, the conception of magic that is involved was analogous to that in other instances. Probably the most important case of this sort is that of Alice Perrers, tried in 1376 for bewitchment of Edward III. Alice was reputed to have obtained the services of a Dominican sorcerer, who employed incantations, juices from powerful herbs, and wax effigies of both his client and the king. In this instance the amorous relation was indeed real, though the magical explanation was no doubt devised for political purposes.[77]

Contact with magical substances was also used as a means for inducing love. A sorcerer in Florence copied out a psalm on a piece of parchment and left it in a spot where he thought a certain woman would pass by.[78] A sorceress tried at Todi employed hairs for a similar purpose,[79] and when Institoris went to Innsbruck he found a woman who attained the same effect through use of an object taken

from the body of a hanged man.[80] One might include in the same
class the use of images when they were placed in proximity to the
persons seduced, as was done at Todi.[81] In some instances the
application of the magical substance was peculiarly intimate, if not
indeed obscene. A woman tried at Reggio had allegedly recommended
that women smear their mouths with chrism and then kiss their
husbands, to arouse passionate love.[82] In lieu of chrism, specifically
sexual secretions would arouse passion when applied in the same
way.[83] Barring the possibility of coincidence, it seems that the substances placed in contact with the prospective lover served on
occasion to undermine his bodily wellbeing. A Florentine sorceress
of the late fourteenth century placed an assortment of objects—
bread, charcoal, salt, and a coin bearing an engraved cross—in the
bed of her neighbor to arouse his love. Apparently the only result,
however, was that the neighbor began to feel pains in his heart and
elsewhere.[84]

Incitement of love was not the only sort of manipulation of
affection sought by sorceresses. In a few cases the goal was to arouse
hatred or bring about impotence. A young man of Todi wanted to
marry a certain girl, but her relatives made arrangements for her to
wed someone else. The lover went to a sorceress and asked for a way
to make his beloved and her bridegroom incompatible. She told him
to take a blessed candle, light it, and carry it to a crossroads; at the
time of the wedding he should extinguish it, recite a diabolical
prayer, break it, and leave its remains in a hiding-place. As long as
the broken candle stayed at this spot the couple would be unable to
consummate their marriage.[85] Stories of impotence through bewitchment survive also—though without such detailed elaborations
—from the superior records of Durham and Innsbruck.[86] It was
evidently easier for sorcery to effect a decrease in passion among
males, though occasionally it could work among females as well.
One sorcerer, punished at Florence in 1404, anointed his own
genitals with an unguent before having intercourse with his mistress,
to assure that she would not be attracted by other men.[87] Far more
commonly, however, magical means were thought to have stimulat-
ing effect on sexual behavior. One may well wonder what the
sources were of the pathological fantasies of the *Malleus maleficarum*
—for example, the story of the nest full of castrated yet animated
male members, which ate oats fed to them presumably by the witch
who had removed them.[88] They may come entirely from the febrile

mind of Institoris, whose senility was attested by a contemporary observer.[89] If they derive at all from popular belief they are wholly atypical.

WEATHER MAGIC

There is evidence of a general climatic transformation throughout Europe, beginning around the year 1300.[90] Severe winters were frequently followed by cool and wet summers. Violent storms occurred through the area of the North and Baltic seas, and repeated destructive rains brought the severe famine of the early fourteenth century. Rivers such as the Thames and the Po froze over for weeks or months. The crop failures in Norway made Norwegians dependent on grain imported from the North German plains. Icelandic glaciers extended further south than they had in more than a millennium; the Viking settlements in Greenland suffered poor harvests, and in the course of the fourteenth century the Norse settlers underwent attack by the Eskimos as the latter moved southward along with the ice. The effects remained in the fifteenth century. Around 1430, changes in the circulation of oceans caused the herrings to stop spawning in the Sound between Denmark and Sweden. One scholar has calculated that these transformations arose from a change in the tide-generating power of the sun and moon, which reached a peak in 1434.

Given such conditions, it is not surprising that contemporaries sought to explain natural disasters in terms of sorcery. The long-range climatic change may not have been detected as such, but there were many devastating calamities that called for explanation. What is surprising is that the charge of weather magic occurs as seldom as it does in the superior sources. It arises more often in the inferior texts; in the superior ones it appears only twenty times, mostly in Switzerland or areas near the Swiss border.[91] It is tempting to conjecture that this distribution is a result of the distinctive geography of the Alpine country—of the ordinary harshness of mountain climate, combined with the special rigors of weather during this period. Yet the area of concentration only partially overlaps the Alps, and includes a great many more cases from non-mountainous areas of the Swiss midlands and southern Germany.

The relative infrequency of weather magic as a charge in the superior documents is comprehensible when one considers that

accusations of sorcery usually stemmed from personal antagonism
between the accuser and the suspect, and that the accuser felt personally and directly aggrieved by the malice of the sorcerer.[92] An
individual, particularly in an agrarian village, might suffer from
damage to his crops, but since the entire community would undergo
the same loss he would not feel that it was directed specifically
against him, and he would not attribute it to a personal enemy. It is
interesting to note in this connection that Keith Thomas found few
examples of such sorcery in early modern England, and gave an
explanation closely analogous to that here proposed: 'An accusation
of witchcraft originated with someone living in close proximity to
the suspect, and was meant to explain some local and personal mis-
fortune.' Thus, it was only if witches were seen as a 'devil-worshipping sect,' as on the Continent, that it became plausible 'to regard
them as enemies of society in general . . . and hence to blame them
for storms or plagues, in the way that sometimes happened in
Europe.'[93] The evidence from the fourteenth and fifteenth centuries
allows one to take this analysis one step further: as will be seen in
the next chapter, even in continental Europe the allegation of
weather magic arose more commonly in the course of judicial
interrogation, under coercion, than it did in the original accusations.

Perhaps the accusation had been equally infrequent in antiquity:
it was forbidden in the penitential of the Pseudo-Theodore, which
prescribed penance for a 'stirrer of storms,'[94] but in the Norse sagas
it was conceived as an exotic practice, engaged in specifically by
Finnish sorcerers.[95]

The superior records of the period 1300–1500 give only meager
details about the way in which this sorcery was worked, and the
damage that it brought about. A sorceress at Lucerne performed
some kind of ritual at a pond, after which there was mist on the pond
for an entire day, and then a great storm.[96] Another witch of the
same city was supposed to have raised a hailstorm by performing a
rite three times in succession: standing with her back to a well, she
put her hand into the water and drew the water over her head.[97] In
Bern, similar results were allegedly accomplished by a ritual involving sheaves of hay, birds, and frogs.[98] When the records speak of the
precise character of the torrents, they more frequently speak of
hailstorms than of rain, thunderstorms, or snow. From both
superior and inferior texts it is clear that the standard way to ward
off this magic was to ring the town bells.[99] In one exceptional case

the magically induced storm was intended to raise a siege,[100] but in other instances the only apparent purpose was the destruction of crops. It may be noted in passing that the superior records of this period contain virtually no reference to destruction of property other than by weather magic. During one trial in Lucerne it was revealed that a witch had gone through her neighbor's garden cursing the onions and making them shrivel, but this case stands alone.[101]

THEFT

The one remaining objective accomplished by sorcery, theft, plays only a very minor role in the trials from 1300 to 1500. The few cases that do occur are almost all from Germany. Occasionally a woman was accused of being 'a witch and a thief,' though it is unclear in such cases whether the suspects' theft was thought of as accomplished through sorcery or whether the charges were separate.[102] A woman of Breslau was banished along with her daughter for stealing money from altars through sorcery,[103] and a church-robber at Gnechwitz used magical plants to gain entry into buildings.[104] Other sorcerers are supposed to have obtained money by magic, either stealing it or transforming other substances into money.[105]

One kind of sorcery that appears in the records with surprising infrequency is that of stealing milk from cows through magic. Burchard of Worms in the eleventh century had condemned women who believed they could accomplish this theft.[106] The theoretical literature of the late Middle Ages noted this form of sorcery, and indicated that the theft was carried out by sticking a knife into a wall and then milking the knife.[107] And Jacob Grimm alluded to modern remnants of belief in sorcery of this kind.[108] In the superior records of the period under consideration, however, the offence is rare. It occurs only four times, exclusively in Switzerland and Germany.[109] And in two of these cases it is not even clear whether the witches were supposed to have stolen the milk or merely rendered cows incapable of producing it. (The latter was definitely the case in two trials at Lucerne, where sorceresses had allegedly afflicted cows so that they gave blood instead of milk.)[110]

In a few further trials it was not objects but persons who were removed through sorcery. In three trials, all in fifteenth-century Germany, sorcery was employed to release prisoners from jail.[111]

Likewise, when Enguerrand de Marigny was exiled to Cyprus in 1315, his wife and certain associates are supposed to have used magic to obtain his liberation.[112] Perhaps these cases belong in a separate category; in any event, a class of this kind would be numerically insignificant.

MEANS OF SORCERY

Discussion of the techniques of maleficent magic has up to now been subsidiary to treatment of the sorcerers' ends. The procedures are of some importance in their own right, however, and deserve some independent consideration.

In a handful of cases the extant records refer to the means used even when they fail to cite the results. For example, a sorceress at Oldenburg took slivers of wood from a gallows, soaked them in beer, and then gave the beer to a man. But the document does not indicate whether she expected him to die or to fall passionately in love with her.[113] Similarly, a sorceress at Breslau was in the habit of giving men her own urine and perspiration to drink, and while the actual results may easily be conjectured, the intended outcome remains obscure.[114] The eucharist was commonly thought efficacious for both beneficent and maleficent magic. A person who had a consecrated host in his pocket when he was cast into water was supposedly immune from drowning. In the twelfth century a woman is supposed to have kissed her husband while holding a host in her mouth, so as to gain his love.[115] The eucharist likewise served as an implement of sorcery in occasional late medieval trials, in which the purpose of the sorcerer was not specified.[116] In other instances the records speak of powders,[117] bits of clothes from executed criminals,[118] and other objects as means for accomplishing unspecified acts of sorcery (if indeed the purpose in all these cases was maleficent). Far more commonly, though, the sources give the results of sorcery while neglecting the techniques employed, and in a large number of instances they specify neither means nor ends.

Still, the evidence reveals basic patterns that would probably be confirmed if further documents gave relevant information. The most significant features of the witch trials, viewed in this aspect, are three. First, the most common techniques for bodily harm and love magic were image magic and, most especially, ingestion of magical substances. As suggested earlier,[119] the dominance of material techniques for sorcery may have been caused in part by the incidence of the plague throughout the later fourteenth and the fifteenth century. In the case of herbal specialists who turned to illicit pursuits (or were thought to do so), the reason for the choice of magical substances is particularly obvious. Second, the methods for weather magic and for magical theft are seldom specified. In a few cases weather magic involved water rituals, as one might expect. And in one instance a sorcerer accomplished burglary through the wholly inexplicable use of plants. But otherwise the records for these forms of sorcery fail to indicate the techniques. Third, incantation (or the chanting or inscription of a magical spell or curse), which figures as a dominant mode of sorcery in some cultures, occurs rarely in the trials between 1300 and 1500, and almost never as an independent procedure. In some instances it occurred in conjunction with other forms of magic. For example, an Italian sorceress advised one woman to twist a shirt and simultaneously recite a formula indicating that her husband's heart should be twisted, or constrained to love her.[120] In a case of this sort the simple incantation seems to derive its power mainly from its association with the homeopathic ritual. In other cases, sorceresses or their clients recited incantations over herbs before using them in magic.[121] And when the Florentine sorcerer Niccolò Consigli attempted image magic to effect bodily harm he recited spells over the wax images, and inscribed words on them, as well as pricking them and suffocating them with incense. He also instructed his client to cut out the heart from a chicken, reciting the words, 'I do not extract the heart of a chicken, but of Martino and his son.'[122] Use of incantation by itself, however, was virtually unknown.[123]

The rarity of incantation is particularly puzzling because it was of paramount importance in Germanic and Graeco-Roman (and probably also Celtic) antiquity. The words for sorcery and magic in these cultures are frequently derived from roots meaning 'to sing,' as with the Old Norse *galdr* or the Latin *fascinatio*. The Twelve Tables of ancient Rome specified punishments for one who had sung *malum carmen*, and one of the most common kinds of magic throughout antiquity was the recitation or intonation of verbal formulas. These formulas were also important in the practice of defixion (the nailing-down of an enemy's name, usually written on a lead tablet), despite the essentially homeopathic nature of this magic.[124] The place of these incantations in Germanic tradition was so large that

Jacob Grimm reserved a distinct chapter of his *Teutonic Mythology* for spells and charms.[125] In a few of the beneficent Anglo-Saxon charms (or curative formulas) there are corrupt Celtic phrases;[126] these do not demonstrate that incantation was of central importance in Celtic maleficent magic, but the mere presence of the druids, whose learning was transmitted orally, would if anything tend to reinforce the prevalence of this method, which seems to be common among Indo-European peoples.[127] How, then, does one explain its insignificance in the fourteenth and fifteenth centuries?

Anthropological work has shown important relations between the forms of sorcery in various cultures and the social structures of these cultures. E. E. Evans-Pritchard has analyzed the spells used by the Azande and by the Trobriand islanders, and found them significantly different.[128] Whereas the Trobrianders use spells with rigidly fixed ritual wording (what Evans-Pritchard calls 'formula' spells), the Azande are largely free to improvise on the form of their spells (which the anthropologist designates as 'saying' spells). This distinction is explicable in terms of the social system of the two peoples. The Trobrianders live in villages, which perform both mundane and magical tasks in common, and which maintain and guard their rituals with a certain jealousy. The Azande, on the other hand, live in scattered homesteads; they engage in few communal tasks, and they transmit their forms of magic freely within their families or among families. The more rigorous the transmission of magic, the more control there is over the magical ceremony itself.

The form of maleficent magic in Europe can in large part be explained by comparing the position of the sorcerer in pre-Christian antiquity and in the period 1300–1500. Before the conversion to Christianity, low (or practical) magic was not clearly despised by any segment of society. The political and religious leaders proscribed maleficent magic at most; the techniques of magic, which could be turned to either salutary or harmful purpose, were not viewed as necessarily and inherently wrong, and were not consistently prosecuted.[129] Thus, there was little chance that these leaders could control the employment of magic, and if someone decided to use it for evil means, even if the endeavor was detected and punished, the proclivity towards use of magic could not be significantly limited. Nor were there effective social sanctions. The sagas might portray old women as feared and shunned on account of their sorcery, yet anyone could perform magic with honor so long as he did so in a manly way.[130] If he brought harm, the grievance could be redressed in various ways, but in a society given to perpetual feud, such as Iceland, the prospect of retaliation does not seem to have been a deterrent. Neither in Germanic nor in Graeco-Roman tradition was sorcery distinctive to the lower classes. The testimony of the *defixionum tabellae* shows clearly that maleficent magic in the Mediterranean world was common among literate individuals. It was illegal, to be sure, but it was still widely practiced. Thus, for two main reasons pre-Christian society was able to maintain incantation as an important form of sorcery. First, though there is obviously no statistical basis for judgment, the lack of effective sanctions probably allowed frequent practice of sorcery, so that verbal formulas could be shared and transmitted from one sorcerer to another. Second, maleficent magic was practiced freely by literate as well as illiterate classes, so that such formulas could likewise be passed on through the written medium.

The *Eyrbbygia Saga* mentions that most people 'lost their power of sorcery when they were baptized.'[131] Clearly this is an exaggeration, but not a wholly meaningless one. For beneficent purposes, Christian prayer might serve as well as overtly magical formulas and rites. There were no doubt many people who still entertained maleficent intentions. But in some instances Christian priests may have restrained uncharitable behaviour, and principles of Christian ethics may have permeated the masses enough to make some people more reluctant to speak of their sorcery than they would have been before conversion. The political and intellectual élites, in any case, would be less inclined to use it than they had been earlier. Explicit low magic was thus in large part relegated to the lower classes, or to the 'little tradition.'[132] After the passage of centuries, sorcery was no longer so common and so open that it could be shared communally. The general notions of sorcery—the ideas that there are such things as plants, words, and rites that can have maleficent effect—no doubt persisted, even when they were not acted upon. But the specific information requisite for practice did not necessarily survive. As will be seen in a later chapter,[133] sorcerers in the fourteenth and fifteenth centuries were more often than not individual, isolated practitioners; even when two or three of them were apprehended together, there is no evidence that they stood in an ongoing tradition of commonly shared techniques for sorcery. Specific forms of sorcery were thus in large part not possessed but improvised, not traditional but spontaneous. Given the basic idea of image magic, it would be relatively easy for a person to devise specific types of image and ideas for mutilation of them. Likewise, if one has heard of love potions or substances that will induce death, it is not difficult to find materials that are generally viewed as ominous—menstrual blood, bits of clothes from an executed man, herbs, etc.—with which one can experiment. But improvisation of verbal formulas presents special problems. One can use words and phrases from ordinary discourse, but these generally have no communally recognized magical power. One can invent one's own words, but *a fortiori* these will lack general recognition as magically efficacious, and the individual who contrives them is not likely to place much confidence in them. An alternative possibility is to adapt Christian prayers and maledictions to the ends of sorcery, as seems to have been done widely in early modern England.[134] But even if such adaptation began before the sixteenth century, it was evidently not widespread enough to occasion anxiety and prosecution. Hence, the position of the sorcerer within society— his isolation from a common stock of maleficent techniques—made incantation less viable than other forms of sorcery.

The character of sorcery during the fourteenth and fifteenth centuries as the sporadic activity of isolated individuals is shown also in the experimental nature of many maleficent acts. Occasionally the word *experimentum* is used as tantamount to *maleficium*, or 'bewitchment.'[135] On certain occasions sorcerers carried out experimental killings before proceeding to their main prey. Conspirators against Pope John XXII are supposed to have tested their image magic by first using it to assassinate Jacques de Via, the pope's favourite nephew. When they found that the sorcery worked they went ahead with their plans.[136] Likewise, when the sorcerer and his assistant at Coventry attempted in 1324 to murder the king of England and other political lords, they first tried their techniques on an experimental victim, driving him mad by piercing the forehead of his image, and then killing him by stabbing the image in the heart.[137] If the methods of sorcery had been derived from long-standing tradition, shared and commonly employed throughout society, this kind of experimentation would scarcely have been necessary. Those sorcerers who recognized that their procedures were fundamentally those of trial and error may have found it relatively easy to reconcile themselves to the failure of their endeavors. There are numerous recorded instances of sorcery that did not work as it was intended.

In one case a Florentine administered powdered bird-bones to a woman in hopes of seducing her, but found that the procedure did not work; if it had, he explained, he would then have used it to seduce a more attractive woman.[138] Doubtless there were many more instances of failure that have escaped historical notice because there was no occasion for anyone to take the would-be culprits to court. To be sure, even in societies where sorcery is more routine, and where standard methods are commonly taught, there are ways of accounting for failure.[139] But the attitude of experimentation that one finds among certain sorcerers of the fourteenth and fifteenth centuries seems to imply a special willingness to recognize failures as an inevitable part of their life.

INVOCATION

The essential features of invocation have been stated above in the Introduction; examples have been discussed in the last chapter. In its goals invocation does not differ from sorcery, and examples survive of invocation used to effect bodily harm, to manipulate affections, and to achieve other goals similar to those of sorcery. The range of goals may have been somewhat broader in the case of invocation, and may have included attainment of knowledge or skills that would not normally be sought through sorcery. One man at Lucerne, for example, gave himself to an evil spirit to obtain success in playing games.[140] Yet the only difference in principle is in the means used to attain one's goal: by definition, invocation involves reliance upon the power of the devil. Even the techniques, though, could easily be combined with those of sorcery. The Provençal defendant Catherine David was supposed to have used a potion obtained from a demon;[141] her offense was thus partly sorcery and partly invocation. A priest of Tournai likewise combined sorcery and invocation by taking the names of demons from a book and invoking them while using image magic to seduce a girl.[142] In another trial for a similar offense, although there was still a magical element it was much reduced. A notary named Geraud Cassendi went before inquisitors at Carcassonne on the charge of taking gold threads from a picture of the Blessed Virgin, placing them in his shirt, and then reading a formula of invocation from a book. Immediately a swarm of demons appeared, filling him with terror. He threw a shoe at them and commanded them to depart, which they did. Yet on another occasion he invoked demons seven times. At least one of the purposes of this invocation was the endeavor to debauch women and girls.[143]

While invocation could be even more serious an offense than sorcery, its participants seem not infrequently to have viewed it with an attitude of levity, as a way of duping their fellow townsmen. One swindler in Florence extracted sums of money from various people, promising that he would have demons obtain vast fortunes for them.[144] And a case in Yorkshire showed a strangely undignified conception of the devil. A man named John de Ithen sold the devil to one Robert de Roderham for three pence halfpenny, and then failed to meet the terms of the contract. When Robert took the swindler to court the judge dismissed the case on the grounds that Christians should refrain from agreements of this sort, and adjourned both parties 'to the infernal regions, there to hear their judgment'.[145] In a trial in Norfolk, on the other hand, the devil himself was the victim of a hoax. Two men had the devil reveal to them a hidden treasure, on the understanding that they would repay the favor with a human sacrifice. They tricked him by baptizing a cock and immolating it as a substitute victim.[146]

The charge of invocation appears occasionally in the original depositions of lay witnesses, but it seems to have been most common in trials involving clerics. Thus, although it was not in principle distinctive to learned tradition it was evidently more popular among educated men than with the unlearned masses. Those clerics who performed or abetted invocation often added their own refinements —use of inscriptions, sacraments and sacramentals, and so forth— though they shared with the laity the fundamental idea of calling upon the devil. In a case at Château-Landon, in which derelict monks and canons regular participated along with laymen, a live cat was buried under a crossroad for three days. The transgressors provided a system of tubes to prevent suffocation. They also furnished a supply of bread mixed with chrism, holy oil, and holy water. Their intention was to exhume the animal after three days, skin it, and lay strips of its hide in a circle, within which a person could stand and invoke a demon named Berich. (The informant solemnly asserted that the invocation would be in vain unless the person entering the circle first took remnants of the cat food and placed them in his posterior.) While buried, however, the cat attracted the attention of a pack of dogs, whereupon the authorities sought out the perpetrators and delivered them to various punishments.[147]

Although invocation was never widespread or frequent among the laity during the period in question, its significance will become clear in the next chapter: it was a notion rooted in popular thought that could easily serve as a stepping-stone to learned ideas of diabolism. In its goals it shared much in common with sorcery, but the border between use and veneration of demons was a tenuous one, and easy for a judge to disregard.

RIDING ON WOLVES

One further phenomenon, which seems to occur exclusively in Swiss trials, calls for discussion. It is not actually included in witchcraft proper, but sometimes occurs in judicial records alongside charges of witchcraft. In a small number of trials, witnesses reported that they had seen the accused riding on wolves. There is no recorded case of lycanthropy in the superior records for witchcraft; so far as the sources reveal, the accusers did not think of the wolves as human beings in bestial form. Nor is there the slightest suggestion in the superior texts that the wolves were actually demons. Why the witches were riding on wolves remains in all cases obscure, as does the question where, if anywhere, they were going. In two cases there were explanations for these alleged excursions. One witch of Lucerne pleaded that she had not been riding a wolf, but merely walking her dog.[148] And in a trial at Zürich, child witnesses accused a woman of riding over meadows, hedges, and graves on a wolf, and staying dry even during a storm, but adults with presumably more accurate perception stated that the animal had actually been an ass.[149] A man at Basel alleged that a woman mounted on a wolf had charged towards him, and presumably a more plausible account of this episode could easily be devised.[150] As mentioned earlier, a sorceress of Lucerne is supposed to have kept pet foxes and wolves, and fed them when her husband was away.[151] In this instance there was no explicit mention of her riding on the creatures, but the testimony clearly arose out of the same typically Swiss association between witches and wolves.

If these incidents are in any way important, it is because of their potential for misinterpretation. Like invocation, the idea of riding on the back of a wolf could easily suggest further, more bizarre charges. In particular, the wolf could easily be thought of as a devil.[152] Given the judicial means for imposition of learned tradition, to which we now must turn, the possibilities for this misunderstanding were great indeed.

Chapter V

The Imposition of
Learned Notions

In 1428 a woman named Matteuccia Francisci appeared before an inquisitor at Todi.[1] The inquisitor had evidently conducted extensive inquiry into her activities, and had obtained charges against her from numerous former clients. He routinely specified the precise place and year in which Matteuccia had performed sorcery for these clients, or given them recipes or advice. Many of these patrons were women whose husbands no longer loved them, and the sorceress prescribed a wide variety of folk remedies for this complaint. Many of these cures involved use of herbs; others centered about rituals in which wax images were placed over fire; still others involved use of incantations. Though the records specify that Matteuccia gave such prescriptions 'at the instigation of a diabolical spirit,' many of her incantations called upon members of the Trinity, the Virgin, and various saints. The woman appears to have been something of a specialist in folk medicine, and on one occasion prescribed a contraceptive for the concubine of a local priest. The bulk of the trial contains no hint of diabolism. Toward the end, however, one can discern a clear caesura: the tone of the allegations shifts abruptly, and one finds Matteuccia confessing to all the crimes perpetrated by members of the devil's sect. The emphasis is still largely upon bewitchment, but the maleficent acts are different in kind from those in the earlier part of the trial, and from those in records of witnesses' depositions. Rather than employing magical substances and rituals, the subject is supposed to have anointed herself with unguents made, among other things, from the fat of babies. She then recited a formula, whereupon a demon appeared in the shape of a goat, transporting her to the assemblies over which he presided. On countless occasions she is supposed to have gone to the homes of people in various towns and sucked the blood out of their babies, so that their fat might be employed in the manufacture of unguents.

Though there is no mention in the record that the later admissions were made under judicial coercion, it is difficult to account for the abrupt change by any other hypothesis. Clearly in this trial the notions of diabolism were superimposed on earlier charges in the course of judicial interrogation.

Another trial suggests the same interpretation: The chronicler Cornelius Zantfliet mentions that in 1456 two women were burned at Cologne, one for killing a man and the other for her ability to raise winds, hail, and storms in the company of her associates.[2] The latter woman had come from Metz, where she had raised inclement weather on one occasion and destroyed all the crops within two miles. The citizens of Cologne wanted to know whether the abilities she claimed were real, so they asked her for a demonstration. When a cup of water was brought to her she promptly made it turn so hard that it could not be cut even with the sharpest knife. In addition to the chronicler's account there are letters exchanged between the authorities of Cologne and those of Metz, which shed further light on this trial. Having heard that the woman from Metz had relatives still in that vicinity, and that her sister was presently in captivity, the burgomaster and council of Cologne wrote to the government at Metz requesting information about the suspect's background. The authorities of Metz replied that the woman in question had fled from their town under suspicion of witchcraft. Other women, who had killed infants, raised storms, and flown through the air, had implicated her in their misdeeds. They claimed that the suspect had given each of them a box of ointments, presumably for use either in casting bewitchments or in flying to Sabbaths. The fact that similar suspicions arose in both cities suggests clearly that the woman did engage in weather magic of some kind. In Metz, however, the authorities did not content themselves with this accusation of sorcery. Pressing further, and probably employing some form of judicial coercion, they convicted the suspects of certain elements of diabolism. The discrepancies between the charges in Metz and those in Cologne can best be explained on the supposition that, unlike their counterparts at Cologne, the officials at Metz used coercive measures to superimpose the learned notion of diabolism on the popular charge of sorcery.

In all respects, then, these cases are analogous to those discussed in Chapter II, in which witnesses' charges of sorcery were followed by judicial interrogation, in which charges of diabolism were extracted from the suspects. Indeed, all valid and relevant evidence indicates that this pattern was typical. This is not to say that all members of the learned élite believed in diabolism and interjected it into the charges. Recent historians have made clear that there were divergent strains in thought concerning witchcraft. Certain educated people, particularly those with humanist backgrounds, seem to have been less inclined to credulity than others.[3] Yet a relatively skeptical attitude could serve only to suppress the popular charges of witchcraft or to leave them as they stood, without the addition of further, more elaborate concepts. It is only those educated people who did believe in diabolism, therefore, who imposed distinctively learned notions upon the substratum of popular belief. This latter group of intellectuals was significant because of the effect they had on judicial proceedings. Even if they were numerically unimportant in 1300 (and they probably were), they seem to have increased dramatically by 1500. In any event, it is their ideas that call for separate attention.

The task that remains for understanding the context of witch accusations is fourfold. First the distinctive features of the imposed learned tradition must be examined. Second, the reasons must be ascertained why members of the intellectual élite felt it necessary to devise notions more fantastic than those of the populace, and to place these ideas in the mouths of suspects. Third, the way in which judges carried out this imposition must be explained. And fourth, the influence of learned concepts upon popular belief must be studied, to the extent that the sources allow.

It would be superfluous to examine the learned notions of witchcraft in comprehensive detail. They are fundamentally the same whether seen in witch hunting manuals or in the charges brought forth in court. They have been studied extensively by numerous historians—perhaps at greater length than their historical significance requires. It will suffice here to suggest some of the ways in which learned tradition as shown in the trials differed from folk belief.

The most essential point to be conveyed is that learned influence did not merely juxtapose the notion of diabolism with that of sorcery. In basic ways it transformed the conception of sorcery as well. In only rare instances does one find sorcery precisely as described in the last chapter included in a document along with diabolism, in the same stage of the judicial proceedings.[4] Almost invariably the sorcery that accompanies diabolism is radically distinct. Whereas the sorcerer or sorceress in popular tradition is usually an enemy of an individual accuser, or a set of specific accusers, the devil-worshipper is an adversary of a broader and less personal society. The sorcerer in the superior document, whose offenses are specified by the victim, attacks out of personal motives having to do with the victim.[5] The devil-worshipper, whose crimes are suggested by judges (individuals not affected in any directly personal way by the suspect's actions), inflicts evil out of sheer malice. This distinction is clearest, as Keith Thomas has suggested in a different context,[6] in trials for weather magic. Because destructive storms were not clearly directed against specific individuals, there was little inclination for private accusers to press charges of weather magic. In the superior documents the accusation arises with moderate frequency in Switzerland and in Upper Germany, but virtually never in other regions. Even in inferior texts, where it occurs more frequently,[7] it is not universal; it does not appear in Italian trials for diabolism, perhaps because of relatively stable climate, but it does arise frequently in France.[8] The relative frequency of the charge in inferior sources seems natural. When a suspect was under interrogation, and when judges were looking for offences that could plausibly be attributed to him or her, it might frequently have been easier for them to recall a damaging storm from the recent past than to call to mind a death, illness, or love affair that seemed incomprehensible in natural terms.

Storms were not the only means that witches had to destroy crops, according to the inferior sources. They also accomplished this goal by filling the skin of a cat with various grains, soaking it in a spring for three days, then drying and pulverizing the mixture, and strewing it to the winds from a mountain top. Whatever fields the powder fell on would be rendered sterile.[9] For destruction of property, witches in certain Swiss trials are also supposed to have created avalanches.[10]

Oddly, one does not find plague ascribed to witches in the inferior documents, though this also would be a crime against society in general. Probably the closest approximation to this notion is a charge against witches in or near Savoy: that they formed a powder from the innards of murdered children and the bodies of venomous animals, and scattered the concoction through the air during a mist. Those towns to which the deadly substance was carried by the wind would suffer heavy mortality, while neighboring areas would be spared.[11] From the very onset of the plague in the mid-fourteenth century, however, this disease had been widely attributed not to maleficent action of witches but to the malice of Jews or to the wrath of God. These alternative explanations evidently preempted the suggestion that outbreaks of the affliction could be blamed on devil-worshippers. To be sure, there were two incidents in which the populace held sorceresses responsible for epidemics,[12] but the diseases in these cases do not appear to have been plague (particularly not in the case of Boucoiran, where the disease affected animals and children specifically).

In any case, the specifically antisocial nature of devil-worshippers is borne out by further aspects of their maleficence. They attacked infants far more commonly than did mere sorcerers. The records frequently give as motive for infanticide the need of infants' fat as an ingredient in unguents, or the consumption of their flesh at Sabbaths.[13] Likewise, the attribution of stillbirth and miscarriage to witches seems to be a distinctive feature of the inferior documents.[14] In both these ways the sheer malevolence of devil-worshippers, not directed against specific personal enemies, is revealed. Furthermore, the most clearly personal offense of witches, love magic, is conspicuously lacking in most of the inferior texts.[15] This may be surprising to readers of the *Malleus maleficarum*, which dwells in lurid detail on the sexual bewitchments of witches, and which claims that God permits them special power over the sexual act.[16] Yet earlier theologians had not demonstrated the same measure of concern for this kind of sorcery, and apparently neither had judges. Canonists had had to consider whether impotence resulting from bewitchment was grounds for annulment of marriage, but their concern evidently does not indicate general preoccupation with the matter among the intellectual élite.[17]

The acts of sorcery narrated in inferior texts are more commonly carried out through direct, overtly physical contact than are those in superior sources. Neither image magic nor placement of magical substances in proximity to the victim plays a prominent role in the inferior sources.[18] Instead, one finds devil-worshippers incessantly approaching people (especially babies) directly, particularly during the night, and either pressing them on their chests in such a way as to wound them or else smearing them with magical unguents. One witch, having quarreled with a certain man over a debt, took vengeance by rubbing the man's daughter on the hand with an unguent that the devil had given her. The daughter at once grew ill, and five days later died. The same witch avenged another grievance by bewitching a man's cow with certain powders, again given to her by the devil.[19] A witch in the diocese of Lausanne entered through a window one night and strangled his own granddaughter, and used her remains to make a lethal powder and an unguent that would cause a broom or stick to fly through the air.[20] In the mid-fifteenth century the devil gave a male witch in the same diocese an unguent, and told him to place it between the testicles of a certain John of Mossel and see what would happen. The witch, concealed in a cloud, approached the victim from behind and anointed him with the unguent. Immediately John began raging about the fields in a mad frenzy, unable to bear the pain.[21] In numerous other circumstances witches used magical poisons to afflict both men and animals. One witch at Boucoiran killed a one-year-old girl by putting magical powders in her bowl as she sat eating on her doorstep. Likewise, she put powders into the troughs from which pigs fed; a man testified in court that his pigs had in fact died, though he had not known the cause.[22]

The most fundamental distinction between the popular and learned notions of sorcery, however, is that in learned tradition the devil had a necessary role in all bewitchment. The devil dispensed powders and unguents to his followers at the Sabbaths, ordered them to work as much harm as they could, and instructed them in the arts of sorcery. On one occasion a witch refused to carry out this order,[23] but typically they complied with their master's will. One subject confessed that he and his companions had been rendered invisible, and had gone behind farmers as they sowed their fields, snatching up the seeds. Asked why they had done this, he said merely 'that their master had ordered them to do so, and that the evils and harms that they inflict on others redound to his purposes.'[24] In other contexts the powders and unguents used by witches were concocted 'by diabolical art,' or 'through diabolical mystery.'[25] In short, learned ideas were not merely added to popular beliefs, but were thoroughly intermingled with them, and altered them.

Why did the judges bring about this radical transformation of the charges? If diabolism had been the original charge against the suspects, one would have to explain the preoccupation with it as the result of a morbid, pathological fear or fascination. But from all the valid evidence available it appears that diabolism was not the original charge, but was superimposed in the courtroom on some prior accusation, usually sorcery. The introduction of diabolism can thus more plausibly be construed as resulting from a desire of the literate élite to make sense of the notion of sorcery. On this interpretation the concern with diabolism arose more from intellectual needs than from psychological grounds. Psychological factors no doubt played an important subsidiary role, particularly in the case of a pathological soul such as Henry Institoris. Whether some further kind of amorphous collective psychosis played a major part in the formulation of ideas about witchcraft is highly dubious.

The motives for the transformation are clearer in the witchcraft treatises than in the court records. Essentially, the authors of this literature opposed a religious interpretation of sorcery to a magical one. They could not entertain seriously the notion that acts of sorcery and maleficent words or substances had inherent power to bring evil results, without the mediation of demons. There was no place in their world-view for causation that was neither natural nor fully supernatural. As H. R. Trevor-Roper has pointed out, it was predominately Aristotelians rather than Neo-Platonists who encouraged the concern with witchcraft,[26] and it was Aristotelians who elaborated the specific notion of diabolism. Granted, they did not invent the concept, and there was no necessary connection between their metaphysics and belief in diabolism. Accusations of devil-worship occurred sporadically long before Aristotelian influence emerged in western Europe, and strict Aristotelians never held a monopoly on this concern. Yet there was a close affinity between Aristotelian concepts and recourse to the idea of diabolism specifically as a way of explaining sorcery. Thus, it was perhaps natural that those who had been nurtured in the Aristotelian tradition inclined more than others toward this preoccupation. Neo-Platonists might readily accommodate in their world-view the idea of various kinds of mysterious powers, both individual spirits and non-individuated forces, susceptible of human manipulation. But the Aristotelian conception was more parsimonious. It recognized matter and distinguishable spirits, but nothing further that was not a property of a material substance or of a spirit. It could not acknowledge the efficacy of preternatural, magical forces except by postulating that they were in the control of spiritual beings, whether angels or devils. Even the movement of the celestial spheres was entrusted to angels.

The Aristotelianism of the medieval schools was unwilling to recognize magic as an independent type of reality, and had to interpret it in religious terms. In the mid-fifteenth century, Johannes Wünschelburg argued by analogy with the Church's sacraments and rituals: just as these rites have efficacy as signs, whose use is the occasion for God's bestowal of grace, so also the words and formulas of the sorcerer are merely signs to the devil.[27] In neither case is the result strictly magical. Whatever effect is attained comes about only because of the pact that binds natural and supernatural orders together. The populace might misinterpret the sacraments as having inherent, magical power, independent of divine action. And the Church's doctrine that the sacraments worked *ex opere operato*, independently of human effort, could easily be misconstrued to support this erroneous conception. But from the viewpoint of the intellectual élite neither sacraments nor sacramentals could take effect without God's cooperation. Likewise, from their viewpoint there could be no sorcery without involvement of the devil. One might even suggest that they conceived sorcery as a kind of negative, diabolical sacrament.

In principle it might have been sufficient even for Aristotelians to view sorcery as entailing an implicit pact alone. Furthermore, this pact could have been of the contractual type required for invocation, rather than the submissive pact of diabolism. For many members of the learned élite, these less extravagant notions may in fact have sufficed; their views, which would accord closely with those of the populace, would not be evident in the sources because they would not be distinctly learned. Yet a large and apparently growing section of the educated élite found it more satisfying to explain sorcery as an offshoot of diabolism. Why they should opt for this view is not immediately apparent. One might be tempted to conjecture that the idea of overt diabolism appealed more to the imaginations of late medieval theologians than did that of invocation or that of sorcery accomplished through merely implicit pact; diabolism offered a broader wealth of titillating detail. Even as a means of explanation, however, the notion of diabolism had a certain superiority, since it suggested countless specific ways in which the devil could inspire and abet his worship by performing sorcery. To take merely one example, it became relatively easy to grasp the motive for a gratuitous act of bewitchment such as unprovoked infanticide if one posited a Satanic banquet in which devil-worshippers ate the flesh of babies.

From the judges' viewpoint it was enough to grant the mere possibility of diabolism. When judges pressed for admissions they would naturally want to extract all relevant confessions, and the suspicion that a witch had more than merely implicit or contractual relations with the devil could readily be confirmed under coercion. It should be borne in mind that in explanation of judicial developments the strict requirements of the Aristotelian world-view were not so important as the impression that this system of thought would leave on the minds of men such as judges, who, though not professional theologians, would have contact with learned men. One can readily understand how they would incline towards the more extreme of the two possibilities: assumption of diabolism, rather than mere invocation.

The statements of contemporary writers on the connection between sorcery and diabolism may be discussed in three groups. First there were questions regarding demons' role in sorcery: how far does the power of witches extend independent of diabolical aid? And how far does the power of the materials of bewitchment (charms of various sorts) extend without such aid? What role do demons play in the carrying out of bewitchment, and why do they need to play such a role? Second, there are questions regarding the role of witches: could demons execute the bewitchments that they perform without the cooperation of witches? And if so, why do they rely on witches at all? Precisely what function do witches play in the demonic scheme of things? Third, there are questions regarding the bond between witches and demons: how is this bond formed? What sort of force does it have? In what ways are demons subject to witches, and witches to demons? These questions had not been subject to significant debate prior to the later Middle Ages, but from the thirteenth century on they commanded sustained attention.

For the theory of the role of demons in carrying out sorcery, the work of Johannes Nider is relevant. Writing about 1435, Nider quoted a verbal exchange between a judge and a male witch, named Staedlin, who was active in the Swiss town of Boltingen. The judge asked Staedlin how he went about stirring up storms and hail. Staedlin replied that he and his accomplices went out to a field and with a certain formula implored the prince of demons to send one of the lesser demons to their aid. When the requested demon arrived, the witches sacrificed a black chicken to him at a crossroads, throwing the chicken into the sky so that the demon could catch it. After this ceremony the demon brought on the inclement weather, not always in the places designated, but wherever God permitted.[28] This example may be based on an element derived from popular tradition: the notion of killing a fowl at a crossroads and casting it into the air sounds likely enough as a popular means for bringing rain.[29] Yet the rationalization is surely a learned addition. It is apparent that Nider thought there had to be a demon who somehow fulfilled the witches' bidding and executed the desired effect.

There are other examples in which authors attempted to specify the mechanism involved in maleficent operations. The *Malleus maleficarum*, for example, indicates that a witch who wishes to steal milk will thrust a knife into a wall and go through the motions of milking the knife. Then the witch summons her demon, 'who always works with her in everything,' and instructs him to obtain milk from a specified cow. The devil transports the milk from the animal's udder to the place where the witch is stroking the knife, and releases the fluid as if it were emanating from the knife.[30] Two assumptions underlie this explanation: that the devil has powers of locomotion applicable to material objects, and that he can affect the vision of minds of men so that they cannot see objects (in this case milk) in transit. That the devils had such powers was not a controversial question, though there might be incidental disagreement among theologians regarding the way in which the power was implemented. The *locus classicus* concerning the devil's power of locomotion was a passage from Thomas Aquinas' commentary on Job, establishing the possibility of the atmospheric turbulence mentioned in the book of Job. Though Thomas granted that neither angels nor devils have power over corporeal matter *ad susceptionem formarum*, it was nonetheless clear from the example of man, who can move his body by a mere act of will, that spirits possess powers of local motion over material objects.[31] Nor was this by any means their only relevant power. According to Francisco de Toledo, there are fundamentally three ways in which demons can carry out the desires of witches: by local motion, by application and acceleration of natural causes, and by delusion.[32] What is of interest here, though, is not so much the argument that demons could interfere in the processes of nature, but rather the preoccupation with the fact that they do so at the bidding of witches. It is this carefully rationalized notion of witchcraft, with meticulous specification of the role of demons in the execution of sorcery, that is significant for present purposes.

The witchcraft literature abounds in passing, incidental references to the role of demons as witches' accomplices. It is demons who affect men's bodies to make them impotent when witches have bewitched them.[33] It is the same demons who devastate crops. The anonymous author of the *Errores Gazariorum* speaks of a powder, concocted in diabolical fashion, which when spread over cultivated lands acts as a form of sacrifice to the devil. 'They say that [this powder] brings sterility, and that the devil, on account of this sacrifice, consumes the fruits of the land over which the powders are spread.'[34] The devil sometimes aids in even the most trivial problems, readily soluble through natural expedients. Thus, as one author explains, it is possible for witches to enter houses at night to kill infants, because they do so through the guidance of demons.[35]

In addition to these incidental references to the devil's role there are several passages in the witchcraft literature in which this role becomes a matter of central attention. Francisco de Toledo defines *maleficium* as 'the art of harming others by the power of a demon';[36] amatory witchcraft is effected by the devil's use of phantasms and his motion of the imagination, whereas 'venefic' witchcraft is accomplished either by poisons which the demon provides to the witch or else by the direct action of the demon in the service of the witch.[37] The author gives an example to show precisely how the demon's power may be applied. When a sorcerer does injury to a figurine representing an intended victim, it is not the act of the sorcerer that injures the victim. Rather, the demon reproduces on the victim the same harm that the sorcerer inflicts on the image.[38] And it is no argument to the contrary that witches often confess having done such things of their own accord, 'for the demon deceives the witches themselves.'[39] This passage, as well as similar ones in other works, highlights the divergence between the popular and learned ideas of witchcraft. The populace adhered to the simpler belief in the power inherent in a witch or her actions, whereas the learned élite insisted repeatedly that the witch of herself has no magical power, and that all she does, she does through the mediation of demons.

Just as the witchcraft literature emphasizes that the witch has no inherent magical powers, likewise it stresses that the charms, unguents, and powders employed by the witch have no power in and of themselves. If these materials have any effect, this must be attributed to the devil. 'The effects which follow the means or curses of evil persons are not caused by these means or curses themselves, but they have another causal agent [viz., the devil].'[40] Geiler von Kaiserberg, writing in 1508, refers to the action or material that witches use as signs (*zeichen*), indicating to the devil what the witches wish to have done; when the devils observe these signs they know what they are supposed to do, and act accordingly. He gives the example of a witch who sprays water over her head by means of a broom cast into a stream, in order to cause hail. Neither the spraying of the water nor the words that the witch speaks cause the hail, but the devil sees and hears the witch's signs and attends to her wish.[41] The same notion is brought out clearly in the *Malleus maleficarum*, in Johannes Vincentii, and in Johannes Wunschilburg.[42] Along with the other notions to similar effect, it may be classed as a noncontroversial element in the witch treatises.

There is a variation on this theme, already touched upon above in the discussion of Francisco de Toledo. The devil's role is not restricted to that of an executor of the wish expressed by the witch's 'sign.' He also is often responsible for having given the witch the material means that she uses. Peter Mamoris speaks of 'unguents received from the demon.'[43] Another author mentions the possibility of witches' destroying crops through application of material given by demons, in such a way that the demons act upon the signs that they themselves have provided.[44] The variety of roles played by demons is suggested by the anonymous *La Vauderye de Lyonois en brief*, which speaks of sorcery administered 'on the suggestion and instruction of the devil'; of powders 'made by the artifice of a demon'; of herbs 'expressly specified by a demon as food for working bewitchment'; and of an unguent 'prepared by diabolical art.'[45]

In short, the notion of diabolical mediation was an essential part of the mainstream of the theory of sorcery. It was either taken for granted or stated so confidently that the possibility of argument is scarcely conceivable. The point should be emphasized, however, that this interpretation was distinctive and in a way innovative. There is no indication that the subtleties of causal connection had greatly concerned people in the lower strata of society; the repeated insistence in the witchcraft literature that curses and charms have no inherent power suggests that the authors were arguing against a deep-set popular conviction that such inherent power did obtain. If this suggestion is correct, the notions of the early European populace were no different from those in non-Western cultures, in which one seldom encounters the idea that supernatural agents have a role in carrying out magic.[46]

While emphasizing on the one hand the role of the devil, the writers of most witchcraft treatises were equally emphatic in showing the role played by the witch. Lorenzo Anania argued that tempests, floods, conflagrations, sickness, and so forth, can be brought about by demons only when they make use of a human agent.[47] The authors of the *Malleus maleficarum* conceded that there are some things that devils can accomplish on their own: they can effect a darkening of the understanding; when God grants them power they can exercise a certain control over certain earthly matters; and they can reveal information in divination, independently of any contact with a witch.[48] In another passage the devil is allowed a broader repertoire of independent activities: injury to men's bodies only, injury to men's bodies and inner faculties, inward and outward temptation, deprivation of the use of reason, and transformation into the forms of beasts.[49] There is little, it seems, that the devil cannot accomplish on his own. Yet he prefers whenever possible to engage witches as his associates in malice. The main reason for this preference seems to be the obvious one: by acting in connection with a witch he can bring about the perdition of that witch. A further, equally evident motive is that God is more deeply offended when one of his creatures is thus corrupted. But the authors of the *Malleus* proceed to give a third reason, which struck H. C. Lea as 'a singular example of wrongheadedness': that when God is offended, he permits the devil more power to injure men.[50] This conception of divine retribution is merely an extension of that which views natural catastrophes as punishments sent by God. Thus, although it is the aristocracy that sins through feudal warfare, God punishes this offense by inflicting the *ignis sacer* on all of society.[51] Likewise, though it is witches who are offending God, all of mankind bears the punishment of diabolical maleficence. Once one has granted that the just may suffer along with the unjust in reparation for sin, the reasoning of the *Malleus* becomes comprehensible.

Some of the authors stressed the responsibility of witches as a justification for punishing them. Arnaldo Albertini argued that, even though the demon is the principal cause of *maleficia*, still these crimes are rightly attributed to witches—attributed, presumably, in the sense that witches are legally responsible for the crimes committed.[52]

The same theme occurs in the *Malleus*. The authors give two examples to illustrate their point. When a witch produces rain by dipping a twig into water and then sprinkling the water in the air, even though it is the devil who produces the rain, it is she who is to be held responsible for the deed: 'she herself nevertheless deservedly bears the blame,' since it is she who has occasioned the devil's work. The same is the case when a witch does injury to an image formed in molten lead cast on water; even though this act in itself does not cause the injury to the person whose image is mutilated, the injury is justly attributed to the witch. Thus, one cannot exculpate her on the grounds that the devil is the real agent of the crime. 'For without her God would never allow the devil to inflict the injury, nor would the devil on his own account try to injure the man.'[53]

In a later section of their work, Institoris and Sprenger give an example which demonstrates how little the witch actually needed to do to give what Geiler von Kaiserberg called a sign. Certain witches captured at Ravensburg had bewitched horses and cattle by placing bones under the threshold of the stable door, 'in the name of the devil and all the other devils.' But upon inquiry one of the witches revealed that she had done nothing but dig a small hole, into which the devil had placed certain objects—presumably magical powders and similar substances—unknown to her. Thus, the extent of the witch's cooperation may be minimal: 'only a touch or a look' may suffice to engage her along with the devil in the act of sorcery.[54]

Historians have viewed the diabolical pact as one of the most important elements in the notion of witchcraft. Yet this concept can receive only brief attention here. The details of how the pact was established between the devil and the witch—the ceremonies attendant on its confirmation, the devil's mark bestowed on the witch as a sign of the pact, etc.—are irrelevant for present purposes. It is important, however, to recognize the prime significance of the pact as a means for placing the devil at the service of the witch, so that the witch's desires might be carried out with an almost mechanical regularity by the devil.

Apart from those passages in the witchcraft literature that speak specifically of the pact, there are numerous references to the connection between the pact and the witches' sorcery. Thus, the *Malleus maleficarum* states that witches are able to work harm 'by the help of the devil, on account of a compact which they have entered into with him.'[55] And John of Frankfurt makes essentially the same point when he says that acts of sorcery 'occur by virtue of a pact with the demons.'[56] The pact is thus represented as the real basis for the powers of the witch, and the assurance from the demon that the witch's desires will be fulfilled. The pact spoken of here is not so much the written agreement as the act of submission on the part of the witch. The written covenant is merely a formal sign of the spiritual relation, less necessary than a written contract in civil law, and often viewed as replaceable by a mere tacit pact.[57] Still, a pact of some kind is requisite. Nicholas Jacquier states explicitly that the pact is a necessary condition for sorcery: the power to bewitch is itself evidence that the pact has been established.[58]

The precise connection between the pact and the working of bewitchment is twofold. On the one hand the witch's right to have the devil execute her wishes is established by the contractual element in the pact. As stated in the sixteenth century by Francisco de Toledo, the pact is the promise by man to demon and by demon to man. The man pledges to obey the demon and deny God's precepts and sacraments; the demon promises to aid in sorcery.[59] On the other hand, it is in association with the pact (immediately after it has been formed, one may conjecture) that the devil and witch form an understanding as to the signs by which she will make her wishes known. In the words of John Geiler of Kaiserberg, 'The devil has made a pact with certain men, and given them words and signs; when they make the signs and use the words, he does what they request; thus, the devil does it for their sake.'[60] As writers on the subject frequently pointed out, however, the pact did not give the witch powers of coercion over the devil. And if the devil seemed coerced, this was merely a clever trick on his part, the better to ensnare the witch and keep her from repenting. Nicholas of Jauer insists that herbs, magic circles, images, verbal formulas, characters, figures, signs, and adjurations are all incapable of forcing demons to present themselves and to act as the witch bids them: 'but if they come, they come without coercion.'[61] There is even a theological reason for the impossibility of coercing demons. As John of Frankfurt states it, a spirit, having intellect and will, cannot be forced by another spirit, even if it can be acted upon by that other spirit.[62] There is, however, one exception to this general principle: a higher demon, according to Francisco de Toledo and Raphael de la Torre, may have powers of coercion over a lower demon. And a witch may be able to secure control over the lower demon by her influence with the higher one. But in this case it is still the higher demon who has powers of coercion, and not the witch herself.[63] In any case, there is generally little need for such coercion of malign spirits, for witches and demons are united, according to the authors of these treatises, in the common cause of perpetuating evil. John Trithemius sums up the matter thus cynically: 'It is not cause for wonder that witches seem to command demons, to whom their perverse impiety makes them similar, so that by a mutual inclination they are joined in seeking evil for the human race.'[64]

As should be clear from this sampling of citations, the connection between sorcery and diabolism was more than an occasional concern of theologians. It forms a dominant theme in the witchcraft literature. To be sure, there were still members of the educated élite who maintained skeptical or reserved attitudes towards notions of diabolism, and who distrusted the persecutors. But to the majority of those who reflected on witchcraft, and especially those who attempted to analyze it within an Aristotelian framework, the link between sorcery and diabolism seemed apparent. This literary association of diabolism with sorcery, though, would be of little relevance to this work if it had been only a theological exercise. But it quickly became more than that: its impact on judicial proceedings was pronounced. The question that arises at this juncture is how the judges who had assimilated such notions succeeded in imposing them on their subjects. Mere accusation was not enough; in most instances the judges insisted that the suspects confess their involvement in diabolism, and they commonly succeeded in obtaining this admission. But how did they do so?

The role of torture, though perhaps overemphasized in the historical literature, was surely great. There are many known cases in which suspects confessed diabolism only after torture. To take merely one example out of many, a Savoyard court apprehended a woman named Antonia in 1477.[65] She denied under oath that she was guilty of 'heresy' (meaning in this case witchcraft). Asked if she knew why she had been detained, she said those who had seized her said it was for reasons of faith. She denied that she had ever been defamed as a witch, or fled to avoid arrest for witchcraft. Evidently she admitted some form of magic, but she insisted that she had never gone to diabolical assemblies, and denied knowledge of what witches did. The inquisitor gave her a formal threefold monition to tell the truth, over a period of three days. He interrogated her further, asking about quarrels she had had with various persons. The procurator of the faith (essentially a prosecutor) requested an interlocutory sentence, which would lead to torture, providing the accused had no valid objections to this measure. Antonia pleaded only that she was innocent of witchcraft, but this was evidently not a legitimate objection. After an interlocutory sentence the woman was taken to the place of torture and raised on the strappado, three cubits from the floor, for about half an hour. She refused to confess, but asked for time to deliberate, and was taken down. Tortured again on the following day, she pleaded that if she were released from torture she would tell the truth. Yet it was only after a further day's deliberation that she broke down and confessed her engagement in diabolism. Her response to these procedures was typical. Virtually all suspects seem to have confessed as much as the judges wanted when they were subjected to torture, or as much as they could imagine themselves as having committed. One alleged witch, having made substantial confessions already, pleaded after torture, 'I know nothing more. Even if you were to tear me to a thousand pieces I would not be able to tell anything further.'[66] But more often than not the extent of the confessions appears to have been directly proportional to the length of torture.

Still, many subjects confessed even without torture. Indeed, there are known instances in which it is clear that subjects admitted their witchcraft before they were coerced in any physical way. In two trials in the diocese of Lausanne in 1461, the subjects confessed freely to having venerated the devil, and it was only afterwards that one of the judges demanded the application of torture to ensure that these confessions were accurate and complete.[67] In these cases, then, the court had no qualms about recording that torture was applied, and one may be confident that the subjects made their prior admissions without suffering physical pressure. Yet overt torture was not the only means of judicial coercion. Sustained imprisonment was sometimes effective as inducement to confession. In one trial for heresy at Eichstätt, in 1381, the heretic claimed that he would never admit guilt, even if heaven and earth poured forth bloody tears, and even if his body were pulverized, burned, or unnerved; but eight days in prison sufficed to convince him that he had been led astray by an evil spirit.[68] In a presumably atypical trial in Italy in the early fourteenth century, the inquisitor Thomas of Aversa deprived a young suspect of food for several days, and then plied him with potent wine, so that in his drunken stupor he convicted himself and his companions.[69] More common was the procedure recommended in the *Malleus maleficarum*, of promising a subject mercy if she confessed her guilt. The authors of the *Malleus* suggested that the judges employ a mental reservation: when they spoke of mercy they were to mean by that mercy to society, which could best be accomplished through the witch's demise.[70] In a well known trial at Arras in the mid-fifteenth century, subjects were falsely promised minor penances if they confessed, but threatened with death if they refused to incriminate themselves. When they admitted their guilt the judges shocked them by releasing them to the secular court for burning.[71] Likewise in one of the trials of 1461 in the diocese of Lausanne the subject's initial confessions came 'voluntarily' when the bishop promised merciful treatment.[72] The promise was not necessarily deceitful. Two subjects in the diocese of Lausanne were allowed to abjure their 'heresy' and receive penance.[73] In a trial at Zürich the judge kept his promise at least nominally: a suspect confessed diabolism when she was assured she would not be executed. The judge sentenced her to life imprisonment in a narrow cell with no windows, and with only a hatch on the ceiling through which she could be given one meal a day. After her death, her corpse was to be burned to ashes.[74] Prisoners subject to such treatment seem to have viewed the judges with justifiable suspicion, and not infrequently vacillated repeatedly between confession and retraction —a mode of behavior which only assured their condemnation.[75]

Information extracted under coercion could derive from a variety of sources. Some kinds of confession were no doubt true, even if made under torture. Others might be purely imaginary. Still others might be created from popular notions of what sorcerers or witches (or other criminals) did. But there was a special tool that was likely to mold the suspect's confessions in accordance with the judges' ideas: the interrogatory. Such lists of leading questions were included in all extensive inquisitorial manuals,[76] and when they were not readily at hand they could easily be assembled either from the information in demonological literature or from the confessions of earlier subjects. Their use in court was by no means restricted to ecclesiastical tribunals: employment of interrogatories was standard in secular courts as well, even for purely secular crimes.[77] As Joseph Hansen pointed out, the manuscript record of a witch trial at

Lucerne in the middle of the fifteenth century has either a small cross or the word *nichil* written in the margin beside each article of the confession, though in a different ink from the articles themselves. These markings indicate clearly that the confessions were used as an interrogatory for a later trial.[78] Sometimes the content of a judicial protocol gives evidence of such procedure. For example, in trials at Biel in 1466 and 1467 the male defendants allegedly confessed to having carried out certain deeds in the company of 'other pythonesses';[79] the word 'pythoness' had been used specifically for female witches, and suggests that the confessions of these male witches were modeled after those of an earlier female subject. Herbert Grundmann has shown the effect that employment of interrogatories had in trials for heresy, in which the words attributed to one heretic might be drawn verbatim from the trial of another heretic, or from a papal document condemning heterodox belief.[80] These techniques suffice to explain the common elements in witches' confessions. The individual features that sometimes occur are likewise entirely comprehensible: once the leading question was posed the subject was free to interject specific details as needed, and to embellish upon the basic story that the question had suggested. Even in relatively minor details, however, one finds stereotyping of subjects' confessions, indicating the heavy hand of the judge or scribe in formulating the confessions. For example, numerous witches in the diocese of Lausanne are supposed to have reported that they found the flesh of babies to taste 'sweet,' or 'good and sweet'—a detail that could scarcely come from any source other than a warped theological imagination.[81]

One might expect that learned notions would gradually spread to the lower classes of society and merge with ideas that were popular in origin. The media for transmission of these notions—especially sermons and public executions—were bound to have eventual impact on popular thought.[82] There is in fact evidence that during the fifteenth century people at large were becoming cognizant of learned concepts of witchcraft. The best evidence of this development comes in the records of interrogations from the diocese of Lausanne, where on occasion the judges asked suspects not what they themselves had done but what they knew about witchcraft. Their responses show some familiarity, albeit vague, with learned ideas. A woman tried in 1477 had heard rumours that witches gathered together, ate the flesh of children, had intercourse *more brutorum*, flew on brooms that they rubbed with an unguent, and refrained from making the sign of the cross. She was unable to give further details, though she had ostensibly seen a great number of mysterious candles about her one night in jail, and duly reported this phenomenon.[83] A woman tried in 1498 gave details similarly reminiscent of learned tradition.[84] But a man questioned in the same year claimed to know virtually nothing about the subject. He knew that witches kill men and animals, but did not know why. He had heard that they gather at synagogues, which he presumed would be held at night, but when asked what transpired at these assemblies he said that he had no way of knowing, since he had never been there.[85] As early as 1448, when a suspect was threatened with torture he sarcastically offered to confess: 'I will say anything that you want. I will admit that I ate children, and will tell about all the evil deeds that you want to hear.'[86]

These bits of evidence suggest that prosecution in this diocese had, over the years, made the population vaguely aware of charges being pressed against witches. No doubt similar spread of learned notions occurred elsewhere, and many people surely took these accusations seriously. But there is still not the slightest evidence that the uneducated people were ready to take their neighbors to court on such charges. As indicated earlier, there are distinct kinds of folklore;[87] the fact that a motif occurs within a given population does not necessarily indicate that the believers expect it to be relevant in their own lives, or that they will take practical action on the basis of this notion. When people in the diocese of Lausanne first heard about devil-worshippers who had been burned they may have believed these charges as they applied to these specific witches. They may also have been willing to grant that there might be other such offenders elsewhere. But there is absolutely no evidence that they, like their learned contemporaries, made an automatic association between sorcery and diabolism. Even in the late fifteenth century superior sources contain sorcery as the exclusive charge. The transmission of learned notions to the populace must thus be broken down into two stages. In the first there was some recognition of the reality of diabolism, but no incentive on a popular level to seek out perpetrators of this offence. The second stage, involving popular zeal to exterminate devil-worshippers, came only after 1500, if at all.[88]

Chapter VI

The Social Context of Witch Trials

The historical importance of diabolism is elusive. It is of some interest in intellectual history; its significance for judicial history lies mainly in the fact that it embellished the charges against many people who were burned, and no doubt led to the execution of some who, on the charge of sorcery alone, would have received more lenient sentences. Yet the allegation of diabolism does not appear to have arisen out of the tensions of society at large, and its relevance to social history is meager. Sorcery, on the other hand, was clearly an offense that aroused widespread anxiety. Prosecution for sorcery is a subject that has furnished important data regarding societies' problems and obsessions. The sources for the fourteenth and fifteenth centuries do not permit exhaustive analysis of the social context of witch accusations and trials. For later periods there is firmer, more abundant, and more diverse documentation: not only are the judicial records frequently informative on matters of social relevance, but supplementary pamphlets and other sources sometimes help to establish the subjects' place in society and relations with the accusers. The documents prior to 1500, however, shed so little light that one can merely probe in the darkness, in hopes that the patterns discerned are more than creations of one's imagination and expectations. In some ways the most one can do is point to analogies to witchcraft in other eras, and such correspondences are never altogether safe. Still, it may prove useful to examine the sources for whatever information they yield on this topic.

Apart from the general paucity of evidence, there are other serious methodological problems in studying the witchcraft of this era against the setting of social history. Records of manorial courts are seldom extant. In some cases the documents of ecclesiastical and municipal courts contain cases from rural areas subject to their authority, but for the most part the documents that survive are from

93

towns and their suburbs, and show trials that arose out of distinctively urban tensions. H. R. Trevor-Roper has suggested that the
European witch-craze began in the pre-feudal societies of the Alps
and the Pyrenees, and only later spread to the feudal society of the
plains.[1] It is true that in the period 1300–1500 there is a preponderance of witch trials from Switzerland. And if one can accept the
evidence that Lamothe-Langon presents, there were numerous trials
in the valley between the Pyrenees and the Cévennes—though as
has been argued above, the authenticity of his sources is highly
dubious.[2] In any event, most of the trials in these lands took place in
or near urban concentrations. The great majority of Swiss trials
occurred not in the Alps but in the urbanized region of the Swiss
midlands, which had a cultural, social, and economic complexion
quite distinct from that of the mountains. There was also a substantial number of trials in the French- and Italian-speaking Alps, but
the connection between mountain culture and witch trials is belied
by the extreme rarity of such trials in the German-speaking Alps.[3]
There were important cases in Innsbruck and Andermatt, but these
were significant (if modest-sized) towns lying along trade routes. If
anything, then, the trials for which records survive arose not out of
a pre-feudal context but out of the post-feudal, or post-manorial,
environment of towns.

It is possible that the rural villages of Europe experienced an
increase in witch trials along with the towns. Certainly in the modern
period witch trials were predominantly rural rather than urban
phenomena.[4] Fuller records might show that the rural cases vastly
outweighed those in the towns, and further information on known
cases might reveal that many urban trials had their origins in sur-
rounding agrarian communities. On the other hand, however, it is
conceivable that witchcraft before 1500 was primarily a preoccupation of townsmen. Recent work has shown that there was a breakdown of the traditional family structure specifically in the towns of
certain parts of Europe during the fourteenth and fifteenth centuries.[5] This kind of social disintegration is precisely the sort of
development to which Keith Thomas ascribes early modern witch
trials.[6] And there is anthropological precedent for witchcraft as a
predominantly urban concern. In his work in Yucatan, Robert
Redfield found that allegations of witchcraft were most common in
the urban areas near the northwest coast of the peninsula.[7] In the
agrarian villages of the southeast there was severe punishment (such

as public execution) for alleged witches, but cases were rare. In the heterogeneous society of the cities, however, accusation of witchcraft was a common phenomenon, resulting from the manifold tensions and quarrels of the complex environment. Anxiety about illness was a frequent source of such accusations. With less fixity in the role of women, and greater insecurity for females, rivalry between two women was another common incentive to charges of witchcraft. In the town of Dzitas, it was estimated that one out of every ten adults had been suspected of witchcraft or had been thought of as a victim of some witch. Likewise in other societies, there is a correlation between social disorientation and charges of witchcraft.[8]

It remains ultimately impossible to prove whether late medieval witchcraft was preponderantly rural or urban. Yet most of the trials for which evidence survives can be explained only as outgrowths of specifically urban developments and tensions. There may have been other trials that arose for other causes, but on this matter the records yield extremely little evidence. Among the urban developments responsible for witch trials, the incipient breakdown of family structure—with the need for reliance on one's own resources and on the aid of potentially hostile neighbors—probably played an important role. The movement into cities during and after the Black Death furthermore created a large class of new town-dwellers who were unaccustomed to urban life.[9] These newcomers did not necessarily sever all ties with their original homes and social systems, but to the extent that they did so they must have suffered profound disorientation, which would help to explain the rise in trials during the late fourteenth century. (Later outbreaks of the plague may have helped to perpetuate this effect.) The opening of new Alpine passes in the thirteenth century may also have intensified this development specifically in Switzerland, by eventually bringing new classes into an urban environment. And as suggested in an earlier chapter,[10] the introduction of inquisitorial procedure into municipal proceedings may have been partly responsible for the rise in witch hunting fervor.

Even in municipal records, important information is frequently lacking. The documents rarely reveal the social class from which an alleged witch came. On occasion they were members of the urban patriciate, as at Basel in 1407,[11] and in some instances the records of judicial confiscations indicate possession of substantial property.[12] In the majority of instances there is no such evidence. This silence itself may serve as *prima facie* evidence that the suspects were from the lower or middle classes, since the prosecution of prominent citizens was likely to occasion special notice of their socio-economic standing. The age of the suspect is seldom given, and when it does appear it suggests no significant pattern of ages. When marital status is indicated, the subject is more frequently married than unmarried or widowed. One is on somewhat firmer ground in speaking of the sex of the accused. Roughly two-thirds of the accused witches for whom personal information is recorded were female, with perhaps a smaller percentage in the early years of prosecution and a higher proportion in the late fifteenth century.

In some instances a suspect's notoriety extended beyond the charge of sorcery or witchcraft. The sorceress at Boucoiran in 1491 was widely known for her immoral life; she had given birth to an illegitimate child, and several witnesses commented on her promiscuity; she and her mother had moved to the town some time before, reputedly for fear of prosecution as witches.[13] In his trial at Innsbruck in 1485, Institoris began questioning one of the suspects about her sexual life, until another member of the tribunal terminated this prurient line of inquiry.[14] The inquisitor may have posed his question out of idle curiosity, but it is likely that he had some reason to suspect the woman of sexual laxity. As early as the mid-fourteenth century, secular authorities implied a connection between sexual immorality and witchcraft.[15] And on more than one occasion, men were bewitched by their own former mistresses.[16] There is evidently more frequent evidence for violation of moral norms by alleged witches in later centuries,[17] but the few relevant cases from before 1500 suggest that this association was already common.

One of the most important features of witch-suspects, as has already been suggested, is that they were most commonly isolated offenders. In roughly two-thirds of the trials, only one witch was brought forth at a time, and even when more than one was detected in the course of a witch hunt there is seldom reason to assume a connection between them. Occasionally the records speak of mothers who taught their arts to their daughters, as at Boucoiran in 1491.[18] In other cases sorceresses are supposed to have given instruction in magic to girls or to other women. Anna Brommenhansinn of Breslau confessed that she had boiled toads in the company of her mother and another woman, and furthermore named a certain woman as her instructor in the black arts.[19] At Innsbruck, both Michel Zimmermannin and Barbara Hufeysen were blamed for leading young women astray.[20] And a priest of Tournai received instruction from an associate named Egidius.[21] It is indeed likely that on occasion herbal lore and folk medicine were thus transmitted, and when the records speak of instruction in magic the content of the instruction was probably of this sort, and seldom dealt with strictly magical matters. In any case, the evidence suggests that, to the extent that sorcery was practiced at all, it was by and large more the sporadic endeavor of isolated individuals than a living, ongoing, commonly shared tradition.

In some instances these individuals were professionals: herbalists or other specialists, rightly or wrongly accused of performing sorcery for the sake of their clients. Sorceresses at Reggio in 1375,[22] at Todi in 1428,[23] and at Brescia in 1480[24] are clear examples of this sort of figure. Likewise, a woman prosecuted at Velay in 1390 had given a lethal drug to a client who had hoped to obtain a love potion.[25] When the town of Olten was being besieged by troops from Bern in 1383, the count of Kyburg raised the siege by summoning a woman to produce the greatest rain that had ever been seen in the land. She performed her magic after being promised by the duke that he would not harm her.[26] The Florentine sorcerer Niccolò Consigli furnished numerous kinds of sorcery for a client, in a futile attempt to injure an enemy and his son.[27] Again at the end of the fifteenth century, the woman who endeavored to kill the bishop of St David's enlisted the help of two other women in making images for the bewitchment.[28] And when a priest of Soissons wished to murder his enemies in 1460, it was a professional sorceress who allegedly instructed him to baptize a toad to be used in the making of a poison.[29] Further examples could easily be cited. Much more often, however, persons accused of sorcery appear to have acted on their own, out of personal malice, without serving as professionals. They may have been habitually inclined towards use of sorcery, and in many cases they were suspected of it by various members of their communities. Dorothea Hindremstein was so notorious that people of the vicinity attempted to avoid all dealings with her.[30] Around 1480, an inhabitant of Lucerne was reluctant to move to a new house that he had bought, because in the meantime a known sorceress had moved into the neighborhood. When a friend asked him why he had not moved in, he exclaimed, 'Let the devil move into that house! I would have to have a witch before my eyes all morning, and she knows well that I recognize her, and I know that she is a witch.'[31] But on the other hand there are many cases in which there was only one accuser, and only one specified offense. Given the obscurity of many of the records, it is impossible to say whether single or multiple offenses were more common, but both patterns were frequent.

One of the clearest lessons that anthropology has drawn in its study of witchcraft in many different societies is that the circumstances giving rise to accusations of witchcraft are not accidental.[32] There are specific kinds of situation that are likely to lead to such charges. Frequently it is possible to show prior animosity between the accuser and the accused—usually in the form of some specific quarrel. Most importantly, in many cases the suspected witch stands in a position of moral superiority in this quarrel, so that the accuser feels guilty, and reverses his guilt by projecting it on to the accused. If he has denied her the hospitality or kindness that he owes her, for example, he relieves his own feeling of guilt by asserting that she is somehow morally culpable. If appropriate circumstances arise, he will charge her specifically with bewitchment of him or a member of his family.[33]

There are numerous examples of this mechanism in the witch trials of the fourteenth and fifteenth centuries. Though the moral guilt of the accuser is not always clear, the importance of the quarrels is obvious. In 1450 at Péronne, an accused witch is supposed to have had a quarrel with her accuser, in which she threatened him with bewitchment. The reasons for the conflict are not specified, and one may doubt that the threat was fully overt, but conceivably the sorceress may have wished to impress upon the accuser the dangers of quarreling with her.[34] Dorothea Hindremstein, at Lucerne, likewise became embroiled in an argument. One of her children was fighting with a playmate one day, and was pushed into the mud. When Dorothea arrived she scolded the offending child angrily, and threatened that he would never forget his misdeed. In less than half a day, swelling developed on the body of the child, and he lay ill for three weeks. Having heard Dorothea's threat, the mother of the sick boy deduced that she had bewitched her son.[35] Perrussone Gapit, in the diocese of Lausanne, was accused by her sixty-year-old husband and by her stepson. The stepson had somehow gotten into a dispute with her, and she had allegedly threatened him, whereupon he fled from home for three weeks. Even when he returned, he distrusted her, and refused to eat anything she had prepared. On one occasion he relaxed his vigilance and ate four pears that she had cooked, and predictably he had become gravely ill.[36] A woman at Lucerne was tried later in the fifteenth century on the testimony of numerous witnesses. One of them had come into conflict with the woman, whereupon his cows gave nothing but blood. Another had recently arrived in the community, and planted a garden that was better than hers; out of spite, she went through his garden one day cursing the plants in it, and from then on his onion crop was blighted. The same woman, with an obvious bent for contention, quarreled with numerous other neighbors, and when circumstances arose they readily identified her as a sorceress.[37] In two cases sorcery is supposed to have been in retribution for adultery. A girl in fifteenth-century Todi fell sick with an apparently uncurable disease after having an affair with a married man. The natural suspicion was that the man's wife had bewitched her.[38] In an inferior text from Biel, in 1466, a sorcerer confessed that he had knocked a certain man off his horse (evidently through sorcery) because this man had committed adultery with his wife.[39]

In a case at Lucerne in 1489, accusations arose because the subject was unwanted in the boarding house or inn where she was staying. She had just been released from the jail at Unterwalden (the reason for her detention is not specified), and her son had taken her to this inn for lodging. The proprietor took her in reluctantly. After a few days someone else came and recommended that the innkeeper remove her, since she was a witch. The innkeeper had the woman's son promise that he would take her away, but he failed to do so. Soon afterward three more persons came and suggested that she be forced to leave, before she ruined the entire region. Although she was old and feeble, the innkeeper saw her one day on a narrow ledge outside the inn, and this experience did little to reassure him that he should allow her to stay. Other witnesses told that they had come across her one day in a creek bed while they were out hunting wolves, and when they asked her what she was doing there she reproached them bitterly. Obviously an eccentric old woman, she inspired fear in all who met her. She evidently cultivated this image studiously. Apart from the incidents already mentioned, when she was about to leave the inn she suggested to the proprietor that he purify the house with blessed palms and holy water, lest evil befall him. He asked her not to harm him or his cattle. Though she said she would not inflict harm on them, she warned that evil would come upon them soon. As expected, all of his cattle died or became ill shortly afterward.[40] Anthropologists have suggested that in certain cases elderly women may have claimed preternatural powers so as to gain respect from those with whom they came in touch.[41] The present instance seems to fall within this category.

Three of the accused sorceresses at Innsbruck in 1485 had been in similar conflicts.[42] One of the witnesses found that her garden had been damaged one day, and the footprints leading from the garden continued up to the house of a notorious sorceress. When the latter went and asked the witness whether she held her responsible for the damage, a confrontation ensued, and shortly afterward the witness grew seriously ill. For some period of time she was even deprived of her powers of reason. Another woman had had numerous altercations with the same suspect. On one occasion they had met in a narrow street, when the sorceress was carrying a bundle on her head, and the accused woman abruptly began addressing the witness in foul terms—without provocation, according to the witness's account. When the witness proposed to take the matter to court, the sorceress threatened that her health and possessions would be ruined. The next day the witness became ill, and remained sick to the time of her deposition. To obtain relief, she sent two other women to speak with the sorceress, who answered the request by saying, 'If I had not inflicted the disease on her, I would still.' The witness then asked these intermediaries to take the matter to court, but they refused to have anything further to do with the evil woman. Only two months before the witness's deposition, the accused had passed her on the street and spat on the ground, crying out, 'You are not worthy that I should look at you.'

In most of the instances so far discussed, the sorceress appears to have been at least as culpable as the accuser—though this circumstance may derive from the fact that it was the accuser who told the recorded details in court. In certain other cases, there are clearer reasons why the accuser might feel guilt. In two Parisian trials from the late fourteenth century, women who had formerly been mistresses were tried for bewitching their lovers after these men had left them and married other women.[43] In two of the inferior texts from the fifteenth century, there is record of witches who inflicted curses after being refused alms;[44] despite the inferiority of the documents, there is no reason to believe that details of this sort would have been devised by the judges and falsely placed in the subjects' mouths. In a case at Lucerne at the end of the fifteenth century, the accuser seems to have recognized that he was in some way guilty for his treatment of the accused. The accuser had been ill for ten weeks altogether. After six weeks of his disease, he asked a seer for advice. The seer acknowledged that he knew who had bewitched him, but would not tell the sorceress's name. The accuser then sent his wife to the suspect, and had the suspect come to him. Having arrived at his house, she complained that she too was ill. He begged her to forgive him if he had ever aggrieved her, and when she made the same request he gave her his forgiveness. Apparently they had an extended history of mutual inhospitality. After she had forgiven him, his sickness was cured—and as a result of the healing he knew for sure that she was the one who had bewitched him, as he had suspected all along.[45]

Inquisitors and secular judges were apparently aware of this social mechanism as an important cause of accusations. In a trial at Boucoiran the judge asked repeatedly whether the sorceress had quarreled with the persons she afflicted. She protested that she herself had not fought with them, but one of her associates, with whom she had carried out the misdeeds, had come into conflict with the aggrieved families.[46] In other cases there is a similar manifestation of judges' interest in the minor disputes that had given rise to enmity.

One insuperable difficulty in discussion of the social context of sorcery is that the historian can seldom ascertain with confidence whether an accusation had basis in fact. There clearly were instances in which the people accused of maleficent magic did genuinely attempt to bewitch their neighbors. On occasion the magical substances that they employed were detected and identified.[47] At times these substances may have been misconstrued, but when the persons afflicted found wax images beneath their thresholds with pins sticking through them there was little room for doubt. In cases of this sort, where there actually was attempt at sorcery, the social mechanism that led to that attempt need not have been the same as the mechanism involved in false accusation. It is plausible that any kind of quarrel might lead an unscrupulous person to use sorcery —particularly a person who felt powerless against her neighbors, such as an old and neglected woman who felt unable to redress grievances in more orthodox ways. False accusations, on the other hand, probably arose from specific types of quarrel—particularly the sort in which the accuser recognized, clearly or vaguely, that he was in some measure morally culpable for an offense against the accused.

If the hypotheses made in this chapter are valid, then one must see a high degree of continuity between the witch trials of 1300–1500 and those in the early modern era. Social factors such as growing mobility, with its impact on family structure and style of life, provoked the first surge of witch accusations in the fourteenth and fifteenth centuries. The intensified social disruption of the sixteenth century produced the witch-craze of the early modern period. In neither era was the pattern of witch hunting wholly distinctive.

Chapter VII   Conclusion

Historians have typically viewed the Continental witch trials as fundamentally different from those in England. Some have suggested that the specifically popular notion of witchcraft was the same on both sides of the Channel, but differences have unquestionably received more emphasis than similarities. On one point there has been unanimity, either express or tacit: that if there *were* popular witch accusations on the Continent analogous to those in England, they are lost to history, buried under the excrescences of learned tradition. It is this last thesis that the present work seeks to overturn. It has been suggested here that one can distinguish certain types of record that are superior to others as sources of popular belief, and that by using these documents as touchstones for analysis one can separate folk notions from ideas of the intellectual élite.

The most basic distinctive feature of popular witch beliefs is their thoroughgoing preoccupation with the threat of sorcery. It was in response to this threat that the populace took suspects to court. The cosmological assumptions of the populace were relatively fluid. Long inured to religious practices that seemed to have magical effect, unsophisticated people accepted magical causality alongside natural and religious causal factors; without requiring any detailed explanation of how magic worked, they were willing to accept it as efficacious, and to experiment with various forms of magic. Educated people, on the other hand, and especially those bred on Aristotelian thought, could not accept the idea of distinctively magical causes. When the populace pointed to instances of maleficent magic, growing numbers of intellectuals could only see the influence of Satan. When these learned individuals entered the courtroom, they convicted suspects of diabolism—a charge more serious than that of sorcery, more sensational, and probably punished more frequently with death. First prominent in the Italian courts, the charge of

103

diabolism became important throughout Europe from about 1435 on, in response to the theological literature on witchcraft.

These basic findings are scarcely revolutionary; many historians have assumed for some time that popular and learned notions differed in this way. The contribution that this study attempts to make, however, is twofold. First, it seeks to provide methodologically sound verification for what many scholars have merely presumed on *a priori* grounds. Without such concrete evidence, one cannot validly exclude those alternative positions that certain other historians have taken for granted: that the people at large were concerned with both sorcery and diabolism, or that diabolism actually was practiced on a wide scale. Second, the present work endeavors to draw further and more detailed comparisons between popular and learned tradition. Reflecting directly the conceptions of theological literature, the accusations set forth by judges portray the witch as closely allied with the devil: he gives her the material means for bewitchment (unguents, powders, etc.), instructs her in their use, orders her to employ them to afflict her neighbors, and otherwise aids and abets her malfeasance. This involvement of the devil in the act of sorcery is almost wholly absent from texts which bear the mark of popular tradition. Invocation of the devil was known in folk belief, but only rarely occurred; when it did arise, the devil was more a servant of the invoker than a leading force inspiring maleficence. Certain kinds of sorcery, such as love magic, appear more commonly in folk tradition than in learned thought. More direct physical assault, on the other hand, while virtually unknown in popular accusation, comes forth frequently in the allegations introduced during judicial interrogation. In both popular and learned sources one finds emphasis on material means for bewitchment: powders, potions, images, and other such objects. The verbal method of incantation, important though it was in European antiquity, played virtually no role in late medieval sorcery. This shift may be explained in terms of the social position of the sorcerer: usually an isolated figure (or at most the member of a very small group), and unable in most cases to obtain information from written sources, he improvised his procedures in large part, rather than inheriting them from a stock of commonly shared techniques of maleficent magic. He thus experimented with those objects which by common consensus were thought of as in some way ominous.

In a few cases witch trials developed out of prosecution for heresy, or for participation in popular rites or festivals. The suspects may at times have been eccentric, self-professed devil-worshippers. The bulk of known documents, though, suggests that three occasions gave rise to the vast majority of witch trials: actual use of sorcery; use of beneficent magic or folk medicine; and altercation between the accuser and the accused. In any of these instances, the charge brought forth by the accuser would be that of sorcery; the further charge of diabolism would arise, if at all, only in the court.

While the sources prior to 1500 do not permit extensive analysis of the social background for witchcraft or witch accusations, the trials suggest that social mechanisms were at work analogous to those found in later eras and in other cultures. Quarrels of all kinds, intensified by the concentration of disoriented persons in the towns, frequently led either to actual attempts at sorcery or to suspicions of witchcraft. When a person felt guilty because of the quarrel, he might accuse the other party of witchcraft even when there was no real foundation for the charge.

The results of this study suggest a reflection on a question that has long exercised historians: whether the witch persecutions were essentially the responsibility of the masses or of the élite. One must surely conclude that the drastic increase in trials for sorcery came about primarily because of anxieties felt throughout society. The more fantastic charge of diabolism, then, built on a foundation that was already laid. The jurists and theologians who suggested this charge supplied a new dimension to the craze that was already under way, adding fuel to an already blazing fire. The masses and the intellectual élite combined their energies in a task of common concern—and demonstrated that the fruits of such cooperation are by no means necessarily salutary.

Calendar of
Witch Trials

The following calendar is intended for two purposes: first, as a supplement to the Notes, so that readers desiring further information on trials cited in the present book may find relevant works; second, as a general reference guide for scholars interested in witchcraft. It includes those trials in which sorcery, invocation, or diabolism (as defined above in the Introduction) was alleged. It also incorporates trials for heresy or magic in which circumstances indicate that witchcraft was a charge; for example, it contains trials for magic in which a sentence of execution suggests that the magic was maleficent, even though this is not an absolutely necessary conclusion. Trials for clearly beneficent magic and for simple divination are excluded.

Although archival material has been used for some of the cases, it should be stressed that the contents of archives throughout Europe still need systematic investigation before a full list of ascertainable witch trials can be made. Especially in England there are abundant judicial records that await scrutiny. Even for the Continent, however, early historians overlooked relevant materials from major archives, as recent work (eg, by Gene Brucker for Florence, and by Hartmut Kunstmann for Nürnberg) has made clear. Further cases will undoubtedly come forth in the research of local historians. The following calendar is therefore merely a provisional tool, reflecting the present state of research.

Three kinds of material are given in square brackets: first, those whose relevance is in doubt, such as trials for magic or divination that may have included witchcraft but probably did not; second, those in which it is not certain that accusation led either to official investigation or to judicial proceedings; third, those whose occurrence is doubtful or not confirmed by evidence cited by previous historians. In some instances historians have given incorrect dates for trials; in the event that readers may look for these cases under the incorrect dates, cross-references are given under these dates, in brackets. Material in brackets is not included in the enumeration of trials given in the text.

Whenever possible, the following information is given: date, place, number and sex of subjects, outcome of proceedings, court, and charges. In many instances, however, the sources do not give all these details. It has also been difficult in many cases to state the precise charges, because the terms used in the original sources are frequently vague. The general terms for witch and witchcraft are particularly nebulous; even words cognate with 'sorcery' can in different contexts apply to diabolism or to beneficent magic. Whenever such terms are ambiguous the language of the original documents is included, so that the reader can either judge on his own their precise meaning or else recognize their ambiguity.

Bibliographic references are separated into primary sources ('S') and secondary literature ('L') which refers to the trials in question. Full bibliographic information for a particular work, when not given in the calendar, may be obtained from the list of abbreviated titles, which follows the calendar.

Trials for any given year are listed in the following order:

(1) Trials occurring before or during the specified year—eg., '1450 (at latest), Lucerne'
(2) Trials occurring entirely within the specified year—eg., '1450, Lucerne'
(3) Trials occurring around the specified year—eg., 'c. 1450, Lucerne'
(4) Trials beginning during the specified year but continuing past it—eg., '1450–5, Lucerne'

Within each of these groups, the order is alphabetical. Multiple trials for a single place in a given year are distinguished by lower case letters.

For the sake of brevity, executions resulting from ecclesiastical proceedings are referred to as occurring 'by inquisitor' or 'by ecclesiastical court'. It should not be overlooked that the actual execution was carried out by secular authorities, to whom the subjects were released.

[1300, Freiburg i.B: Reference to witch trial in Midelfort, *Witch Hunting*, 201, not borne out in source there cited.]

1300, Nürnberg: Man banished by municipal court for incantation and other offenses. S: Schultheiss, *Acht-, Verbots-, und Fehdebücher*, 18. L: Kunstmann, *Zauberwahn*, 27.

1301–3, England: Walter Langton (bishop of Coventry) tried by ecclesiastical court for diabolism; acquitted. S: *Flores historiarum*, ed. Henry Richards Luard (Rolls Series, XCV), III (London, 1890), 305f.; Rymer, *Foedera*, I, pt IV, 27f. (reprinted in part in Hansen, *Quellen*, 2). L: Lea, *History of the Inquisition*, III, 451; Kittredge, *Witchcraft*, 241f.; Ewen, *Witchcraft and Demonianism*, 28f.; Rose, *Razor*, 64f.; Alice Beardwood, 'The Trial of Walter Langton, Bishop of Lichfield, 1307–12', *Transactions of the American Philosophical Society*, N.S., LIV, pt III (Philadelphia, 1964), esp. 7f. (with further sources cited in notes).

1302, Exeter (a): Trial for defamation; man had called woman a 'wicked witch and thief'. L: Wright, 'Municipal Archives', 307 (from MS); Kittredge, *Witchcraft*, 50f.

1302, Exeter (b): Woman tried by municipal court for dealing with witches and enchanters. L: Wright, 'Municipal Archives', 307 (from MS); Kittredge, *Witchcraft*, 51; Ewen, *Witchcraft and Demonianism*, 29.

1303–11, France: Boniface VIII charged with invocation, consultation of diviners, and other offenses, by officials of Philip IV. S: Pierre Dupuy, *Histoire du différend d'entre le pape Boniface VIII et Philippes le Bel* (Paris, 1655), 101–6, 324–46, 350–62. L: Lea, *History of the Inquisition*, III, 450f.; Hansen, *Zauberwahn*, 251; Russell, *Witchcraft*, 187; Cohn, *Europe's Inner Demons*, 180–5; Karl Wenck, 'War Bonifaz VIII. ein Ketzer?' *Historische Zeitschrift*, XCIV (N.S., LVIII) (1905), 1–66; Robert Holtzmann, 'War Bonifaz VIII. ein Ketzer?', *Mitteilungen des Instituts für österreichische Geschichtsforschung*, XXVI (1905), 488–98.

1304, Mons-en-Pevèle: Sorcerer charged before secular court with responsibility for death of Count William of Jülich. S: *Monumenta Germaniae historica*, *Scriptores*, XVI, 587f.; reprinted in Hansen, *Quellen*, 516f. L: Hansen, *Zauberwahn*, 393; Cauzons, *Magie*, II, 302.

1306–14, France (primarily): Prosecution of Templars by ecclesiastical and secular authorities for immorality, blasphemy, and diabolism. L (selection): George Archibald Campbell, *The Knights Templars: Their Rise and Fall* (London, 1937); Julius Gmelin, *Schuld oder Unschuld des Templerordens: Kritischer Versuch zur Lösung der Frage* (Stuttgart, 1893); Lea, *History of the Inquisition*, III, 238–334; Cauzons, *Magie*, II, 221–300; Russell, *Witchcraft*, 195–8; Cohn, *Europe's Inner Demons*, 75–98.

1308, Paris: Lord of Ulmet tried by secular court for poison and sorcery to kill wife, with aid of concubine; concubine and other involved woman burned. S: Hansen, *Zauberwahn*, 354 n. 2. L: Hansen, *Zauberwahn*, 354; Lea, *History of the Inquisition*, III, 451; Cauzon, *Magie*, II, 302f.

1308–13, France: Guichard (bishop of Troyes) tried by secular and ecclesiastical authorities for sorcery (killing of queen and others by image magic and potions), invocation, and other offenses. L: Abel Rigault, *Le procès de Guichard évêque de Troyes, 1308–1313* (Paris, 1896) (with documents); Guillaume Mollat,

'Guichard de Troyes et les révélations de la sorcière de Bourdenay', *Moyen Age*, XXI (ser. 2, XII) (1908), 310–14; Eubel, 'Vom Zaubereiunwesen', 29–31; Hansen, *Zauberwahn*, 335f.; Kittredge, *Witchcraft*, 76, 108f.; Cauzons, *Magie*, II, 303f.; Lehugeur, *Histoire de Philippe le Long*, 415; Lerner, *Free Spirit*, 69f.; Cohn, *Europe's Inner Demons*, 185–92.

1311, London: Investigation (by episcopal authority) of sorcery, enchantment, magic, divination, and invocation. L: Kittredge, *Witchcraft*, 51f.

1314 or 1315, England: Man hanged for attempt to gain crown through diabolical aid; had served devil more than three years. L: Kittredge, *Witchcraft*, 242.

1314–15, Paris: Woman condemned (evidently by secular court) for sorcery; two men accused by her given royal rehabilitation. S: Arthur Auguste Beugnot, ed., *Les olim, ou registres des arrêts rendus par la cour du roi*, II (Paris, 1842), 619. L: Lea, *History of the Inquisition*, III, 451; Kittredge, *Witchcraft*, 76f.; Russell, *Witchcraft*, 172.

1315, France (a): Enguerrand de Marigny hanged, and female associate burned, while others imprisoned, for image magic against Louis X and Charles of Valois; male associate committed suicide in jail. S: *Recueil des historiens*, XX, 612f., 618, 693–6, 700; XXI, 42f., 659–61; XXII, 158–60; Paris, *Les grandes chroniques*, V, 206–20. L: Jean Favier, *Un conseiller de Philippe le Bel: Enguerran de Marigny* (Paris, 1963); Eubel, 'Vom Zaubereiunwesen', 629; Hansen, *Zauberwahn*, 356; Lea, *History of the Inquisition*, III, 451; Kittredge, *Witchcraft*, 76f.; Russell, *Witchcraft*, 172.

[1315, France (b): Pierre de Latilly, bishop of Châlons-sur-Marne, tried for killing Philip IV (by witchcraft?); released. S: *Recueil des historiens*, XX, 613, 696; XXI, 43. L: Langlois, 'L'affaire du cardinal Francesco Caetani', 71 n. 1.]

1315, Krems: Trial of heretics, accused *inter alia* of antinomianism and Luciferanism. L: Bernard, 'Heresy', 50–4; Russell, *Witchcraft*, 177–9; Lerner, *Free Spirit*, 28f.

1315, Paris: Three women burned for killing bishop of Châlons-sur-Marne with potions. S: *Recueil des historiens*, XX, 614.

1316, France: Cardinal Francesco Gaetani investigated by royal court for image magic against king, his brother, and 2 cardinals. S: Raynaldus, *Annales*, a.a. 1316, no. 11; Langlois, 'L'affaire du cardinal Francesco Caetani' (with commentary). L: Lehugeur, *Histoire de Philippe le Long*, 416f.; Hansen, *Zauberwahn*, 356f.; Eubel, 'Vom Zaubereiunwesen', 628; Russell, *Witchcraft*, 172.

1317, Avignon: Hugues Géraud (bishop of Cahors) burned by ecclesiastical court, and others tried, for attempt on life of John XXII and certain cardinals through sorcery. S: Raynaldus, *Annales*, a.a. 1317, no. 52f. L: Edmond Albe, *Autour de Jean XXII: Hugues Géraud, évêque de Cahors: L'affaire des poisons et des envoûtements en 1317* (Cahors, 1904) (with documents); Guillaume Mollat, 'Un évêque supplicié au temps de Jean XXII', *Revue pratique d'apologétique*, IV (1907), 753–67; Guillaume Mollat, *The Popes at Avignon, 1305–1378* (English ed., London, 1963), 12f.; Hansen, *Zauberwahn*, 252f.; Lea, *History of the Inquisition*, III, 452f.; Cauzons, *Magie*, II, 318–41; Lehugeur, *Histoire de Philippe le Long*, 415f.; Cohn, *Europe's Inner Demons*, 192.

1317, France: Matilda of Artois tried for sorcery (love magic, killing Louis X); acquitted. L: Lehugeur, *Histoire de Philippe le Long*, 168–74, 415; Hansen, *Zauberwahn*, 357; Russell, *Witchcraft*, 172.

1317, Paris: Man condemned by secular court for killing several persons by invocation and sorcery (wax images baptized by priests). S: M. E. Boutaric, ed., *Inventaires et documents: Actes du Parlement de Paris*, ser. 1, II (Paris, 1867), 199f. L: Lehugeur, *Histoire de Philippe le Long*, 416.

1318, Avignon (a): Proceedings by papal commission against clerics and laymen charged with magic and invocation. S: Hansen, *Quellen*, 2–4. L: Cohn, *Europe's Inner Demons*, 193.

1318, Avignon (b): Proceedings against bishop of Prague for protecting Luciferans in his diocese. S: Joseph Emler, ed., *Regesta diplomatica nec non epistolaris Bohemiae et Moraviae*, III (Prague, 1890), 173–6. L: A. Patschovsky, *Die Anfänge einer ständigen Inquisition in Böhmen* (Berlin, 1975).

1319, Carcassonne: Bernard Délicieux (Franciscan) cleared by ecclesiastical court of charge of sorcery (attempt on life of Benedict XI), but imprisoned for possessing book on necromancy and invocation. L: Barthélemy Hauréau, *Bernard Délicieux et l'Inquisition albigeoise, 1300–1320* (Paris, 1877), 143–65 (sentence: 198–218); Lea, *History of the Inquisition*, III, 451f.; Eubel, 'Vom Zaubereiunwesen', 628f.; Hansen, *Zauberwahn*, 253f.

1319, France: Jeanne de Latilly tried by royal court for sorcery against Charles of Valois; acquitted. L: Lehugeur, *Histoire de Philippe le Long*, 416; Hansen, *Zauberwahn*, 357.

1319, Paris: hearing of woman who confessed sorcery (killing with potions, image magic); had earlier testified in trial of Guichard of Troyes. S: Eubel, 'Vom Zaubereiunwesen', 629f. L: Guillaume Mollat, 'Guichard de Troyes et les révélations de la sorcière de Bourdenay', *Moyen Age*, XXI (ser. 2, XII) (1908), 310–14.

1320, Avignon: Matteo and Galeazzo Visconti charged by ecclesiastical authorities with invocation and sorcery (image magic to kill John XXII). S: Eubel, 'Vom Zaubereiunwesen', 609–25 (with commentary); Michel, 'Le procès de Matteo et de Galeazzo Visconti', 307–26. L: Hansen, *Zauberwahn*, 333f.; Michel, 'Le procès de Matteo et de Galeazzo Visconti'; Cohn, *Europe's Inner Demons*, 192.

1320–6, March of Ancona: Allies of Federico of Montefeltro (count of Urbino) charged by John XXII with idolatry, heresy, and invocation. S: Raynaldus, *Annales*, a.a. 1322, no. 1ff., and esp. 1321, no. 38; Conrad Eubel, ed., *Bullarium franciscanum sive Romanorum pontificum constitutiones* (Rome, 1898–1904), V, no. 405, 455a, 461, 536, 582. L: Hansen, *Zauberwahn*, 334; F. Bock, 'I processi di Giovanni XXII contro i Ghibellini delle Marche', *Bolletino dell'Istituto storico italiano per il medio evo*, LVII (1941), 19–43; Cohn, *Europe's Inner Demons*, 193.

[1320–50, Carcassonne: 400 persons tried by inquisitor for 'magic', and 200 executed. L: Lamothe-Langon, *Histoire de l'Inquisition*, III, 226; cited in Hansen, *Quellen*, 454; Hansen, *Zauberwahn*, 326. See above, pp. 16–18.]

[1320–50, Toulouse: 600 persons tried for witchcraft, and 400 executed. L: Lamothe-Langon, *Histoire de l'Inquisition*, III, 226; cited in Hansen, *Quellen*, 454; Hansen, *Zauberwahn*, 326; Lea, *Materials*, I, 232. See above, pp. 16–18.]

[1321, Pamiers: In proceedings against Cathar and Waldensian heretics, man and 5 women confessed magic; all recanted. S: Hansen, *Quellen*, 446f. L: Hansen, *Zauberwahn*, 311f.; Lea, *Materials*, I, 232.]

1322, Utrecht: Woman banished by municipal court for sorcery and divination. S: Samuel Muller, ed., *De middeleeuwsche rechtsbronnen der stad Utrecht*, I (The Hague, 1885), 60. L: Hansen, *Zauberwahn*, 393 (with erroneous reference to p. 170 of Muller).

c. 1322, Ehingen: Woman burned for use of eucharist in *maleficium*. S: Johann von Winterthur, *Chronica*, 108. L: Hansen, *Zauberwahn*, 388; Russell, *Witchcraft*, 167, 186.

1323, Château-Landon: 2 men sentenced to burning by ecclesiastical court for planning invocation, though one died before execution; associates degraded from orders. S: Paris, *Les grandes chroniques*, V, 269–72; *Recueil des historiens*, XX, 633f., 710–12. L: Lea, *History of the Inquisition*, III, 454f.; Hansen, *Zauberwahn*, 332; Kittredge, *Witchcraft*, 202f.; Russell, *Witchcraft*, 188; Cohn, *Europe's Inner Demons*, 194.

1323, Figeac: Monk investigated on papal order for alchemy, necromancy, augury, image magic, counterfeiting, etc. L: Thorndike, *History of Magic*, III, 29.

[1323, Toulouse: 2 clerics tried by ecclesiastical court for divination. S: Hansen, *Quellen*, 447–9. L: Lea, *Materials*, I, 230.]

[c. 1323–6, Austria: Man charged with invocation to secure release of Duke Frederick III from captivity. S: *Chronica Mathiae de Nuwenburg*, ed. A. Hofmeister (*Monumenta Germaniae historica, Scriptores rerum Germanicarum*, NS IV), I (Berlin, 1924), 125f.; *Chroniken der deutschen Städte*, VIII, 467f. L: Lea, *History of the Inquisition*, III, 456; Russell, *Witchcraft*, 188f.]

1324, Kilkenny: Alice Kyteler tried by ecclesiastical and secular authorities, along with 7 other women and 4 men, for diabolism, invocation, and sorcery (illness and death to own husbands); at least one accomplice executed. S: Wright, *Contemporary Narrative* (with commentary). L: Lea, *History of the Inquisition*, III, 456–8; Hansen, *Zauberwahn*, 341–3; Kittredge, *Witchcraft*, 52f., 94, 122f., 144, 177, 415; Ewen, *Witchcraft and Demonianism*, 30–3; Rose, *Razor*, 65f.; Robbins, *Encyclopedia*, 294f.; Russell, *Witchcraft*, 189–93; Cohn, *Europe's Inner Demons*, 198–204.

1325, Coventry: Robert le Mareschal and 27 clients charged before secular court with sorcery (attempt on life of king and other authorities). S: Wright, *Contemporary Narrative*, xxiii–xxix; excerpt in English transl. in Montague Summers, *The Geography of Witchcraft* (New York, 1927), 82–4, with original text 189f. n. 43. L: Lea, *History of the Inquisition*, III, 458; Kittredge, *Witchcraft*, 77f.; H. G. Richardson, 'Year Books and Plea Rolls as Sources of Historical Information', *Transactions of the Royal Historical Society*, ser. 4, V (1922), 35f.; Ewen, *Witchcraft and Demonianism*, 29f.

1326, Agen: 3 men tried for sorcery and invocation (to procure storms and death); one burned, others handed over to papal commission. S: J. M. Vidal, *Bullaire de l'Inquisition française au XIVe siècle et jusqu'à la fin du Grand Schisme* (Paris, 1913), 118f. L: Cohn, *Europe's Inner Demons*, 193f.

[1326, Austria: Suspicion of sorcery on death of Duke Leopold. L: Hansen, *Zauberwahn*, 387.]

1326, Toulouse: Men tried for sorcery (attempt on life of Charles IV with image magic); nephew of pope accused but absolved. S: Claude Devic and Joseph Vaissete, *Histoire générale de Languedoc*, X (Toulouse, 1885), col. 661–2. L: Eubel, 'Vom Zaubereiunwesen', 628; Lea, *History of the Inquisition*, I, 230; *ibid.*, III, 458; Hansen, *Zauberwahn*, 357.

c. 1326, Cologne: Trial for antinomianism and diabolism, by ecclesiastical court. L: Lerner, *Free Spirit*, 92ff.

[Before 1327, Lombux: Burning of woman, possibly for witchcraft, by ecclesiastical court. S: Hansen, *Zauberwahn*, 386 n. 3.]

1327, Austria: Trial of heretics, accused *inter alia* of antinomianism (and Luciferanism?). L: Russell, *Witchcraft*, 328; Lerner, *Free Spirit*, 26, 30f.

1327, France: Certain clerics tried by ecclesiastical court for sorcery (image magic against Charles IV) and invocation. S: Raynaldus, *Annales*, a.a. 1327, no. 44; further material in Hansen, *Quellen*, 671f. L: Hansen, *Zauberwahn*, 257.

1329, Carcassonne: Peter Recordi (Carmelite) imprisoned by inquisitors for sorcery (love magic, magic to obtain person's release from prison), invocation, and diabolism. S: Lea, *History of the Inquisition*, III, 657–9; cited Hansen, *Quellen*, 449. L: Lea, *History of the Inquisition*, III, 455f.; Hansen, *Zauberwahn*, 312f.; Russell, *Witchcraft*, 186; Cohn, *Europe's Inner Demons*, 194f.

[1330, England: Condemnation of Edmund, Earl of Kent, on political grounds; had obtained important information from demon, through mediation of friar. L: Kittredge, *Witchcraft*, 53.]

[1330, Toulouse: Imprisonment of 8 women by inquisitors for sorcery. L: Lamothe-Langon, *Histoire de l'Inquisition*, III, 211f.; Hansen, *Zauberwahn*, 313f. See above, pp. 16–18.]

1331, Dauphiné: Woman tried by secular court for magic and sorcery (use of amulets to prevent confession under torture). S: Archives Départementales de l'Isère, ser. B, MS 4355, first document. L: Marx, *Inquisition*, 30, 108.

1331, France (a): Group of clerics and laymen tried by ecclesiastical court for sorcery against Philip VI. S: Hansen, *Quellen*, 7f. L: Hansen, *Zauberwahn*, 257; Lynn Thorndike, *A History of Magic and Experimental Science*, III (New York and London, 1934), 31; Russell, *Witchcraft*, 172.

1331, France (b): Count Robert of Artois and female associate charged with attempt on Philip VI and Prince John, and with other sorcery (killing through use of wax images); woman burned. L: Hansen, *Zauberwahn*, 357.

1331, Southwark: Man tried (with a client and his associate) by royal court for sorcery; subjects claimed to have used image magic only to obtain friendship but jury asserted that intent was murder. S: Sayles, *Select Cases*, V, 53–7. L: Thomas, *Religion*, 467.

[1334, Ehingen: Date suggested by Hansen, *Zauberwahn*, 388, for trial listed above, c. 1322.]

[1335, Carcassonne: 74 persons tried by inquisitor for heresy, sorcery (killing, love magic), and diabolism. L: Lamothe-Langon, *Histoire de l'Inquisition*, III, 226–30; excerpts reprinted in Hansen, *Quellen*, 449f., and Cauzons, *Magie*, II, 356–8; Hansen, *Zauberwahn*, 314f.; Lea, *Materials*, I, 230–3; Baroja, *World of the Witches*, 89; Russell, *Witchcraft*, 181f. See above, pp. 16–18.]

[1335, Toulouse: 63 persons tried by inquisitor, including some accused of diabolism. S: Lamothe-Langon, *Histoire de l'Inquisition*, III, 233–41;

excerpts in Hansen, *Quellen*, 450–3; reprinted in Cauzons, *Magie*, II, 349–55; English transl. in Baroja, *World of the Witches*, 84–6. L: Hansen, *Zauberwahn*, 315–17; Lea, *Materials*, I, 231f.; Carlo Ginzburg, *I benandanti: Stregoneria e culti agrari tra Cinquecento e Seicento* (Turin, 1966), 47; Russell, *Witchcraft*, 181–5. See above, pp. 16–18.]

1336, Angermünde: Trial for Luciferanism by ecclesiastical court; 14 burned, others purged selves. S: 'Gesta archiepiscoporum Magdeburgensium', in *Monumenta Germaniae historica, Scriptores*, XIV (Stuttgart, 1883), 434f. L: Lerner, *Free Spirit*, 27f.; Russell, *Witchcraft*, 180; Kurze, 'Ketzergeschichte', 55–62; Cohn, *Europe's Inner Demons*, 35f.

[1336, Austria: Date sometimes given for trial of 1338, Austria, q.v.]

[1336, Avignon: Man tried by papal court for *ars nigromantica*. S: Hansen, *Quellen*, 9. L: Hansen, *Zauberwahn*, 258f.]

1336, diocese of Langres: 5 men and unspecified number of women tried by ecclesiastical court for *sortilegium* and necromancy. S: Hansen, *Quellen*, 8f. L: Hansen, *Zauberwahn*, 258.

1336, Paris: Transmission of English necromancer, on papal order, for sorcery (use of magical tablets). S: Hansen, *Quellen*, 8. L: Hansen, *Zauberwahn*, 258, 362; Kittredge, *Witchcraft*, 53.

1336–7, Avignon: Priest and layman tried by papal court for sorcery and magic. S: Hansen, *Quellen*, 9–11. L: Hansen, *Zauberwahn*, 259.

1337, Béziers: 2 clerics tried for having falsely accused bishop of image magic (during pontificate of John XXII). S: Hansen, *Quellen*, 11f.; Michel, 'Le procès de Matteo et de Galeazzo Visconti', 326f. L: Hansen, *Zauberwahn*, 259f.

[1337, Hatfield: Man tried by manorial court for failure to deliver devil as arranged in commercial transaction; case dismissed. S: Ewen, *Witchcraft and Demonianism*, 33f.]

[1338, Austria: Trial of heretics; charges (as given in chronicle) included antinomianism and possibly diabolism. S: Winterthur, *Chronica*, 144f. L: Lea, *History of the Inquisition*, II, 375; Bernard, 'Heresy', 55f.; Lerner, *Free Spirit*, 25f.; Russell, *Witchcraft*, 179f.; Cohn, *Europe's Inner Demons*, 34f.]

1338, Avignon: 2 women tried by ecclesiastical court for diabolism (and sorcery?). S: Hansen, *Quellen*, 13f. L: Hansen, *Zauberwahn*, 260; Russell, *Witchcraft*, 186f.

[1338, Brandenburg: Alleged trial of Luciferans. S: Johann von Winterthur, *Chronica*, 151. L: Kurze, 'Ketzergeschichte', 56f.; Lerner, *Free Spirit*, 27f.; Cohn, *Europe's Inner Demons*, 35f.; Russell, in *Witchcraft*, 327 n. 19 and 328 n. 25, appears to place too much confidence in precisely what Kurze and Lerner call into question, viz. the reliability of the passage in Johann von Winterthur.]

[1339, monastery of Bolbona: Cleric and 4 monks tried by ecclesiastical court for magic (image magic to obtain treasure). S: Hansen, *Quellen*, 14f. L: Hansen, *Zauberwahn*, 260f.]

[1340, Germany: Impotence from bewitchment used as grounds for annulment of marriage between John Henry of Luxemburg and Margaret Maultasch. L: Hansen, *Zauberwahn*, 387f.]

1340, Salzburg: Trial for Luciferanism. L: Russell, *Witchcraft*, 180.

[1340, Toulouse: Priest imprisoned by inquisitor for magic and blasphemy. L: Lamothe-Langon, *Histoire de l'Inquisition*, III, 242f.; Hansen, *Zauberwahn*, 331; Russell, *Witchcraft*, 187.]

[c. 1340, Novara: Woman tried by ecclesiastical court for diabolism; case known only from forged judicial opinion attributed to Bartolo of Sassoferrato. S: Hansen, *Quellen*, 64-6; cited *ibid.*, 453. L: Hansen, *Zauberwahn*, 334-6; Lea, *History of the Inquisition*, III, 534; Lea, *Materials*, I, 232. See esp. Cohn, *Europe's Inner Demons*, 138-45.]

1347, Mende: Priest imprisoned by episcopal court for sorcery (use of wax tablets) against bishop. L: Edmond Falgairolle, *Un envoûtement en Gévaudan en 1347* (Nîmes, 1892) (with document); Hansen, *Zauberwahn*, 291 n. 1, 362 n. 1.

1347, Nürnberg: Woman banished by municipal court for sorcery. S: Schultheiss, *Acht-, Verbots-, und Fehdebücher*, 70. L: Kunstmann, *Zauberwahn*, 27.

1349, Augsburg: Man banished by municipal court as thief and sorcerer. S: Buff, 'Verbrechen', 225.

[1350, Toulouse: Numerous witches tried by inquisitor, and 22 executed. L: Lamothe-Langon, *Histoire de l'Inquisition*, III, 246f.; cited in Hansen, *Quellen*, 454. See above, pp. 16-18.]

c. 1350, Brünn: 2 women tried by municipal court for sorcery (infliction of death), and allowed purgation. S: Emil Franz Rössler, *Die Stadtrechte von Brünn aus dem 13. und 14. Jahrhundert* (Prague, 1852), 24; reprinted in Hansen, *Quellen*, 517f. L: Hansen, *Zauberwahn*, 390f.; Lea, *Materials*, I, 246.

[c. 1350, Burgundy: Unspecified number of witches burned by inquisitors. L: Lamothe-Langon, *Histoire de l'Inquisition*, III, 245; Hansen, *Zauberwahn*, 332. See above, pp. 16-18.]

[1352, Carcassonne: 48 persons tried by inquisitor for diabolism, invocation, and sorcery, and 8 executed. L: Lamothe-Langon, *Histoire de l'Inquisition*, III, 256-58; cited in Hansen, *Quellen*, 454; Hansen, *Zauberwahn*, 332; Lea, *Materials*, I, 232; Russell, *Witchcraft*, 185. See above, pp. 16-18.]

1353, Strassburg (a): Woman banished by municipal court for sorcery; magical materials discovered in her possession. S: *Chroniken der deutschen Städte*, IX, 1020.

1353, Strassburg (b); 2 women banished by municipal court for sorcery. S: *Chroniken der deutschen Städte*, IX, 1021.

[1353, Toulouse: 68 persons tried by inquisitor for heresy, magic, and invocation; 11 executed. L: Lamothe-Langon, *Histoire de l'Inquisition*, III, 258-61; cited in Hansen, *Quellen*, 454; Lea, *History of the Inquisition*, III, 534; Russell, *Witchcraft*, 185f. See above, pp. 16-18.]

[1357, Carcassonne: 52 persons tried by inquisitor for heresy and witchcraft; 31 executed. L: Lamothe-Langon, *Histoire de l'Inquisition*, III, 265f.; cited in Hansen, *Quellen*, 454. See above, pp. 16-18.]

[1357, Toulouse: Unspecified number of persons tried by inquisitor for heresy, witchcraft, and diabolism. L: Lamothe-Langon, *Histoire de l'Inquisition*, III, 266f.; cited in Hansen, *Quellen*, 454. See above, pp. 16-18.]

1358, Roches: Woman burned by secular court for witchcraft. L: Dumont, *Justice criminelle*, II, 69; Hansen, *Zauberwahn*, 386.

c. 1360, Como: Unspecified number of persons tried (presumably by inquisitor) as members of *secta strigiarum*, according to sixteenth-century treatise. S: Hansen, *Quellen*, 282; cited *ibid.*, 454. L: Hansen, *Zauberwahn*, 337. Cohn, in *Europe's Inner Demons*, 145f., dismisses this case as a fiction; it seems more likely that it is based on an archival reference to action against some form of witchcraft, probably mere sorcery.

[1366, England: Man died after reconciliation to Church, having had pact with devil; no recorded judicial proceedings. S: James Tait, ed., *Chronica Johannis de Reading et Anonymi Cantuariensis, 1346–1367* (Manchester, 1914), 176. L: Kittredge, *Witchcraft*, 242; Russell, *Witchcraft*, 209.]

[1370, Milan: Date given for trial by Russell, *Witchcraft*, 210, evidently in reference to trial of 1390.]

1371, Douai: Woman banished by secular court for witchcraft. L: Villette, 'La sorcellerie dans le Nord', 144.

1371, Salurn: Woman and man tried by secular court for image magic; woman apparently executed. S: Hartmann Ammann, 'Ein Mordversuch durch Zauberei im Jahre 1371', *Mittheilungen des österreichischen Instituts für Geschichtsforschung*, X (1889), 135–8 (with commentary). L: Hansen, *Zauberwahn*, 389.

1371, Southwark: Man tried by royal court for invocation; possessed book for *experimenta*, and Saracen's head for enclosure of demon; disclaimed use of head; released. S: Sayles, *Selected Cases*, V, 162f. L: Thomas, *Religion*, 467.

1372, Halfedanges: Man and woman tried for witchcraft. L: Dumont, *Justice criminelle*, II, 69; Russell, *Witchcraft*, 209.

1372, Metz: Man and 3 women burned for sorcery (wax images, love potions, etc.). S: Huguenin, *Chroniques*, 112; reprinted in Hansen, *Zauberwahn*, 386 n. 2. L: Dumont, *Justice criminelle*, II, 25ff.; Hansen, *Zauberwahn*, 386.

[1373, Utrecht: Man banished by municipal court for sorcery. L: Hansen, *Zauberwahn*, 393 (with erroneous reference to Muller, *Middeleeuwsche rechtsbronnen*, I, 170).]

1375, Florence: Woman tried for love magic by municipal court; sentenced *in absentia* to burning, but sentence later canceled. S: Excerpts translated in Brucker, *Society of Renaissance Florence*, 26of. L: Brucker, 'Sorcery', 9f., 23 (from MS).

1375, Reggio: Gabrina degli Albeti branded and mutilated by municipal court for sorcery (mostly love magic), diabolically instigated curses, and invocation. S: Aldo Cerlini, 'Una strega reggiana e il suo processo', *Studi storici*, XV (1906), 59–68 (with commentary). L: Russell, *Witchcraft*, 209f.

[c. 1375, Florence: Woman tried for magic. L: Cerlini, 'Una dama e una stega', 85; Russell, *Witchcraft*, 210.]

1376, England: Dominican associated with Alice Perrers tried by ecclesiastical court for love magic directed at king. S: *Chronicon Angliae, ab anno Domini 1328 usque ad annum 1388, auctore monacho quodam Sancti Albani* (Rolls Series, LXIV), ed. Edward Maunde Thompson (London, 1874), 97–100. L: Kittredge, *Witchcraft*, 78, 105; Ewen, *Witchcraft and Demonianism*, 34.

1379, Augsburg: Woman banished by municipal council for sorcery and other offenses. S: Buff, 'Verbrechen', 228.

1380, Paris: Provost imprisoned by ecclesiastical court for love magic and other offenses. S: Louis Tanon, *Histoire des tribunaux de l'Inquisition en France* (Paris, 1893), 121f. nn.; excerpt in Hansen, *Quellen*, 454; Paris, *Les grandes chroniques*, VI, 474–6. L: Hansen, *Zauberwahn*, 332; Cohn, *Europe's Inner Demons*, 196.

[1383, Olten: Woman claimed responsible for weather magic during siege of Olten; no record of trial. S: Conrad Justinger, *Die Berner-Chronik*, ed. Gottlieb Studer (Bern, 1871), 156.]

[1383, Siena: Effort by inquisitor to instigate proceedings against group of witches, who allegedly engaged in love magic, invocation (to obtain murder), and especially diabolism; no record of judicial proceedings. S: G. Sanesi, 'Un episodio d'eresia nel 1383', *Bullettino senese di storia patria*, III (1896), 384f. L: Brucker, 'Sorcery', 19f., 23; Russell, *Witchcraft*, 210.]

1384, Florence: Niccolò Consigli executed by inquisitor for illicit exorcism, necromancy, divination, sorcery (infliction of disease, attempt at death, and manipulation of affections), and diabolism. S: Excerpts translated in Brucker, *Society of Renaissance Florence*, 361–6. L: Brucker, 'Sorcery', 13–16, 22f. (from MS).

1384, Milan: Woman tried by inquisitor for attending assemblies with 'Oriente'. L: Verga, 'Documenti', 166f.; Russell, *Witchcraft*, 211.

1384, Prenzlau: 5 men (evidently all Waldensians) tried by ecclesiastical court for Luciferanism; allowed purgation. L: Kurze, 'Ketzergeschichte', 55f., 58f. (see also document, 91–3); Russell, *Witchcraft*, 180f.; Cohn, *Europe's Inner Demons*, 36.

1385, Augsburg: Woman banished by municipal court for sorcery (evidently love magic). S: Buff, 'Verbrechen', 191.

1385, Douai: Man tried by secular court for witchcraft. L: Villette, 'La sorcellerie à Douai', 123f., 170.

[1385, London: 2 men tried by ecclesiastical court for magic. S: *Calendar of Patent Rolls, 1385–1389*, 63; L: Kittredge, *Witchcraft*, 56.]

1385, Saint-Quentin: Woman banished by municipal court for sorcery and *madagogie*. L: La Fons, 'Des sorcièrs', 438 n. 3.

[c. 1387, Spain: Peter IV of Aragon victimized by image magic; no record of judicial proceedings. L: Menéndez y Palayo, *Historia de los Heterodoxos*, II, 437 n. 2; Hansen, *Zauberwahn*, 351.]

1387–8, vicinity of Turin and Pinarolo: Waldensians tried by inquisitor; charges included diabolical assemblies. S: Girolamo Amati, 'Processus contra Valdenses in Lombardia superiori, anno 1387', *Archivio storico italiano*, ser. 3, I, pt 2 (1864), 3–52, and II, pt 1 (1865), 3–61; excerpts in J. J. I. von Döllinger, *Beiträge zur Sektengeschichte des Mittelalters*, II (Munich, 1890), 251–73. L: Hansen, *Zauberwahn*, 411; Lea, *Materials*, I, 204; Riezler, *Geschichte der Hexenprozesse*, 46; Russell, *Witchcraft*, 220f.; Cohn, *Europe's Inner Demons*, 37f.

[1387–1400, Carcassonne: 200 persons tried by inquisitors for heresy and magic; 67 executed. L: Lamothe-Langon, *Histoire de l'Inquisition*, III, 285f.; cited in Hansen, *Quellen*, 454; Lea, *Materials*, I, 232; Russell, *Witchcraft*, 219. See above, pp. 16–18.]

[1388, London: Sir Robert Tresilian found practicing invocation, though executed on other grounds. S: Thomas Favent, *Historia sive narratio de modo et forma mirabilis Parliamenti*, ed. May McKissack, *Camden Miscellany*, XIV

(Camden Society Publications, ser. 3, XXXVII) (London, 1926), 18. L: Kittredge, *Witchcraft*, 54; Russell, *Witchcraft*, 209.]

1389, Brussels: Woman fined by secular court for sorcery. L: Poullet, *Histoire du droit*, 278; Hansen, *Zauberwahn*, 394.

1390 (at latest), Milan: Woman tried, presumably by ecclesiastical court, for attending assemblies with 'Diana'. L: Verga, 'Documenti', 167 (from MS); Russell, *Witchcraft*, 212f.

1390, Laon: Unspecified number of sorcerers tried; released on order of Parlement. L: Lea, *History of the Inquisition*, III, 460f.

1390, Milan (a): Woman executed for diabolism by inquisitor. L: Verga, 'Documenti', 167 (from MS); Russell, *Witchcraft*, 211f.

1390, Milan (b): Woman executed by inquisitor for attendance at assemblies led by 'Diana' or 'Erodiade' or 'Oriente'. L: Verga, 'Documenti', 167 (from MS); Russell, *Witchcraft*, 213.

1390, Paris: 2 women burned by secular court for sorcery (to inflict impotence) and invocation. S: Duplès-Agier, *Registre criminel*, I, 327–62; excerpts in Hansen, *Quellen*, 518–20. L: Lea, *History of the Inquisition*, III, 461–3; Hansen, *Zauberwahn*, 358–60; Russell, *Witchcraft*, 214; Cohn, *Europe's Inner Demons*, 196f.

1390, Velay: Woman executed by secular court for sorcery (infliction of death). S: Augustin Chassaing, ed., *Spicilegium brivatense: Recueil de documents historiques relatifs au Brivadois et à l'Auvergne* (Paris, 1886), 438–46. L: Lea, *History of the Inquisition*, III, 463.

1390–1, Paris: 2 women burned by secular court for sorcery (infliction of illness, manipulation of affections) and diabolism. S: Duplès-Agier, *Registre criminelle*, II, 280–343; excerpts in Hansen, *Quellen*, 520–3. L: Hansen, *Zauberwahn*, 358–60, 362–4; Russell, *Witchcraft*, 214f.; Cohn, *Europe's Inner Demons*, 197.

1392, France: Duke of Orleans accused of sorcery (use of wax image baptized by monk) against Charles VI. L: Hansen, *Zauberwahn*, 364.

1392, Fribourg: Man accused of sorcery against two others; parties reconciled. S: Hansen, *Quellen*, 523.

1392, Nürnberg: Woman imprisoned and subject to public penance for sorcery, by secular court. L: Kunstmann, *Zauberwahn*, 27f. (from MS).

1393, Béarn: Woman tried for witchcraft by secular court. S: Lespy, 'Les sorcières', 59.

1394, Florence: Woman whipped and imprisoned by municipal court for love magic. L: Brucker, 'Sorcery', 10, 24 n. 45.

[1394, Osnabrück: See Hansen, *Quellen*, 545 n. 1.]

c. 1395–1405, Simmenthal: Numerous persons burned by secular judge (according to later clerical author) for diabolism, sorcery (infliction of illness and death on men and animals, theft of grain, etc., raising storms, causing sterility in men and animals), and divination. S: Nider, *Formicarius*, 314–16, 318f., 329–31; reprinted in Hansen, *Quellen*, 91–9; cited *ibid.*, 523. L: Lea, *History of the Inquisition*, III, 535; Russell, *Witchcraft*, 215f.; Cohn *Europe's Inner Demons*, 204f.

[1396, Florence: Man imprisoned by municipal court for attempted divination. L: Brucker, 'Sorcery', 12f., 22, 24 (from MS).]

[1396, Fribourg: Proceedings by provincial of Augustinians against local convent, accused of patronizing diviner to find stolen goods. L: Summarized in Hansen, *Quellen*, 523f.]

1397, Appenzell: Woman executed by secular court for sorcery (infliction of disease on animals). L: Schiess, *Gerichtswesen*, 93 (from MS).

1397, Paris (a): 2 women executed by secular court for witchcraft. L: Foucault, *Les procès de sorcellerie*, 292.

1397, Paris (b): 2 men accused by 2 Augustinians of sorcery (infliction of mental disturbance on Charles VI), but released; Louis of Orleans accused by same Augustinians of same sorcery, but not tried; Augustinians themselves, threatened with torture, admitted sorcery and invocation, then beheaded and quartered. L: Lea, *History of the Inquisition*, III, 465.

1398, Lucerne: Woman charged before municipal court with sorcery (possibly love magic, directed against husband of accuser) and other offenses. S: Hansen, *Quellen*, 524.

1398, Paris: Man executed by secular court for magic (probably sorcery). L: Foucault, *Les procès de sorcellerie*, 293. Cf. account of trial for diabolism, involving 2 men, of whom 1 was executed, in *Chroniken der deutschen Städte*, XXVI, 107.

1399, Basel: Woman banished by municipal court for sorcery (infliction of poverty). L: Buxtorf-Falkeisen, *Baslerische Stadt- und Landesgeschichten*, IV, xii; cited in Hansen, *Quellen*, 524.

1399, Paris: Man burned for sorcery. L: Hansen, *Zauberwahn*, 365.

1399, Portogruaro: Unspecified number of witches burned; court not specified. S: Francesco di Manzano, *Annali del Friuli*, VI (Udine, 1868), 139; reprinted in Bonomo, *Caccia*, 478 n. 1. L: Russell, *Witchcraft*, 209.

1399 or 1400, Berlin: Woman burned by municipal court for sorcery (poisoning). S: Hansen, *Quellen*, 524. L: Hansen, *Zauberwahn*, 395.

1400, Lucerne: Woman tried before municipal court for sorcery. S: Hansen, *Quellen*, 524.

[1401, France: Man accused of sorcery (use of wax statuette) against Count Bernard of Armagnac; no record of judicial proceedings. L: Hansen, *Zauberwahn*, 365.]

1401, Geneva: Woman tried before court of vidame; had allegedly used divination to detect stolen objects, and also invoked the devil, who appeared in form of man; under torture, confessed to having summoned devil so he could tell her the circumstances of thefts; several witnesses testified that they had used her services, but knew nothing about diabolical invocations. S: Hansen, *Quellen*, 524–6. L: Hansen, *Zauberwahn*, 384; Lea, *Materials*, I, 247; Russell, *Witchcraft*, 209.

1401, Paderborn: Papal absolution of priest who had employed *sortilegium* to obtain money. S: Hansen, *Quellen*, 672.

1401–2, Cambrai: Woman tried before secular court for witchcraft. L: Villette, 'La sorcellerie dans le Nord', 144.

1402, Lucerne: Trial for defamation before municipal court; one woman accused that another had called her a thief and a sorceress. S: Hansen, *Quellen*, 526.

1404, Florence: Man sentenced to penance and imprisonment by municipal court for various offenses; had employed love magic (applying unguent to his own genitals before intercourse, leaving inscribed parchment in certain place, and administering pulverized bird-bones) and other forms of magic. S: Excerpts translated in Brucker, *Society of Renaissance Florence*, 266–8. L: Brucker, 'Sorcery', 10f., 22, 24 n. 45 (from MS).

[1404, Paris (a): Report by prévot that bodies hanged on gibbets and bodies of stillborn babies were being stolen; persons responsible were suspect of witchcraft; not clear whether judicial proceedings ensued. L: Foucault, *Les procès de sorcellerie*, 293; Russell, *Witchcraft*, 209.]

1404, Paris (b): 3 men and woman burned for pretense of invocation to cure Charles VI. L: Lea, *History of the Inquisition*, III, 465f.; Foucault, *Les procès de sorcellerie*, 293.

1406, Berlin: Man burned for using sorcery to obtain money. S: Hansen, *Quellen*, 526. L: Hansen, *Zauberwahn*, 395.

1406, Lucerne: Woman charged before municipal court for administering love potion. S: Hansen, *Quellen*, 527.

1406, Nürnberg: 2 women banished by municipal court for use of magical powders to induce love. L: Knapp, *Das alte Kriminalrecht*, 217 (from MS); cited in Hansen, *Quellen*, 526f.; Hansen, *Zauberwahn*, 389f.; Kunstmann, *Zauberwahn*, 28 (from MS).

1406, Viège: Man declared by bailli of Valais to be innocent of *ars sortilegii*. S: Gremaud, *Documents*, VII, 15f. L: Bertrand, 'Notes sur les procès', 176.

1406–7, France: Group of clerics tried for attempt (with image magic and magical objects) on life of Benedict XIII and members of curia. S: Pierre Luc, 'Un complot contre le Pape Benoit XIII (1406–07)', *Mélanges d'archéologie et d'histoire de l'École Française de Rome*, LV (1938), 374–402.

1407, Basel: Numerous women banished by municipal court for sorcery and invocation, especially use of spells and potions to bring about love, illness, and death. S: Buxtorf-Falkeisen, *Baslerische Stadt- und Landesgeschichten*, IV, 1–25; cited in Hansen, *Quellen*, 527. L: Lea, *Materials*, I, 247; Hansen, *Zauberwahn*, 382f.

1407, Mantes: Woman tried by secular court for use of sorcery to harm men. S: DuCange, *Glossarium*, VII, 535; summarized with excerpt in Foucault, *Les procès de sorcellerie*, 293f.

1408, Brussels: Woman given penance by secular court for sorcery (placement of magical substance on threshold). L: Poullet, *Histoire du droit*, 278; Hansen, *Zauberwahn*, 394; Hansen, *Quellen*, 527.

1408, Lorraine: 1 man executed for use of love philtres. S: Bournon, *Coupures*, 23. L: Foucault, *Les procès de sorcellerie*, 294.

1409, Frankfurt: Trial by secular court for sale of child to Jewish sorcerer. L: Kirchner, *Geschichte der Stadt Frankfurt*, I, 504; cited in Hansen, *Quellen*, 527.

1409, Gelderland: 3 women fined for sorcery. S: Fragment in Molhuijsen, 'Bijdrage', 195; reprinted in Hansen, *Quellen*, 527. L: Hansen, *Zauberwahn*, 394.

1409, Pisa: Trial of Benedict XIII at council of Pisa for divination, invocation, sorcery (weather magic), and other offenses. S: J. Vincke, 'Acta Concilii

Pisani', *Römische Quartalschrift für christliche Altertumskunde und für Kirchengeschichte*, XLVI (1938), esp. 185–208. L: Margaret Harvey, 'Papal Witchcraft: The Charges against Benedict XIII', *Sanctity and Society: The Church and the World*, ed. Derek Baker (Oxford, 1973), 109–16.

1410, Carcassonne: Geraud Cassendi (a notary) tried before inquisitorial court for invocation and sorcery (use of ritual to induce love). S: Germain, 'Inventaire', 305; reprinted in Hansen, *Quellen*, 454f. L: Lea, *Materials*, I, 232; Russell, *Witchcraft*, 209; Cohn, *Europe's Inner Demons*, 196.

[1412, Carcassonne: Burning of numerous persons by inquisitor for sorcery and sodomy. L: Lamothe-Langon, *Histoire de l'Inquisition*, III, 299f.; cited in Hansen, *Quellen*, 455. See above, pp. 16–18.]

1412, Florence: Man sentenced to amputation and banishment by municipal authorities for fraudulent claims; had obtained money from certain individuals by promising to invoke devil in their service. S: Excerpts translated in Brucker, *Society of Renaissance Florence*, 268–70. L: Brucker, 'Sorcery', 11f., 24 (from MS).

[1412, Toulouse: 29 persons sentenced to penance or imprisonment for witchcraft and heresy, by inquisitor. L: Lamothe-Langon, *Histoire de l'Inquisition*, III, 300; cited in Hansen, *Quellen*, 455; Russell, *Witchcraft*, 219. See above, pp. 16–18.]

1414, Basel: Woman banished by municipal court for sorcery; magical substances discovered in her possession. L: Buxtorf-Falkeisen, *Baslerische Stadt- und Landesgeschichten*, IV, xii; cited in Hansen, *Quellen*, 527.

1416, Basel: 2 women banished by municipal court for sorcery and attempted suicide. L: Buxtorf-Falkeisen, *Baslerische Stadt- und Landesgeschichten*, IV, xii; cited in Hansen, *Quellen*, 527.

1417, Chambéry: Man beheaded by secular court for attempting murder of duke of Savoy through sorcery; subject had been counselor of duke. L: Victor de Saint-Genis, *Histoire de Savoye d'après les documents originaux*, I (Chambéry, 1868), 400f.; cited in Hansen, *Quellen*, 528; Hansen, *Zauberwahn*, 384.

[1417, Landshut: Woman tried by secular and ecclesiastical authorities for sacrilege, and sentenced to public penance, with threat of excommunication and banishment; not clear that crime involved witchcraft. L: Riezler, *Geschichte der Hexenprozesse*, 77f. (from MS); cited in Hansen, *Quellen*, 527f.; Hansen, *Zauberwahn*, 390.]

[1417, Tournai: Priest sentenced by bishop to pilgrimage for association with diviners. S: Fredericq, *Corpus documentorum*, II, 200–2; cited in Hansen, *Quellen*, 527.]

1417, Utrecht: Woman banished by municipal court for sorcery (*toverie*) and other offenses. S: Dodt, 'Aanteekeningen', 187; cited in Hansen, *Quellen*, 528.

[1418 (at latest), Valais: Lord of Anniviers accused in 1418 of failing to prosecute persons charged with witchcraft (*sortilegium*). S: Grémaud, *Documents*, VII, 269. L: Bertrand, 'Notes sur les procès', 176.]

[1419, Canterbury: Chaplain tried by ecclesiastical court for magic. L: Kittredge, *Witchcraft*, 80.]

1419, England: Joan of Navarre accused by Henry V of attempt to kill him by sorcery; Joan and clerical accomplice imprisoned. L: Kittredge, *Witchcraft*, 79f.; A. R. Myers, 'The Captivity of a Royal Witch: The Household Accounts of Queen Joan of Navarre, 1419–21', *Bulletin of the John Rylands Library*, XXIV (1940), 263–84, and XXVI (1942), 82–100 (largely from MSS, edited in second section).

1419, Lucerne: Man tried by municipal court for witchcraft (*hexereye*); acquitted. S: Schacher, *Hexenwesen im Kanton Luzern*, 64f.; excerpt in Hansen, *Quellen*, 528. L: Lea, *Materials*, I, 247; Hansen, *Zauberwahn*, 385.

1420, Appenzell: Woman beheaded by secular court for sorcery; had killed woman with poisoned apple, and bewitched cows. L: Schiess, *Gerichtswesen*, 93 (from MS).

1420 or 1423, Rome: Woman burned by inquisitor for changing self into form of cat and killing children, with devil's aid. S: Felix Hemmerlin, *Dialogus de nobilitate et rusticitate*, c. 32 (reprinted in Hansen, *Quellen*, 110); Johann Hartlieb, *Buch aller verbotenen Kunst*, c. 33 (reprinted in Hansen, *Quellen*, 131). L: Hansen, *Zauberwahn*, 349f.; Russell, *Witchcraft*, 216; Riezler, *Geschichte der Hexenprozesse*, 68f. Hemmerlin gives the date 1420, while Hartlieb (an eyewitness) gives 1423. The incident may be identical with one in 1424, Rome (q.v.), though Riezler is rightly cautious about making this identification.

[1421, Bamberg: Man banished by municipal court for claiming ability to detect stolen goods. S: 'Ein Bamberger Echtbuch (*liber proscriptorum*) von 1414– 1444', *Berichte über Bestand und Wirken des Historischen Vereins zu Bamberg*, LIX (1898), 38; cited in Hansen, *Quellen*, 529. L: Hansen, *Zauberwahn*, 390.]

[1421, Florence: 2 women penanced by municipal court for contriving sorcery and incantation to recruit personnel for brothel. L: Brucker, 'Sorcery', 11, 24 n. 45 (from MS).]

1421, Kempten: Woman tried for love magic by municipal court. S: Carl Heinrich von Lang, ed., *Regesta, sive rerum Boicarum autographa*, XII (1849), 364; cited in Hansen, *Quellen*, 529. L: Hansen, *Zauberwahn*, 390.

1422, Venice: Franciscans tried by ecclesiastical-secular commission for sacrificing to demons. L: Lea, *History of the Inquisition*, III, 547; cited in Hansen, *Quellen*, 455; Hansen, *Zauberwahn*, 338 n. 1.; Russell, *Witchcraft*, 210.

1423, Berlin: Woman burned by municipal court for sorcery (*pulveres et toferyge*). S: Hansen, *Quellen*, 529.

[1423, Carcassonne: Various sorcerers and magicians suspect of heresy burned or imprisoned by inquisitor. L: Lamothe-Langon, *Histoire de l'Inquisition*, III, 307f.; Lea, *Materials*, I, 232; Russell, *Witchcraft*, 219 (with erroneous reference to Toulouse). See above, pp. 16–18.]

1423, Nieder-Hauenstein: Woman executed for witchcraft; had allegedly ridden on wolf. L: Daniel Brückner, *Versuch einer Beschreibung historischer und natürlicher Merkwürdigkeiten der Landschaft Basel*, XII (Basel, 1755), 1366; cited in Hansen, *Quellen*, 529; Lea, *Materials*, I, 247; Russell, *Witchcraft*, 211 (though reference to *maleficium* is not borne out in source).

1423, Putten: Woman fined for sorcery against priest. S: Molhuijsen, 'Bijdrage', 195; reprinted in Hansen, *Quellen*, 529. L: Hansen, *Zauberwahn*, 394.

1423, Sursee: Woman burned by secular court, presumably for witchcraft. S: Hansen, *Quellen*, 529. L: Hansen, *Zauberwahn*, 385.

1423, Utrecht: Midwife banished by municipal court for sorcery and other offenses. S: Dodt, 'Aanteekeningen', 187. L: Hansen, *Zauberwahn*, 394.

1424, Lucerne: Municipal court obtained (presumably on occasion of trial for witchcraft at Lucerne) letter from provost at Interlaken, indicating that Jacob Schurchen had been found guilty there of minor offenses but not witchcraft. S: Hansen, *Quellen*, 530. L: Hansen, *Zauberwahn*, 385.

1424, Rome: Woman burned by unspecified court for killing children and bewitching people. S: Hansen, *Quellen*, 529f. L: Hansen, *Zauberwahn*, 349f.; Lea, *History of the Inquisition*, III, 535; Riezler, *Geschichte der Hexenprozesse*, 68; Russell, *Witchcraft*, 216. Cf. 1420 or 1423, Rome, for date.

1424, Zwickau: Woman banished by secular court for sorcery and theft (*czubernisse und duberey*). L: Ernst Fabian, 'Hexenprozesse in Zwickau und Umgegend', *Mitteilungen des Altertumsvereins für Zwickau und Umgegend*, IV (1894), 123; cited in Hansen, *Quellen*, 530; Hansen, *Zauberwahn*, 394.

1426, England: 2 men plus unspecified number of associates accused of sorcery (illness and attempt at death), thus provoking inquiry at royal direction. S: *Calendar of Patent Rolls, 1422–1429*, 363. L: Kittredge, *Witchcraft*, 80; Ewen, *Witchcraft and Demonianism*, 36.

1426, Fribourg (a): Man detained by secular authorities to force him to cure bewitched man and woman; woman tried by secular court for sorcery. S: Hansen, *Quellen*, 530. L: Berchtold, *Histoire du canton de Fribourg*, I, 530.

1426, Fribourg (b): Trial for sorcery. L: Jean Berchtold, *Histoire du canton de Fribourg*, I (Fribourg, 1841), 238; cited in Hansen, *Quellen*, 530.

1427, Appenzell: Woman tried by secular court for sorcery; had brought illness and death on animals. L: Schiess, *Gerichtswesen*, 93f.

[1427, Benevento: Date given in Russell, *Witchcraft*, 338; applies only to sermon given by St Bernardino, with reference to undated story about witchcraft.]

1427, Florence: Woman beheaded by secular court for love magic and invocation. L: Brucker, 'Sorcery', 16f. (from MS).

1427, Zürich: Priest tried by municipal court for making man lame through sorcery. L: Hansen, *Quellen*, 531 (cited from MS); Schweitzer, 'Hexenprozess', 26 (from MS); Hansen, *Zauberwahn*, 385f.

1428 (at latest), Valais: Man executed (probably by ecclesiastical court) for witchcraft (*multa sortilegia et crimen sortilegie*). S: Grémaud, *Documents*, VII, 531f. L: Bertrand, 'Notes sur les procès', 176f.

[1428, La Tour du Pin: Date given in Russell, *Witchcraft*, 256, for trial of 1438, q.v.]

1428, Todi: Matteuccia Francisci burned by municipal court for witchcraft; in first part of trial, charged with various forms of sorcery (mostly love magic), incantation, and beneficent magic; in second part, charged with diabolism and killing children as *strega*. S: Candida Peruzzi, 'Un processo di stregoneria a Todi nel '400', *Lares: Organo della Società di Etnografia Italiana–Roma*, XXI (1955), fasc. I–II, 1–17 (with commentary). L: Bonomo, *Caccia*, 119.

1428, Valais: Burning of numerous subjects (supposedly more than 100) by secular court; judicial records speak of *sortilegium*; chronicle speaks of sorcery to induce murder, counter-sorcery, theft of milk from cows, destruction of crops, and diabolism. S: Grémaud, *Documents*, VI, 549–51 (judicial records); Hansen, *Quellen*, esp. 533–7 (chronicle). L: Lea, *Materials*, I, 247f.; Bertrand, 'Notes sur les procès', 176f.

1428–47, Dauphiné: 110 women and 57 men executed by secular court for witchcraft, especially diabolism. S: Archives Départementales de l'Isère, ser.

B, MS 4356 (*Quintus liber fachureriorum*); Hansen, *Quellen*, 539–44; Chevalier, *Mémoire historique*, 131–5; Marx, *L'Inquisition en Dauphiné*, 213–29. L: Marx, *L'Inquisition en Dauphiné*, esp. 32–47, 84, 110, 125–36 (from MSS); Hansen, *Zauberwahn*, 440f.; Russell, *Witchcraft*, 216–18.

[1430, Fribourg: Trial for Waldensianism; one woman tried for magic. L: Ochsenbein, *Aus dem schweizerischen Volksleben*, 258, 302 (from MS); Hansen, *Zauberwahn*, 417.]

1430, London: 7 women imprisoned for attempt on king's life through sorcery. L: Kittredge, *Witchcraft*, 83.

1430–1, Neuchâtel: Trials for witchcraft, presumably by ecclesiastical court. L: Chabloz, *Les sorcières*, 51; Frédéric-Alexandre Jeanneret, *Les sorcièrs dans le pays de Neuchâtel au 15e, 16e, et 17e siècle* (Locle, 1862), has not been accessible to me.

1430–2, London: Apprehension of woman and 2 men for sorcery, by secular government. S: Rymer, *Foedera*, IV, pt 4, pp. 177f.; Nicolas Harris, ed., *Proceedings and Ordinances of the Privy Council of England*, IV (London, 1835), 114. L: Wright, *Contemporary Narrative*, xi–xii; Lea, *History of the Inquisition*, III, 467; Kittredge, *Witchcraft*, 83; Ewen, *Witchcraft and Demonianism*, 37.

1431, Faido: Woman tried by secular court for sorcery (killing); acquitted. L: 'Le streghe nella Leventina', 144f.; account reprinted in Hansen, *Quellen*, 544.

1431, Rouen: Burning of Joan of Arc by ecclesiastical court; witchcraft included in original accusations. S: *Procès de condamnation de Jeanne d'Arc*, ed. Pierre Tisset, I (Paris, 1960). L (most recent works only): Regine Pernoud, *Joan of Arc: By Herself and Her Witnesses* (New York, 1966); John Holland Smith, *Joan of Arc* (London, 1973); Walter Sidney Scott, *Jeanne d'Arc* (New York, 1974); Pierre Tisset, 'Capture et rançon de Jeanne d'Arc', *Revue historique de droit français et étranger*, XLVI (1968), 63–9; Russell, *Witchcraft*, 261f.

1432, Constance: 1 person executed for witchcraft. L: Midelfort, *Witch Hunting*, 201.

1432, Faido: Woman tried by inquisitor, confessed invocation. L: 'Le streghe nella Leventina', 145; account reprinted in Hansen, *Quellen*, 456f.; Hansen, *Zauberwahn*, 419; Lea, *Materials*, I, 232f.

[1432, Toulouse: Trial of 112 subjects by inquisitor for heresy and superstitious practices; 16 executed. L: Lamothe-Langon, *Histoire de l'Inquisition*, III, 341f.; Hansen, *Quellen*, 456; Hansen, *Zauberwahn*, 420; Lea, *Materials*, I, 232. See above, pp. 16–18.]

1432–43, England: Accusation before Court of Chancery that priest had injured man's body with sorcery. L: Kittredge, *Witchcraft*, 55f.; Ewen, *Witchcraft and Demonianism*, 37; Thomas, *Religion*, 467.

1433, Barcelona: Trial of woman by inquisitor for witchcraft. L: Menéndez y Pelayo, *Historia de los Heterodoxos*, II, 436; Hansen, *Quellen*, 457.

[1433, Basel: Woman tried by municipal court for riding on wolf. S: Buxtorf-Falkeisen, *Baslerische Stadt- und Landesgeschichten*, IV, xiii; cited in Hansen, *Quellen*, 545.]

1433, Lucerne: 5 persons tried by municipal court for sorcery. L: Schacher, *Hexenwesen*, 34.

1433, Tirol: 2 women tried as sorceresses by secular court. S: Schönach, 'Zur Geschichte', 63.

1434, Barcelona: Woman tried by inquisitor for keeping and venerating familiar spirit; acquitted. L: Menéndez y Pelayo, *Historia de los Heterodoxos*, II, 436; Hansen, *Quellen*, 457.

1434, Nürnberg: Woman exposed in stocks by municipal court for sorcery. L: Knapp, *Das alte Criminalrecht*, 274 (from MS); Kunstmann, *Zauberwahn*, 28 (from MS, with quotation); cited in Hansen, *Quellen*, 545.

1435, Carcassonne: Priest tried by ecclesiastical court for invocation and necromancy. S: Germain, 'Inventaire', 306; reprinted in Hansen, *Quellen*, 457f. L: Hansen, *Zauberwahn*, 420.

1435, Durham: Trial for defamation before ecclesiastical court; 3 men had accused woman of causing impotence through sorcery; woman absolved in ecclesiastical court. S: *Depositions and Other Ecclesiastical Proceedings*, 27. L: Kittredge, *Witchcraft*, 113; Ewen, *Witchcraft and Demonianism*, 37.

[1435, Straubing: Charges set forth (in court?) against Agnes Bernauerin, accused of love magic; subject drowned. L: Sigmund von Riezler, 'Agnes Bernauerin und die bairischen Herzoge', *Sitzungsberichte der königlichen bayerischen Akademie der Wissenschaften*, Historische Classe, 1885, Heft III, 285–354; Riezler, *Geschichte der Hexenprozesse*, 63f.; cited in Hansen, *Quellen*, 545.]

[c. 1435, Cologne: Woman (dressed in male clothes, in imitation of Joan of Arc) tried by inquisitor for magic; excommunicated. S: Nider, *Formicarius*, 332f.; reprinted in Hansen, *Quellen*, 458f. L: Hansen, *Zauberwahn*, 424.]

[1436, Isère: Reference given in Russell, *Witchcraft*, for trial in Dauphiné, for which document is preserved in Archives Départementales de l'Isère; cf. 1428–47, Dauphiné.]

1436, Posen: Woman tried by municipal court for sorcery; trial held originally for defamation, with charges brought by alleged accomplices, but afterward focused upon supposed sorceress. S: A. Werschauer, 'Die älteste Spur eines Hexenprocesses in Posen', *Zeitschrift der Historischen Gesellschaft für die Provinz Posen*, IV (1889), 213–15 (with commentary); cited in Hansen, *Quellen*, 545. L: Hansen, *Zauberwahn* (though reference to acquittal is not borne out in source).

1436, Tirol: Woman tried by secular court for sorcery, and acquitted. S: Schönach, 'Zur Geschichte', 63.

[c. 1436, Osnabrück: Suspicion arose that bishop of Osnabrück had been poisoned by woman or bewitched; some held a deacon responsible; no record whether anyone was tried. L: C. Stüve, *Geschichte des Hochstifts Osnabrück bis zum Jahre 1508* (Jena and Osnabrück, 1853), 341; cited in Hansen, *Quellen*, 545.]

c. 1437 (at latest), diocese of Autun: Unspecified persons tried by inquisitor for sorcery, counter-sorcery, and possibly diabolism. L: Nider, *Formicarius*, 315f.; cited in Hansen, *Quellen*, 456.

1437, Fribourg (a): Woman burned by municipal court for sorcery (infliction of illness). S: Hansen, *Quellen*, 545. L: Ochsenbein, *Aus dem schweizerischen Volksleben*, 366f.

1437, Fribourg (b): Woman executed by municipal court, presumably for witchcraft. S: Hansen, *Quellen*, 546. L: Ochsenbein, *Aus dem schweizerischen Volksleben*, 367.

1437, Mâcon: Man burned by secular court as *enferturier*, diviner, and invoker of demons. S: Hansen, *Quellen*, 546.

1437, county of Nice: Woman burned for witchcraft. L: Aubenas, *La sorcière*, 76.

1438 (at latest), diocese of Lausanne: Jaquetus Mangetaz burned, probably by inquisitor, presumably for diabolism; case known only from reference in later inquisition. S: Archives Cantonales Vaudoises, MS AC 29, fol. 1–3.

1438, Fribourg: Man apprehended by municipal court for *Voudessie*; died (evidently suicide) in jail; woman burned, presumably for same offense. S: Hansen, *Quellen*, 546. L: Hansen, *Zauberwahn*, 441.

1438, La Tour du Pin: Pierre Vallin executed at order of inquisitorial vicar, for diabolism and sorcery (beating spring to induce storms). S: Chevalier, *Mémoire historique*, 135–7; reprinted in Hansen, *Quellen*, 459–66, with further materials. L: Hansen, *Zauberwahn*, 420f.; Lea, *Materials*, I, 233–5; Russell, *Witchcraft*, 256–60.

1438, diocese of Lausanne: Aymonetus (son of Jaquetus Mangetaz) abjured heresy (i.e., diabolism) before inquisitor. S: Archives Cantonales Vaudoises, MS AC 29, fol. 1–3.

1438, Nürnberg: Woman given penance by municipal court for sorcery. L: Hansen, *Zauberwahn*, 431.

c. 1438, Nivernais: Man burned by inquisitor for diabolism. S: Jacquier, *Flagellum*, 55f.; cited in Hansen, *Quellen*, 141, 467.

1439, Neuchâtel: Unspecified number of persons executed by inquisitor for diabolism. S: Chabloz, *Les sorcières*, 80f., 84f.; Frédéric-Alexandre Jeanneret, *Les sorciers dans le pays de Neuchâtel au 15e, 16e, et 17e siècle* (Locle, 1862), has not been accessible to me.

1439, Draguignan: Catherine David tried by inquisitorial court for sorcery; had allegedly manipulated her father's affections by administering potion given by sorcerer (who had received it from demon); acquitted. L: Aubenas, *La sorcière* (with excerpts from MS).

[1439, Paris: Dominican tried by ecclesiastical and secular authorities for magic. L: Félix Aubert, *Histoire du parlement de Paris de l'origine à François Ier, 1250–1515*, I (Paris, 1894), 339f. n. 2; summarized in Hansen, *Quellen*, 467; Hansen, *Zauberwahn*, 421.]

1440, Fribourg: 4 women and 2 (or 3) men tried by municipal court for *le fait des Wodeis*; 4 women and 1 man burned. S: Hansen, *Quellen*, 546.

1440, Nantes: Gilles de Rais executed by ecclesiastical and secular courts for invocation, human sacrifice to devils, sexual perversion, etc. L (selection): Lea, *History of the Inquisition*, III, 468–89; Hansen, *Zauberwahn*, 421f.; Robbins, *Encyclopedia*, 403–7; Russell, *Witchcraft*, 262f.

1440, Péronne: Woman banished by municipal court for sorcery. L: La Fons, 'Des sorciers', 438f.

[1440, diocese of Winchester: 2 persons tried by ecclesiastical court for necromancy and 'sorcery'. L: Thomson, *Later Lollards*, 63.]

1441 (at latest), Bern: 4 trials for witchcraft, mentioned in trial of 1441. S: Türler, 'Hexen- und Zauberwesen', 80.

1441, Bern (a): Trial for defamation before municipal court: one man had called another a male witch (*hachtscher*) and sorcerer. S: Türler, 'Hexen- und Zauberwesen', 80.

1441, Bern (b): Trial for defamation before municipal court; accused had allegedly tried to induce a small girl to incriminate her parents by telling how they used sorcery to raise storms. S: Türler, 'Hexen- und Zauberwesen', 80.

1441, London: Eleanor Cobham (duchess of Gloucester) given penance, Margery Jourdemain burned, and Roger Whiche (or Bollingbroke, a clerk) executed by secular authorities for sorcery. S: Rymer, *Foedera*, V, pt. 1, p. 110; *A Chronicle of London*, ed. N. H. Nicolas, 128 (reprinted in Ewen, *Witch Hunting*, 40, and in Wright, *Contemporary Narrative*, xv–xvi); John Silvester Davies, ed., *An English Chronicle of the Reigns of Richard II., Henry IV., Henry V., and Henry VI.* (Publications of the Camden Society, LXIV) (London, 1856), 57–60; Thomas Wright, ed., *Political Poems and Songs Relating to English History* (Rolls Series, XIV), II (London, 1861), 205–8. L: Lea, *History of the Inquisition*, III, 467f.; Kittredge, *Witchcraft*, 81–4; Notestein, *History of Witchcraft*, 8f.; Ewen, *Witchcraft and Demonianism*, 37f.

1442 (at latest), Dauphiné: Woman executed as witch and heretic; case known only from later record of confiscation. S: Archives Départementales de l'Isère, ser. B, Ms 4355, second document. L: Marx, *L'Inquisition en Dauphiné*, 126.

1442, Fribourg: 3 men and 5 women burned as witches (*Voudez*) by municipal court. S: Hansen, *Quellen*, 546. L: Berchtold, *Histoire du canton de Fribourg*, I, 239.

1444 (at latest), Valais: Unspecified persons tried for *sortilegium* by major of Rarogne; incident known only from letter of bishop of Sion restricting further prosecution. S: Grémaud, *Documents*, VIII, 267f. L: Bertrand, 'Notes sur les procès', 163.

1444, Fribourg: Woman burned by municipal court, presumably for witchcraft. S: Hansen, *Quellen*, 547. L: Hansen, *Zauberwahn*, 441.

1444, Hamburg: 2 women burned by secular court for divination and incantation (i.e., one referred to as *divinatrix*, the other as *incantatrix*). L: Trummer, *Vorträge über Tortur*, I, 108f.; cited in Hansen, *Quellen*, 547; Hansen, *Zauberwahn*, 433.

1444, Lille: Woman executed by secular court for sorcery. L: La Fons, 'Les médecins', 214.

1444, London: Man placed on pillory by secular court for invocation (dealing with a 'wycckyd spyryte'). S: *The Historical Collections of a Citizen of London in the Fifteenth Century*, ed. James Gairdner (Publications of the Camden Society, N.S. XVII) (London, 1876), 185. L: Kittredge, *Witchcraft*, 59.

1444, Nürnberg: Woman apprehended by municipal court for acquisition of potentially magical substance (piece of executed man's shirt). S: *Chroniken der deutschen Städte*, X, 162. L: Kunstmann, *Zauberwahn*, 29.

1444, Utrecht: 2 women tried by municipal court for sorcery (*toverien*). S: Dodt, 'Aanteekeningen', 207; cited in Hansen, *Quellen*, 547. L: Hansen, *Zauberwahn*, 432.

1445, Perugia: Woman burned by secular court for divination and sorcery. S: 'Cronaca della citta di Perugia dal 1309 al 1419 nota col nome di "Diario del Graziani" ', *Archivio storico italiano*, ser. 1, XVI (1850), pt 1, p. 565; reprinted in Hansen, *Quellen*, 547f.

[1445, Rouen: Suppression of books of magic by provincial council; no indication of judicial proceedings. L: Lea, *Materials*, I, 141f. (with excerpts); Russell, *Witchcraft*, 339.]

[1445, Utrecht: Woman banished by municipal court for divination (detection of stolen goods), referred to as *toverien*. S: Dodt, 'Aanteekeningen', 209; cited in Hansen, *Quellen*, 547. L: Hansen, *Zauberwahn*, 432.]

1445, Verdun: Woman burned, apparently for witchcraft. L: Dumont, *Justice criminelle*, II, 69; summarized in Hansen, *Quellen*, 547.

1446, Berlin: 2 women burned by municipal court for sorcery and incantation (*veneficia et incantationes*); had inflicted blindness. S: Hansen, *Quellen*, 548. L: Hansen, *Zauberwahn*, 432.

1446, Cologne: Woman tried by municipal court for sorcery; acquitted. S: Hansen, *Quellen*, 548. L: Hansen, *Zauberwahn*, 432.

1446, Douai: 2 women burned by municipal court for sorcery; had killed one man and afflicted others. S: Fredericq, *Corpus documentorum*, III, 83f.

1446, Durham: 2 women tried as sorceresses; had allegedly obtained husbands for widows; allowed purgation. S: *Depositions and other Ecclesiastical Proceedings*, 29. L: Kittredge, *Witchcraft*, 107.

1446, Gouda: Woman fined by municipal court for love magic. S: Molhuijsen, 'Bijdrage', 195f.; reprinted in Hansen, *Quellen*, 548. L: Hansen, *Zauberwahn*, 432.

1446, Heidelberg: Several women burned for sorcery. S: Hartlieb, *Buch aller verbotenen Kunst*, 22; also in Hansen, *Quellen*, 132; cited *ibid.*, 467. L: Hansen, *Zauberwahn*, 424; Riezler, *Geschichte der Hexenprozesse*, 70.

[1446, Perugia: Date given in Russell, *Witchcraft*, 339, for trial of 1445, q.v.]

1446, Talloires: Antoine Charrière and others burned for witchcraft (evidently including diabolism) by ecclesiastical tribunal. L: J.-M. Lavanchy, 'Sabbats ou synagogues', 403; cited in Hansen, *Quellen*, 467.

1447, Büren: Anna Vögtlin burned by secular court for witchcraft; primary charge was diabolism; had allegedly worked sorcery (destruction of crops, harm to individuals). S: Schneller, 'Hexenwesen', 367-70; also in Hansen, *Quellen*, 548-51. L: Hansen, *Zauberwahn*, 429.

1447, Rouen: Man tried by secular court for invocation and for dedication of stillborn child to devil. L: Floquet, *Histoire du parlement*, V, 617; cited in Hansen, *Quellen*, 552.

1447, Thalheim: Woman burned by inquisitor, with cooperation of secular authority, for sorcery and diabolism. S: Hartlieb, *Buch aller verbotenen Kunst*, 22f.; also in Hansen, *Quellen*, 132f.; cited *ibid.*, 467. L: Hansen, *Zauberwahn*, 424; Riezler, *Geschichte der Hexenprozesse*, 70.

1447, Valais: Numerous persons tried by secular court as witches (*sortilege*); incident known from letter of bishop of Sion restricting further prosecution. S: Grémaud, *Documents*, VIII, 354-6, 365-8; reprinted in Hansen, *Quellen*, 551f. L: Lea, *Materials*, I, 249; Bertrand, 'Notes sur les procès', 163, 167f., 178.

1447, Wadenhoe: Man excommunicated by ecclesiastical court for necromancy and sorcery. L: R. C. Fowler, 'Secular Aid for Excommunication', *Transactions of the Royal Historical Society*, ser. 3, VIII (1914), 117.

c. 1447, Rouen: Man burned by secular court for recovery of lost goods through diabolical aid. L: Floquet, *Histoire du parlement*, V, 617; cited in Hansen, *Quellen*, 552.

1447 or 1448, Braunsberg: Woman banished by secular court for sorcery. L: J. A. Lilienthal, *Die Hexenprocesse der beiden Städte Braunsberg* (Königsberg, 1861), 114 (from MS); Lea, *History of the Inquisition*, III, 536; Hansen, *Zauberwahn*, 433; cited in Hansen, *Quellen*, 552.

1447 or 1448, Durham: Woman tried by ecclesiastical court as enchanter (*incantatrix*). S: *Depositions and Other Ecclesiastical Proceedings*, 29; reprinted in Ewen, *Witch Hunting*, 10. L: Kittredge, *Witchcraft*, 38.

1448 (at latest), diocese of Lausanne: Woman executed, probably by inquisitor, for witchcraft; incident cited in later trial. S: Archives Cantonales Vaudoises, MS Ac 29, fol. 29–40, *passim*.

1448, Béarn: Woman tried by secular court for sorcery (killing woman); died under torture. S: Lespy, 'Les sorcières', 59f.; cited in Hansen, *Quellen*, 552. L: Hansen, *Zauberwahn*, 428; Lea, *Materials*, I, 251.

1448, Fürth: Trial for defamation before secular court; 2 men and woman had accused 2 women of love magic; offenders fined. S: Werner Sprung, 'Der Eberhardshof und der Muggenhof, zwei ehemalige Weiler vor den Toren der Reichsstadt', *Mitteilungen des Vereins für Geschichte der Stadt Nürnberg*, L (1960), 66; Kunstmann, *Zauberwahn*, 28f. (both with commentary).

1448, Gorze: 2 women and 1 man tried by secular court as witches; 1 woman burned, other branded, man banished. S: Huguenin, *Chroniques*, 261; reprinted in Hansen, *Quellen*, 552f.

1448, diocese of Lausanne (a): Man executed by inquisitor for diabolism and sorcery (infliction of illness and death, raising storms). S: Archives Cantonales Vaudoises, MS Ac 29, fol. 5–28. L: Reymond, 'La sorcellerie', 7, 10, 13.

1448, diocese of Lausanne (b): Woman tried by inquisitor for sorcery (love magic) and diabolism; had been accused by former subjects. S: Archives Cantonales Vaudoises, MS Ac 29, fol. 29–40.

1448, diocese of Lausanne (c): Man tried by inquisitor for witchcraft; given absolution and penances. S: Archives Cantonales Vaudoises, MS Ac 29, fol. 44–55.

1448, diocese of Lausanne (d): Man tried by inquisitor for diabolism and sorcery (raising storms, killing children). S: Archives Cantonales Vaudoises, MS Ac 29, fol. 56–68. L: Reymond, 'La sorcellerie', 3, 6, 10, 12, 14.

[1448, Nürnberg: 3 men apprehended for irreligious deeds, described as *zauberliche*, but probably not in sense of specifically maleficent magic. L: Kunstmann, *Zauberwahn*, 29 (from MS).]

1449, Conthey: Man and woman tried by ecclesiastical court for heresy and sorcery; released to secular court; secular authority independently condemned subjects to burning; sentence protested by local secular authorities, claiming judicial autonomy, and protest upheld. L: Bertrand, 'Notes sur les proces', 158f.

1449, Dauphine: Man tried, evidently by ecclesiastical court, for diabolism. S: Archives de l'Isère, ser. B, MS 4355, third document. L: Marx, *L'Inquisition*, 35.

1449, diocese of Lausanne: Man tried by inquisitor for witchcraft. S: Archives

Cantonales Vaudoises, MS Ac 29, fol. 104–13. L: Reymond, 'La sorcellerie', 2f., 5f., 7, 10, 12.

1449, Stade: 4 women tried by municipal court for using sorcery (*des düvels konst*) to release person from jail; 3 executed. S: *Chroniken der deutschen Städte*, XXX, 93f.

1449, Valais: Man tried for *sortilegium* by ecclesiastical court. L: Bertrand, 'Notes sur les procès', 172.

1450, Douai: Woman executed by secular court for witchcraft. L: Villette, 'La sorcellerie à Douai', 170.

1450, Durham: Woman tried by ecclesiastical court for sorcery. S: *Depositions and other Ecclesiastical Proceedings*, 29. L: Kittredge, *Witchcraft*, 38.

1450, England: Jack Cade tried *inter alia* for invocation (summoning devil as black dog). L: Kittredge, *Witchcraft*, 177.

[1450, Ettenheim: Reference in Midelfort, *Witch Hunting*, 201, not borne out in source.]

1450, Péronne: Woman given public penance for sorcery. L: La Fons, 'Des sorcièrs', 439f.

1450, Reimerswael: Woman banished by municipal court for love magic. S: Molhuijsen, 'Bijdrage', 196; portion reprinted in Hansen, *Quellen*, 556.

c. 1450, Lucerne (a): Else of Meersburg tried by municipal court for weather magic, diabolism, invocation, riding on dogs and wolves. S: Hoffmann-Krayer, 'Luzerner Akten', 25–9; reprinted in Hansen, *Quellen*, 553–5. L: Hansen, *Zauberwahn*, 442; Lea, *Materials*, I, 251.

c. 1450, Lucerne (b): Woman tried by municipal court for sorcery (weather magic, love magic, destruction of crops), counter-sorcery, diabolism (including abuse of eucharist). S: Hoffmann-Krayer, 'Luzerner Akten', 30–3; cited in Hansen, *Quellen*, 556. L: Hansen, *Zauberwahn*, 442.

c. 1450, Savoy or vicinity: Unspecified number of witches tried, presumably by ecclesiastical court, for diabolism and sorcery (infliction of illness and death, destruction of crops). S: Hansen, *Quellen*, 118–22; cited *ibid.*, 455. L: Russell, *Witchcraft*, 238–42.

Between 1450 and 1457, diocese of Brixen: 2 women subjected to penance and imprisonment by Nicholas of Cusa for attending diabolical assemblies. S: *Nicolai Cusae Cardinalis Opera* (Paris, 1514), II, fol. CLXXII^r. L: Carl Binz, 'Zur Charakteristik des Cusanus', *Archiv für Kultur-Geschichte*, VII (1909), 145–53; cf. Josef Koch, *Untersuchungen über Datierung, Form, Sprache und Quellen: Kritisches Verzeichnis sämtlicher Predigten* (Cusanus-Texte, I, pt VII) (Heidelberg, 1942), 182f.

1451 (at latest), Basel: Charges raised against unspecified number of witches; case known only from reference in later proceedings. L: Hansen, *Quellen*, 556.

1451, Basel: Woman executed by secular court for witchcraft. L: Buxtorf-Falkeisen, *Baslerische Stadt- und Landesgeschichten*, IV, xiii; cited in Hansen, *Quellen*, 556.

1451, Strassburg: Woman accused of weather-magic before secular court; accuser unable to prove charge, so drowned. L: Hansen, *Quellen*, 556; Hansen, *Zauberwahn*, 431.

[1451 or 1452, Durham: Woman tried by ecclesiastical court for magic. S: *Depositions and other Ecclesiastical Proceedings*, 33.]

1452 (at latest), Chalon-sur-Saône: Vague reference to prosecution by secular and ecclesiastical authorities for heresy, invocation, etc.; precise charges not specified. S: Fredericq, *Corpus documentorum*, I, 333f. L: Russell, *Witchcraft*, 339.

1452, Béarn: Man tried by secular court for sorcery. S: Lespy, 'Les sorcières', 60; cited in Hansen, *Quellen*, 552. L: Hansen, *Zauberwahn*, 428.

1452, Durham: Trial in ecclesiastical court for defamation; one woman had accused another of *sortilegium*, and had spoken of a certain chaplain's profligate infatuation with her (suggestion of love magic?). S: *Depositions and other Ecclesiastical Proceedings*, 33; Kittredge, *Witchcraft*, 38, 60.

1452, Provins: Woman tried by secular court for diabolism and sorcery (weather magic, destruction). S: Félix Bourquelot, 'Les Vaudois du quinzième siècle', *Bibliothèque de l'École des Chartes*, ser. 2, III (1846), 89–93; abridged reprint in Hansen, *Quellen*, 556–9. L: Lea, *History of the Inquisition*, III, 535f.; Hansen, *Zauberwahn*, 443; Lea, *Materials*, I, 251f.

1453, Büsserach: Unspecified number of witches burned. L: Kocher, 'Regesten', 122.

1453, Carcassonne: Woman tried by ecclesiastical court for invocation and sorcery. S: Germain, 'Inventaire', 306; reprinted in Hansen, *Quellen*, 466.

1453, Constance: Woman, man, and boy tried for weather magic by secular court; woman (and boy?) burned. S: Hansen, *Quellen*, 561. L: Lea, *Materials*, I, 253 (erroneously states that man was burned).

1453, Evreux: William Adeline (former professor at Paris) degraded and imprisoned by ecclesiastical court for diabolism; had attended diabolical synagogue to gain favor of certain knight; devil had instructed him to preach that the sect of Vaudois was unreal. S: Hansen, *Quellen*, 135, 211, 241f., 467–72; Martène and Durand, *Veterum scriptorum amplissima collectio*, VI, 11ff. (reprinted in Hansen); Jacquier, *Flagellum*, 27 (cited but not reprinted in Hansen); Friedrich, 'Vauderye', 199f. (excerpt of source printed in full in Hansen). L: Hansen, *Zauberwahn*, 422; Cohn, *Europe's Inner Demons*, 230.

1453, Marmande: 11 or 12 women subject to lynch justice for sorcery (causing epidemic); 5 burned, 2 died under torture. S: 'Exécution faite à Marmande de plusieurs femmes accusées de sorcellerie (1453)', *Bulletin de l'École des Chartes*, ser. 2, V (1848–9), 372–6 (with commentary); reprinted in Hansen, *Quellen*, 559–61. L: Lea, *History of the Inquisition*, III, 536; Lea, *Materials*, I, 252f.

c. 1453, Regensburg: Woman tried by secular court for sorcery and procuring. L: Karl Theodor Gemeiner, *Reichstadt Regensburgische Chronik* (Regensburg, 1800–24), III, 208 n. 385; cited in Hansen, *Quellen*, 561; Hansen, *Zauberwahn*, 430.

1454, Bern and Solothurn: Numerous persons burned as witches. L: Anton von Tillier, *Geschichte des eidgenössischen Freistaates Bern*, II (Bern, 1838), 516; cited in Hansen, *Quellen*, 561.

1454, Ferrara: Woman burned by secular court for love magic. L: Werner L. Gundersheimer, 'Crime and Punishment in Ferrara, 1440–1500', in Lauro Martines, ed., *Violence and Civil Disorder in Italian Cities, 1200–1500* (Berkeley, Los Angeles, and London, 1972), 120f.

1454, Fribourg: Woman and 3 men burned by secular court as *Voudesez*. S: Hansen, *Quellen*, 561. L: Hansen, *Zauberwahn*, 441.

1454, Lucerne: Dorothea Hindremstein sentenced *in absentia* to burning by municipal court for sorcery (infliction of illness on men and animals, infliction of death on animals) and magic. S: Hoffmann-Krayer, 'Luzerner Akten', 33–9; reprinted in Hansen, *Quellen*, 561–5. L: Cohn, *Europe's Inner Demons*, 242.

1455, Douai: 2 women tried by secular court for witchcraft. L: Villette, 'La sorcellerie à Douai', 124f., 170.

1455, Edolo (Val Camonica): Unspecified number of witches accused by inquisitor, who requested aid of secular authority; had allegedly rejected sacraments, immolated children, adored devil. L: Cesare Cantù, *Gli eretici d'Italia*, III (Torino, 1868), 143; summarized in Hansen, *Quellen*, 472; Hansen, *Zauberwahn*, 419; Lea, *Materials*, I, 235.

1455, Locarno: Woman burned by secular court for witchcraft. S: 'Una strega nel 1455', *Bollettino storico della Svizzera italiana*, III (1881), 62; cited in Hansen, *Quellen*, 565.

1455, Talloires: 2 men burned by ecclesiastical court for witchcraft. L: Lavanchy, 'Sabbats ou synagogues', 398f.; cited in Hansen, *Quellen*, 467.

1455, Torcy: Man (2 men?) and woman tried, apparently by secular court, for sorcery (illness and death to animals). S: DuCange, *Glossarium*, VII, 535; brief excerpt reprinted in Hansen, *Quellen*, 565. L: Lea, *History of the Inquisition*, III, 537f.

1456, Breslau: 2 women drowned by secular court for sorcery (love magic, infliction of death). S: Klose, *Darstellung*, 100f.; cited in Hansen, *Quellen*, 569. L: Hansen, *Zauberwahn*, 433.

1456, Cologne: Woman tried by municipal court for sorcery (weather magic, destruction) and magic; associated with witches at Metz who had confessed diabolism. S: Martène and Durand, *Veterum scriptorum amplissima collectio*, V, 491; reprinted in Hansen, *Quellen*, 566–9, with further materials. L: Lea, *History of the Inquisition*, III, 457; Hansen, *Zauberwahn*, 432; Lea, *Materials*, I, 253f.

1456, Como: Man tried for witchcraft and invocation by inquisitor; absolved. L: Vittorio Spinetti, *Le streghe in Valtellina* (Sondrio, 1903), 56–8.

[1456, Dordrecht: Man given public penance by municipal court for divination. S: Hansen, *Quellen*, 569.]

1456, Falaise: Robert Olive burned by unspecified court for diabolism; had killed children and committed arson. L: Jules Garinet, *Histoire de la magie en France* (Paris, 1818), 108; cited in Hansen, *Quellen*, 565.

1456, Metz and vicinity: Numerous persons tried for sorcery (weather magic, infliction of death) by secular court; further burning by inquisitor; in trial at Cologne in same year, information given showing that witches at Metz confessed to diabolism (flight through air, use of ointments). S: Huguenin, *Chroniques*, 285; reprinted in Hansen, *Quellen*, 565f., and cf. *ibid.*, 567–9, 673. L: Hansen, *Zauberwahn*, 443f.; Lea, *Materials*, I, 235, 253.

1456, Valais: Woman burned by secular court as witch. L: Hansen, *Quellen*, 569.

1456, Vic: 'N., dit le Vieux-Saint', executed for witchcraft. L: Dumont, *Justice criminelle*, II, 69.

1457, Aubenas (a): Woman condemned to death by secular court as heretic *arte diabolica imbuta*. L: Régné, 'La sorcellerie en Vivarais', 481.

1457, Aubenas (b): Man condemned to death by ordinary court as sorcerer. L: Régné, 'La sorcellerie en Vivarais', 482.

1457, Breslau: Woman banished by secular court for frequent use of sorcery; magical substance found in her possession. S: Klose, *Darstellung*, 101; summarized in Hansen, *Quellen*, 569. L: Hansen, *Zauberwahn*, 433.

1457, Douai: Woman tried by secular court for witchcraft. L: Villette, 'La sorcellerie à Douai', 170 (from MS).

1457, France: Woman tried by inquisitor for diabolism. S: Jacquier, *Flagellum*, 56; cited in Hansen, *Quellen*, 141, 467.

1457, Fribourg: Man burned by secular government for bestiality, diabolism, and sorcery (weather magic). S: Jean Nicolas Elisabeth Berchtold, 'Supplément à l'histoire de la sorcellerie dans le canton de Fribourg', *Archives de la Société d'histoire du Canton de Fribourg*, I (1850), 494f. L: Hansen, *Quellen*, 569; Hansen, *Zauberwahn*, 441.

[1457, Hertford: Man abjured necromancy and heresy. L: Kittredge, *Witchcraft*, 38.]

1457, Metz: 4 persons burned for diabolism by secular and ecclesiastical authorities. S: Huguenin, *Chroniques*, 287; reprinted in Hansen, *Quellen*, 569f. L: Hansen, *Zauberwahn*, 443f.; Lea, *Materials*, I, 254.

1457, Milan: Man burned by secular court as *stregone*. L: Hansen, *Quellen*, 569.

1457-9, Faido: 32 persons tried by secular court for sorcery (weather, affliction of men and animals) and diabolism; most burned. L: 'Le streghe nella Leventina', VI, 169-71, 233-5, 262f.; *ibid.*, VII, 61f., 82-4, 113-15, 146-9, 170f., 191-4; Hansen, *Quellen*, 570; Hansen, *Zauberwahn*, 442f.; Lea, *Materials*, I, 250f.

1458 (at latest), France: Prosecution for diabolism by inquisitor. S: Jacquier, *Flagellum*, 58; cited in Hansen, *Quellen*, 467.

1458, Chamonix: Man and 2 women burned by ecclesiastical court for heresy, idolatry, and apostasy. S: Hansen, *Quellen*, 472-4. L: Hansen, *Zauberwahn*, 418; Lea, *Materials*, I, 235f.

1458, Constance: Man burned by secular court for sorcery (weather magic, theft of milk from cows). S: Hansen, *Quellen*, 570f. L: Hansen, *Zauberwahn*, 430.

1458, Dillenburg: 2 women tried by secular court for sorcery; 1 burned. L: J. von Arnoldi, *Geschichte der Oranien-Nassauschen Länder*, III, pt 2 (Hadamar and Coblenz, 1816), 78; Hansen, *Quellen*, 571; Hansen, *Zauberwahn*, 433.

1458, France: Man and woman (and probably others) tried by inquisitor for diabolism; man had been initiated into diabolical sect c. 1403-4 (not 1410, as in Hansen) by own mother. S: Jacquier, *Flagellum*, 39f., 56; cf. *ibid.*, 43, 47; partially reprinted in Hansen, *Quellen*, 137.

[1458, Fribourg: Man tried by secular court for divination. S: Hansen, *Quellen*, 570.]

1458, Gnechwitz: Man burned by secular court for sorcery (magical entrance into buildings). S: Klose, *Darstellung*, 101; cited in Hansen, *Quellen*, 571.

1458, Hamburg: Woman burned by secular court, presumably for witchcraft. L: Trummer, *Vorträge über Tortur*, I, 109; cited in Hansen, *Quellen*, 571; Hansen, *Zauberwahn*, 433.

1458, diocese of Lausanne: Man burned by ecclesiastical court for diabolism and killing of children. S: Archives Cantonales Vaudoises, MS Ac 29, fol. 72–87, 91. L: Reymond, 'La sorcellerie', 7; Reymond, 'Cas de sorcellerie', 81–3.

1459 (at latest), Dauphiné and Gascony: Unspecified number of persons tried by ecclesiastical courts for witchcraft. S: Hansen, *Quellen*, 148; cited *ibid.*, 466.

1459, Andermatt: Kattryna Simon beheaded by municipal court for diabolism, sorcery (causing avalanches, inflicting illness, inflicting death on animals and infants), and transformation of self into animal. S: Hansen, *Quellen*, 571–5. L: Hansen, *Zauberwahn*, 443.

1459, Avalon: 4 women and man tried by secular court for witchcraft; witnesses spoke primarily of sorcery, but confessions dealt with diabolism; all but one woman condemned. S: Archives Départementales de l'Isère, ser. B, MS 4355, fifth document, fol. 1ʳ–49ᵛ. L: Marx, *L'Inquisition en Dauphiné*, 36–42, 84f., 108 (cf. edition of excerpt, 230).

1459, Chamonix: Woman burned by ecclesiastical court for heresy, idolatry, and apostasy. S: Hansen, *Quellen*, 474–6. L: Lea, *Materials*, I, 236f.

1459, diocese of Lausanne: Woman tried by inquisitor for diabolism. S: Archives Cantonales Vaudoises, MS Ac 29, fol. 92–100.

1459, Pecquencourt: Woman tried by secular court for witchcraft. L: Villette, 'La sorcellerie dans le Nord', 144.

1459, Valais (a): Woman tried by ecclesiastical court for witchcraft. L: Bertrand, 'Notes sur les procès', 172.

1459, Valais (b): Man tried by ecclesiastical court for diabolism. L: Bertrand, 'Notes sur les procès', 159f.

1459–60, Nivelles: Woman tried by secular court as *valdoise*. S: Fredericq, *Corpus documentorum*, II, 265.

1459–62, Arras and vicinity: 34 persons tried by ecclesiastical court for diabolism; sorcery (harm to men and animals) alleged in one case; 12 subjects burned; appeal ended 1491. S: Fredericq, *Corpus documentorum*, I, 345–97 (cf. 460–2); *ibid.*, II, 263–6; *ibid.*, III, 89–113; excerpts in English transl. in Baroja, *World of the Witches*, 90f. L: Arthur Duverger, *La Vauderie dans les états de Philippe le Bon* (Arras, 1885); Lea, *History of the Inquisition*, III, 519–34; Wright, *Contemporary Narrative*, xii–xiv; Hansen, *Zauberwahn*, 422f.; Russell, *Witchcraft*, 245; Cohn, *Europe's Inner Demons*, 230–2; dissertation being prepared by Gordon Andreas Singer, University of Maryland (College Park).

1460, Lille: Woman tried by secular court as witch. L: La Fons, 'Les médecins', 208; reprinted in Fredericq, *Corpus documentorum*, II, 265f.

1460, Lucerne: Unspecified number of persons burned as witches by secular court. S: Hoffmann-Krayer, 'Luzerner Akten', 39; cited in Hansen, *Quellen*, 576.

1460, Soissons: Woman burned by secular court for sorcery. S: Hansen, *Quellen*, 575. L: Lea, *Materials*, I, 255.

1460, Soissons/Maroilles: Woman tried, presumably by secular court, for witchcraft. L: Villette, 'La sorcellerie dans le Nord', 145.

1460, diocese of Soissons: Woman burned for sorcery (infliction of death), performed for sake of clerical client. L: La Fons, 'Des sorciers', 437f.

c. 1460, Lyonnais: Unspecified number of persons tried, presumably by ecclesiastical court, for diabolism and sorcery (infliction of illness and death to men and animals, abortion, love magic, weather magic). S: Friedrich, 'Vauderye', 193–9; Hansen, *Quellen*, 188–95 (superior ed.); cited *ibid.*, 467.

[c. 1460–70, Milan, Como, Turin: Hansen, *Quellen*, 476, deduces from the treatises of Girolamo Visconti, Ambrose de' Vignate, Bernard of Como, and Sylvester Prierias that these cities witnessed witch trials during this decade; while the treatises do imply familiarity with recent proceedings, any specification of time and place remains speculative; cf., however, the reference to Mendrisio, c. 1457, in Hansen, *Quellen*, 281.]

1461, diocese of Lausanne (a): Woman burned by ecclesiastical court for diabolism and sorcery (killing children). S: Archives Cantonales Vaudoises, MS Ac 29, fol. 120–35. L: Reymond, 'Cas de sorcellerie', 86f.

1461, diocese of Lausanne (b): Man tried by ecclesiastical court for diabolism and sorcery (weather magic, destruction of crops, infliction of death on children and animals). S: Archives Cantonales Vaudoises, MS Ac 29, fol. 136–51. L: Reymond, 'La sorcellerie', 4, 7f.; Reymond, 'Cas de sorcellerie', 83–6.

1461, Putten: Woman fined for love magic by secular court. S: Molhuijsen, 'Bijdrage', 195; reprinted in Hansen, *Quellen*, 576. L: Hansen, *Zauberwahn*, 432.

1461, Willisau: Unspecified number of witches burned by secular court. S: Hoffmann-Krayer, 'Luzerner Akten', 40; cited in Hansen, *Quellen*, 576.

1462, Alpnach: Woman charged with witchcraft. S: Hansen, *Quellen*, 576 (partly paraphrased); summarized in Hoffmann-Krayer, 'Luzerner Akten', 40.

[1462, Ascanio and Bologna: References given in Russell, *Witchcraft*, 339, to a letter of Mariano Sozzini, in which Sozzini relates a story about a witch; the action of the story is not dated, and is fanciful; there is no evidence of judicial action.]

1462, Chamonix: 8 persons burned for diabolism and sorcery (death and destruction) by ecclesiastical court. S: Hansen, *Quellen*, 477–84. L: Hansen, *Zauberwahn*, 418.

1462, Fribourg: Man and woman executed by secular court, presumably for witchcraft. S: Hansen, *Quellen*, 576. L: Hansen, *Zauberwahn*, 441.

1462, Valais: Man executed by ecclesiastical court for witchcraft. L: Bertrand, 'Notes sur les procès', 160.

1462, Zürich (a): Woman tried by municipal court for sorcery (harm to men and animals). L: Hansen, *Quellen*, 576; Hansen, *Zauberwahn*, 430; Schweizer, 'Der Hexenprozess', 26f.

1462, Zürich (b): Woman banished by municipal court for sorcery. L: Hansen, *Quellen*, 576; Hansen, *Zauberwahn*, 430; Schweizer, 'Der Hexenprozess', 27.

1463, Lucerne (a): Woman tried by municipal court for teaching love magic. S: Hoffmann-Krayer, 'Luzerner Akten', 22f.

1463, Lucerne (b): Woman tried by municipal court for love magic. S: Hoffmann-Krayer, 'Luzerner Akten', 23.

[1463–4, Milan: Reference given in Bonomo, *Caccia*, 143; sources cited are letters, which do not give details of prosecution.]

1464, diocese of Lausanne: Perrussone Gapit executed by ecclesiastical court;

witnesses accused her of sorcery (infliction of illness, killing of infant); under interrogation, confessed sorcery (weather magic, killing children) and diabolism. S: Archives Cantonales Vaudoises, MS Ac 29, fol. 160–86. L: Reymond, 'Cas de sorcellerie', 87–90.

1464, Nürnberg: 2 men and woman imprisoned by municipal court for familiarity with sorceress who had afflicted one of these same men; released. L: Kunstmann, *Zauberwahn*, 29f. (from MS).

1465, Lucerne: Woman tried by municipal court for sorcery (love magic?). S: Hoffmann-Krayer, 'Luzerner Akten', 23f.

1465, Norfolk: 2 men tried by royal court for invocation to find treasure. L: Augustus Jessopp, *Random Roaming and Other Papers* (2nd ed., London, 1894), 109–12; Kittredge, *Witchcraft*, 94, 206.

1465, Péronne: Jean de Bourgogne (count of Nevers) subject to dispossession and imprisonment for political purposes, on pretext of image magic; later restored by court of peers. L: La Fons, 'Des sorcièrs', 439 n. 4.

[c. 1465, Porlezza: Reference given in Russell, *Witchcraft*, 339; source is undated petition from citizens of Porlezza to Francesco Sforza, requesting prosecution of witches responsible for bewitching townsmen; no record of consequent judicial action. S: Luigi Fumi, 'L'Inquisizione romana e lo stato di Milano', *Archivio storico lombardo*, ser. 4, XIII, anno 37 (1910), 106.]

1466, vicinity of Assisi: Ecclesiastical trial of heretics, accused *inter alia* of holding diabolical assemblies. S: Franz Ehrle, 'Die Spiritualen, ihr Verhältniss zum Franziskanerorden und zu den Fraticellen', *Archiv für Literatur- und Kirchengeschichte des Mittelalters*, IV (1888), 110–34. L: Hansen, *Zauberwahn*, 412; Cohn, *Europe's Inner Demons*, 44–9.

1466, Biel: Man tried by secular court for diabolism and sorcery (causing avalanches, weather magic, harm to men and animals, death to animals, harm to buildings). L: Kämpfen, *Hexen und Hexenprozesse*, 25 (from MS); summarized in Hansen, *Quellen*, 576f.; Lea, *Materials*, I, 249.

1466, Douai: Man executed by secular court for witchcraft. L: Villette, 'La sorcellerie à Douai', 153, 170.

1466, Ely: Man given public and private penance by bishop for invocation. L: Kittredge, *Witchcraft*, 207.

1466, Siegen: Woman tried by secular court for sorcery. L: Heinrich von Achenbach, *Geschichte der Stadt Siegen* (Siegen, 1883), I, pt 3, p. 33; cited in Hansen, *Quellen*, 576; Hansen, *Zauberwahn*, 433.

1466, Solothurn: Woman tried as witch by secular court. S: Hansen, *Quellen*, 577; cf. also Kocher, 'Regesten', 122.

1467 (at latest), Bern: Woman burned by municipal court for witchcraft. S: Tobler, 'Zum Hexenwesen', II, 59f.; reprinted in Hansen, *Quellen*, 577f. L: Hansen, *Zauberwahn*, 430, 434; Lea, *Materials*, I, 255.

1467, Biel: Man tried by secular court for diabolism and sorcery (weather magic; infliction of death, stillbirth, and illness upon men; infliction of harm on animals). L: Kämpfen, *Hexen und Hexenprozesse*, 25, 49 (from MS); summarized in Hansen, *Quellen*, 577.

[1467, Brescia: Man tried by inquisitor for heresy; allowed abjuration; later charged with diabolism, 1480, but record does not specify that this charge arose 1467. S: Guerrini, *Cronache bresciane*, 185.]

[1467, Holland: Woman tried by secular court for divination. S: Scheltema, *Geschiedenis der heksenprocessen*, 117; reprinted in Hansen, *Quellen*, 577.]

[1467, Rome: Fraticelli tried for holding nocturnal orgies and making sacramental powder from ashes of children. L: Lea, *Materials*, I, 203f.; Russell, *Witchcraft*, 339.]

[1467–80, Italy: Reference given in Russell, *Witchcraft*, 339; not borne out in source there cited.]

1468, Bologna: Prior tried by secular court for maintaining succubi in brothel, and offering sacrifice to them. L: Jakob Burckhardt, *The Civilization of the Renaissance in Italy*, transl. S. G. C. Middlemore (New York, 1929), II, 502 n. 2; cited in Hansen, *Quellen*, 578; Lea, *Materials*, I, 255 ('This seems to be the acme of the superstition').

1468, Breslau: Man and wife banished by secular court for sorcery performed by woman; she had earlier received mercy from court. S: Klose, *Darstellung*, 101; cited in Hansen, *Quellen*, 578; Hansen, *Zauberwahn*, 433.

1468, Bruges: Man tried by secular court for *sortilège* and superstition. S: Fredericq, *Corpus documentorum*, II, 266f.

[1468, Holland: Man condemned by secular court for crimes, including *transforming* (apparently not in conjunction with diabolism). S: Scheltema, *Geschiedenis der heksenprocessen*, 117.]

1468, Nürnberg: Woman exposed in public, branded, and banished by secular court for sorcery. S: *Chroniken der deutschen Städte*, X, 306; reprinted in Hansen, *Quellen*, 578. L: Knapp, *Das alte Nürnberger Kriminalrecht*, 274; Kunstmann, *Zauberwahn*, 30 (partly from MS).

[1469, Augsburg: Man tried by secular and ecclesiastical authorities for magic. S: Hansen, *Quellen*, 578f. L: Hansen, *Zauberwahn*, 431.]

1469, diocese of Lausanne: Woman tried by ecclesiastical court for diabolism. S: Archives Cantonales Vaudoises, MS Ac 29, fol. 196–200.

1469, Lucerne: Woman tried by secular court for witchcraft. S: Hoffmann-Krayer, 'Luzerner Akten', 24.

1470, Béarn: Woman tried for witchcraft by secular court. S: Lespy, 'Les sorcières', 60.

1470, England: Trial for defamation before royal court; man had accused duchess of Bedford of image magic. S: *Calendar of Patent Rolls, 1467–1477*, 190; Wright, *Contemporary Narrative*, xvi–xx. L: Kittredge, *Witchcraft*, 84f.; Notestein, *History of Witchcraft*, 9; Ewen, *Witchcraft and Demonianism*, 38 (misdated).

1470, Luxemburg: Woman and 2 men tried by secular authorities for witchcraft. S: Hansen, *Quellen*, 579. L: Hansen, *Zauberwahn*, 428.

1470–1, Burgundy: Woman burned by ecclesiastical and secular authorities for witchcraft. S: Hansen, *Quellen*, 484f. L: Hansen, *Zauberwahn*, 423; Lea, *Materials*, I, 237.

1470–6, Dauphiné: Various persons tried by secular court for witchcraft. S: Archives de l'Isère, ser. B, MS 4355, sixth document.

1471, Bern (a): Woman burned by municipal court for witchcraft. S: Tobler, 'Zum Hexenwesen', II, 60; excerpt in Hansen, *Quellen*, 579.

1471, Bern (b): Woman tried by municipal court for witchcraft. S: Tobler, 'Zum Hexenwesen', II, 60; excerpt in Hansen, *Quellen*, 579.

[1471, Frankfurt: 3 women tried by secular court for beneficent magic and divination; 1 given public penance, 2 banished. L: Grotefend, 'Hexen in Frankfurt', 72f.; Hansen, *Quellen*, 579; Hansen, *Zauberwahn*, 431.]

1471, Nürnberg: Woman banished by municipal court for sorcery (theft and poisoning). L: Kunstmann, *Zauberwahn*, 30 (from MS).

1472 (at latest), diocese of Cambrai or vicinity: Deacon condemned by ecclesiastical court for diabolism. S: Fredericq, *Corpus documentorum*, I, 439.

1472 (at latest), Tournai: 2 men tried by ecclesiastical court for love magic and invocation. S: Fredericq, *Corpus documentorum*, I, 428f.

[1472, Cawnton: Vicar resigned office on inculpation for sorcery. L: Kittredge, *Witchcraft*, 38.]

1472, France: Imprisonment of abbot for sorcery against Duke Charles of Guienne; devil allegedly appeared to abbot in prison. L: Hansen, *Quellen*, 579; Hansen, *Zauberwahn*, 428.

1472, Holland: Man condemned by secular court for invocation. S: Scheltema, *Geschiedenis der heksenprocessen*, 117.

1472, Val Canavese: 3 women burned by ecclesiastical court for witchcraft. L: Vayra, 'Le streghe del Canavese', esp. 256ff., 658ff.; cited in Hansen, *Quellen*, 485.

1472, Zutphen: Woman burned by secular court for sorcery. S: Molhuijsen, 'Bijdrage', 196; reprinted in Hansen, *Quellen*, 579. L: Scheltema, *Geschiedenis der heksenprocessen*, 120.

1473, Aargau: Woman burned for love magic. L: Bader, *Hexenprozesse*, 179.

1473, Bern (a): 2 women tried by municipal court for weather magic. S: Tobler, 'Zum Hexenwesen', II, 60; reprinted in Hansen, *Quellen*, 580.

1473, Bern (b): 14 men and women condemned by vogt of Grasburg as witches. S: Tobler, 'Zum Hexenwesen', II, 60; reprinted in Hansen, *Quellen*, 580. L: Hansen, *Zauberwahn*, 440.

1474, Nürnberg: Woman banished by municipal court for love magic. L: Knapp, *Das alte Nürnberger Kriminalrecht*, 217; summarized in Hansen, *Quellen*, 580; Hansen, *Zauberwahn*, 431.

1474–5, Val Canavese (a): 2 women tried by ecclesiastical court for witchcraft. L: Vayra, 'Le streghe del Canavese', esp. 228–36; excerpt in Hansen, *Quellen*, 485–7; Lea, *History of the Inquisition*, III, 516f.

1474–5, Val Canavese (b): 5 women burned by ecclesiastical court for witchcraft. L: Vayra, 'Le streghe del Canavese', esp. 228; excerpt in Hansen, *Quellen*, 485–7; Lea, *History of the Inquisition*, III, 518f.

1475, Braunschweig: Woman banished by municipal court for sorcery. L: Jacobs, 'Der Brocken', 793; cited in Hansen, *Quellen*, 580; Hansen, *Zauberwahn*, 433 (with erroneous reference to Hildesheim).

1475, Bressuire: Woman executed by secular court for diabolism, sorcery (infliction of death and illness with image magic), and beneficent magic. S: René Filhol, 'Procès de sorcellerie à Bressuire (Août-Septembre 1475)', *Revue historique de droit français et étranger*, ser. 4, XLII (1964), 77–83.

c. 1475, Heidelberg and Zent: Unspecified number of persons burned, presumably by ecclesiastical court, for sorcery (illness and impotence) and beneficent magic; 2 burned at Zent in 1475. S: Hansen, *Quellen*, 235. L: Hansen, *Zauberwahn*, 431; Riezler, *Geschichte der Hexenprozesse*, 72f.

1476, Aargau: Woman punished for witchcraft, then released. L: Bader, *Hexenprozesse*, 179.

[1476, Brescia: Man tried by inquisitor for relapse into heresy; released; later charged with diabolism, 1480, but record does not specify that this charge arose 1467. S: Guerrini, *Cronache bresciane*, 185f.]

[1476, Diersberg: Date sometimes given for trial of 1486.]

[1476 (at latest), Milan: Woman accused of magic; illicitly absolved by Dominican posing as inquisitor. S: Hansen, *Quellen*, 487. L: Hansen, *Zauberwahn*, 419f.]

1476, London: Trial for defamation in secular court; man had defamed neighbors in matters of sorcery. S: Hale, *Series of Precedents*, 15f. L: Kittredge, *Witchcraft*, 36.

1476, Péronne: Woman banished by secular court for sorcery directed against small boy. L: La Fons, 'Des sorcièrs', 440f.

1477 (at latest), diocese of Lausanne: Man tried, presumably by ecclesiastical court, for witchcraft; case known only from reference in later trial. S: Archives Cantonales Vaudoises, MS Ac 29, fol. 233.

1477, Bar: Woman burned by secular court for witchcraft. L: Dumont, *Justice criminelle*, II, 69; cited in Hansen, *Quellen*, 580.

1477, Béarn: Woman tried for witchcraft by secular court; died under torture. S: Lespy, 'Les sorcières', 60f.

1477, Fribourg: 2 men executed by secular court, presumably for witchcraft. S: Hansen, *Quellen*, 580. L: Hansen, *Zauberwahn*, 441f.

1477, Hildesheim: 2 women burned for sorcery (poison), evidently by secular court. S: Ludwig Haenselmann, ed., *Henning Brandis' Diarium* (Hildesheim, 1896), 35; reprinted in Hansen, *Quellen*, 580. L: Jacobs, 'Der Brocken', 793.

1477, diocese of Lausanne (a): Woman tried by ecclesiastical court for diabolism. S: Archives Cantonales Vaudoises, MS Ac 29, fol. 208–20, 225. L: Reymond, 'La sorcellerie', 11f.; Reymond, 'Cas de sorcellerie', 90f.

1477, diocese of Lausanne (b): Man tried by ecclesiastical court for diabolism and sorcery (weather magic, killing people and animals). S: Archives Cantonales Vaudoises, MS Ac 29, fol. 228–43, 251–3.

1477, diocese of Lausanne (c): Man tried by ecclesiastical court for witchcraft. S: Archives Cantonales Vaudoises, MS Ac 29, fol. 254–8.

1477, Lucerne: Man banished by municipal court for dedicating self to evil spirit. S: Hoffmann-Krayer, 'Luzerner Akten', 24.

1477, Nürnberg: Man apprehended by municipal court for knowledge of (and presumably complicity in) parents' magical theft of neighbor's milk; released; mother then tried and acquitted. L: Kunstmann, *Zauberwahn*, 30f. (from MS).

1477, Villars-Chabod: Antonia tried by inquisitor for witchcraft; before torture, denied sorcery and magic; after torture, confessed diabolism, sorcery (illness and death to men and animals), and diabolical cure. S: Lavanchy, 'Sabbats ou synagogues', 424–40; reprinted in Hansen, *Quellen*, 487–99. L: Hansen, *Zauberwahn*, 418; Lea, *Materials*, I, 238–41.

1478 (at latest), Schlettstadt: Woman burned for witchcraft, presumably by municipal court; trial known only from reference in later proceedings. L: Kunstmann, *Zauberwahn*, 23.

1478, Bern: Woman tried by secular court for witchcraft. S: Tobler, 'Zum Hexenwesen', IV, 227; reprinted in Hansen, *Quellen*, 580.

[1478, England: Date given in Ewen, *Witchcraft and Demonianism*, 38, for trial of 1470, q.v.]

1478, Nördlingen: Midwife tried for witchcraft by municipal court; acquitted on claim that accusation arose from personal enmity. L: Kunstmann, *Zauberwahn*, 23.

[1478, Valais: Reference given in Russell, *Witchcraft*, but not borne out in Hansen or Tobler.]

1479, Bern (a): Man tried by secular court for deeds of witchcraft (*handlung der hexen*); acquitted. S: Tobler, 'Zum Hexenwesen', IV, 237.

1479, Bern (b): Woman tried by secular court for witchcraft. S: Tobler, 'Zum Hexenwesen', IV, 237.

1479, Fribourg: Man and 4 women tried by municipal court for *Voudesie*. S: Hansen, *Quellen*, 581.

1479, diocese of Lausanne: Man tried by ecclesiastical court for diabolism and killing children. S: Archives Cantonales Vaudoises, MS Ac 29, fol. 264–73.

1479. Mâcon: Priest executed by secular court for witchcraft. L: Foucault, *Les procès de sorcellerie*, 301.

1479, Scotland: Earl of Mar executed for employing witches to kill James III. L: Ewen, *Witch Hunting*, 42.

1480, Aubenas: 2 women charged with witchcraft before secular court. L: Régné, 'La sorcellerie en Vivarais', 482.

1480, Bern: Unspecified number of persons tried by municipal court as witches (or heretics?); case taken from episcopal jurisdiction. S: Tobler, 'Zum Hexenwesen', IV, 237 (with commentary on following page). L: Hansen, *Zauberwahn*, 440.

1480, Brescia (a): Maria 'Medica' tried by ecclesiastical court for diabolism, sorcery and invocation (love magic, killing), divination, and cures. S: Guerrini, *Cronache bresciane*, I, 183–5. L: Bonomo, *Caccia*, 121; Russell, *Witchcraft*, 260f.

1480, Brescia (b): Man tried by ecclesiastical court for diabolism. S: Guerrini, *Cronache bresciane*, I, 185f.

1480, diocese of Lausanne (a): Woman tried by ecclesiastical court for diabolism. S: Archives Cantonales Vaudoises, MS Ac 29, fol. 276–96.

1480, diocese of Lausanne (b): Man tried by ecclesiastical court for diabolism and child-killing. S: Archives Cantonales Vaudoises, MS Ac 29, fol. 303–10. L: Reymond, 'La sorcellerie', 3, 8f.

c. 1480, Lucerne: Woman tried by municipal court for sorcery (harm to men, animals, and crops; death to animals; weather magic). S: Hoffmann-Krayer, 'Luzerner Akten', 81–6.

[1480–9, Sardinia: Reference in Russell, *Witchcraft*, 339, not borne out in source given.]

Between 1480 and 1515, England: Woman tried by Court of Chancery for sorcery. S: Martin, 'Clerical Life', 376.

Between 1480 and 1515, St David's: 3 women (Tanglost and 2 others) tried by Court of Chancery for image magic. S: Martin, 'Clerical Life', 374–6. L: Kittredge, *Witchcraft*, 85f.; Thomas, *Religion*, 467.

Between 1480 and 1515, Southwark: Woman tried by Court of Chancery for image magic. S: Martin, 'Clerical Life', 373f.; Kittredge, *Witchcraft*, 85.

1481, Bern: Woman tried by municipal court for witchcraft. S: Tobler, 'Zum Hexenwesen', IV, 237.

1481, Breslau: Woman executed by municipal court for sorcery (killing). S: Klose, *Darstellung*, 101; cited in Hansen, *Quellen*, 582. L: Hansen, *Zauberwahn*, 433.

1481, London: Woman tried by commissary's court for love magic. L: Hale, *Series of Precedents*, 7; Kittredge, *Witchcraft*, 107.

1481, Lorraine: Woman executed for witchcraft. L: Dumont, *Justice criminelle*, II, 69.

1481, Lugano: Unspecified number of men burned by secular court as witches. L: Hansen, *Quellen*, 581.

1481, Mâcon: Woman executed for sorcery (child-killing) by secular court. S: Foucault, *Les procès de sorcellerie*, 302.

1481, Metz and vicinity: 12 women tried by secular court for weather magic; reference made to 'master' (implying diabolism?); 9 executed, 2 died in prison. S: Huguenin, *Chroniques*, 442f.; Hansen, *Quellen*, 581f. L: Lea, *Materials*, I, 254.

1481, Neuchâtel: 4 men executed by ecclesiastical court for diabolism. S: Chabloz, *Les sorcières*, 51–80 (with commentary, and partly in paraphrase); summarized in Hansen, *Quellen*, 499f. L: Hansen, *Zauberwahn*, 418f.; Lea, *Materials*, I, 241; Frédéric-Alexandre Jeanneret, *Les sorcièrs dans le pays de Neuchâtel au 15e, 16e, et 17e siècle* (Locle, 1862), has not been accessible to me.

[1481, York: Man tried by ecclesiastical court for incantation. L: Kittredge, *Witchcraft*, 38.]

1482, Appenzell: Woman tried by secular court for theft and sorcery, but released. L: Schiess, *Gerichtswesen*, 94f.

1482, Bern (a): Man tried by secular court as witch. S: Tobler, 'Zum Hexenwesen', IV, 237; cited in Hansen, *Quellen*, 583.

1482, Bern (b): Trial for defamation before municipal court; one man had claimed that another's family was given to witchcraft (*von hexen geslecht komme*); offending party made retraction. S: Tobler, 'Zum Hexenwesen', IV, 238.

1482, Breslau: Woman banished by municipal court for theft of money from altars; her daughter had likewise used magic, and had obtained money through its employment. L: Klose, *Darstellung*, 101; cited in Hansen, *Quellen*, 583; Hansen, *Zauberwahn*, 433.

1482, Fribourg: Man and woman tried by municipal court as *Vouldez* and *Vouldese*. S: Hansen, *Quellen*, 582.

[1482, Hamburg: Woman executed, presumably by secular court, for magical abuse of eucharist. L: Trummer, *Vorträge über Tortur*, I, 109f.; cited in Hansen, *Quellen*, 582; Hansen, *Zauberwahn*, 433.]

1482, diocese of Lausanne: Man executed by ecclesiastical court for diabolism, child-killing, and invocation. S: Archives Cantonales Vaudoises, MS Ac 29, fol. 313–27. L: Reymond, 'La sorcellerie', 4, 11.

1482, Liestal: Woman burned by secular court, probably as witch. L: Hansen, *Quellen*, 582 (from MS).

1482, Lucerne (a): Woman banished by municipal court for witchcraft and sorcery. S: Hoffmann-Krayer, 'Luzerner Akten', 24, no. 6.

1482, Lucerne (b): Woman tried by municipal court for witchcraft and sorcery. S: Hoffmann-Krayer, 'Luzerner Akten', 24, no. 7.

1482, Lucerne (c): Woman tried by municipal court for witchcraft; had abused eucharist. S: Hoffmann-Krayer, 'Luzerner Akten', 87; cited in Hansen, *Quellen*, 582f.

1482, Lucerne (d): Woman taken to Lucerne as witch, and presumably tried by municipal court. S: Hoffmann-Krayer, 'Luzerner Akten', 40.

1482, Lucerne (e): Unspecified number of persons burned by secular court as witches; had performed weather magic. S: Segesser, *Eidgenössische Abschiede*, 120; reprinted in Hansen, *Quellen*, 582f.; Anshelm, *Berner-Chronik*, I, 224.

1482, Monthureux-sur-Saône and Sénones: Woman and 3 men burned for witchcraft. L: Dumont, *Justice criminelle*, II, 69; summarized in Hansen, *Quellen*, 582.

1482, Murten: Woman burned by secular court for witchcraft (evidently including diabolism). S: Anshelm, *Berner-Chronik*, I, 224. L: Hansen, *Quellen*, 583; Hansen, *Zauberwahn*, 430.

1482, Solothurn: Woman tried by municipal court for witchcraft; believed to have connections with witches in Lucerne. L: Hoffmann-Krayer, 'Luzerner Akten', 86; cited in Hansen, *Quellen*, 582f.

1482–6, diocese of Constance: 48 persons tried for witchcraft by Henry Institoris (including 8 mentioned below, 1484, Ravensburg). S: Sprenger and Institoris, *Malleus maleficarum*, 95, 119, 122, 158, 174 (Summers ed., 91f., 111, 114, 146, 160); cited in Hansen, *Quellen*, 500. Summers erroneously translates place name as Ratisbon (or Regensburg).

1483, Cologne: Woman sentenced to death by municipal court for sorcery (removal of person from prison); died in jail. S: Hansen, *Quellen*, 583. L: Hansen, *Zauberwahn*, 432.

1483, England: Jane Shore and another woman tried by ecclesiastical court for sorcery (alleged harm to Richard III). S: Thomas More, *The History of Richard III* (The Complete Works of St Thomas More, II), ed. Richard S. Sylvester (New Haven and London, 1963), 48. L: Kittredge, *Witchcraft*, 60f.; Notestein, *History of Witchcraft*, 9; Ewen, *Witchcraft and Demonianism*, 38.

1483, Mâcon: Woman burned by secular court for diabolism. S: Foucault, *Les procès de sorcellerie*, 302.

1483 or 1484 (at latest), diocese of Lausanne: Man and woman executed for witchcraft, probably by ecclesiastical court; case known only from reference in later proceedings. S: Archives Cantonales Vaudoises, MS Ac 29, fol. 336, 339, 341.

1483 or 1484, diocese of Lausanne: Man tried by ecclesiastical court for diabolism. S: Archives Cantonales Vaudoises, MS Ac 29, fol. 333–41.

1484, Ravensburg: 8 women tried by inquisitor Henry Institoris for diabolism and sorcery (harm to men and animals, weather magic); 2 executed, some later released. S: Karl Otto Müller, 'Heinrich Institoris, der Verfasser des Hexenhammers, und seine Tätigkeit als Hexeninquisitor in Ravensburg im Herbst 1484', *Württembergische Vierteljahrshefte für Landesgeschichte*, N.S. XIX (1910), 397–417 (with commentary); T. Hafner, *Geschichte der Stadt* (Ravensburg, 1887), 414; see also sources given above for 1482–6, diocese of Constance.

[1484, Toulouse: 11 persons tried by inquisitor for witchcraft and magic; 2 executed. L: Lamothe-Langon, *Histoire de l'Inquisition*, III, 379; excerpt in Hansen, *Quellen*, 500; Hansen, *Zauberwahn*, 424; Lea, *Materials*, I, 241. See above, pp. 16-18.]

1484-6, Dauphiné: Various persons tried by ecclesiastical court for witchcraft. S: Archives de l'Isère, ser. B, MS 4355, seventh document; ed. Marx, *L'Inquisition*, 235f.

1485, Bormio: 40 persons executed by inquisitor for witchcraft. S: Sprenger and Institoris, *Malleus maleficarum*, 68, 105, 119, 248 (Summers ed., 66, 99, 111, 230); cited in Hansen, *Quellen*, 502. L: Hansen, *Zauberwahn*, 420; Lea, *History of the Inquisition*, III, 540.

1485, Breslau: Woman banished by municipal court for sorcery. L: Klose, *Darstellung*, 101f. (from MS); cited in Hansen, *Quellen*, 583; Hansen, *Zauberwahn*, 433.

1485, Chauny: 3 persons tried by ecclesiastical court for witchcraft; 2 burned, 1 beaten and banished. S: Hansen, *Quellen*, 500f. L: Hansen, *Zauberwahn*, 424; Lea, *Materials*, I, 241.

1485, Innsbruck: 48 women and 2 men tried by inquisitor Henry Institoris for sorcery of virtually every variety, invocation, and blasphemy; evidently all released; further proceedings against 7 women on similar charges; allowed purgation. S: Hartmann Ammann, 'Der Innsbrucker Hexenprocess von 1485', *Zeitschrift des Ferdinandeums für Tirol und Vorarlberg*, ser. 3, XXXIV (1890), 1-87 (with commentary); cited in Hansen, *Quellen*, 501f. L: Riezler, *Geschichte der Hexenprozesse*, 90-4; Hansen, *Zauberwahn*, 426; Ludwig Rapp, *Die Hexenprozesse und ihre Gegner in Tirol* (2nd ed., Brixen, 1891), 9-20.

1485, Röthenbach: Woman tried by secular court for *hexenwerk* (sorcery); acquitted. S: Sigmund Riezler, ed., *Fürstenbergisches Urkundenbuch*, IV (Tübingen, 1879), 42f.; summarized in Hanzsen, *Quellen*, 584. L: Riezler, *Geschichte der Hexenprozesse*, 78, 102; Hansen, *Zauberwahn*, 431; Lea, *Materials*, I, 255.

1485, Talloires: Woman burned for witchcraft by ecclesiastical court. L: Lavanchy, 'Sabbats ou synagogues', 398f.; cited by Hansen, *Quellen*, 502.

[1485-7, Brescia: Reference given in Russell, *Witchcraft*, 339; not borne out in source there cited.]

1486 (at latest), diocese of Regensburg: Unspecified number of 'heretics' burned by episcopal court. S: Sprenger and Institoris, *Malleus maleficarum*, 248 (Summers ed., 229). L: Riezler, *Geschichte der Hexenprozesse*, 63; Hansen, *Zauberwahn*, 424.

1486, Bern: Woman tried by municipal court for witchcraft; acquitted. S: Tobler, 'Zum Hexenwesen', IV, 238.

1486, Brescia: Unspecified number of persons condemned by ecclesiastical court for heresy; Hansen interprets the offense (probably rightly) as witchcraft. S: Hansen, *Quellen*, 29f.; cited *ibid.*, 502. L: Lea, *History of the Inquisition*, III, 547.

[1486, Cologne: Man accused of magic; gave surety that he would appear if summoned before ecclesiastical or secular court. S: Pauls, 'Zauberwesen und Hexenwahn', 237; excerpt in Hansen, *Quellen*, 584.]

1486, Diersberg: 2 women strangled and burned by secular court for diabolism and sorcery (illness and death to men, theft of milk). S: Felix Freiherr Röder von Diersburg, 'Mittheilungen aus dem Freiherrl. v. Röder'schen Archiv', *Freiburger Diöcesan-Archiv*, XV (1882), 93–100 (with commentary); reprinted (with significant abridgements) in Hansen, *Quellen*, 584–5. L: F. Eckstein, 'Zum Diersburger Hexenprozess vom Jahre 1486', *Zeitschrift für die Geschichte des Oberrheins*, XL (1927), 635f. (from MS, with correction of published ed.); Hansen, *Zauberwahn*, 444; Lea, *Materials*, I, 255; Kittredge, *Witchcraft*, 163.

1486, Frankfurt: Man drowned by secular court as sorcerer. L: Kirchner, *Geschichte der Stadt Frankfurt*, I, 504 (from MS); cited in Hansen, *Quellen*, 584; Hansen, *Zauberwahn*, 431.

1486, Lucerne (a): Woman tried by municipal court for sorcery (weather magic, theft of milk). S: Hoffmann-Krayer, 'Luzerner Akten', 87f.; cited in Hansen, *Quellen*, 586.

1486, Lucerne (b): Woman tried by municipal court as witch. L: Schacher, *Hexenwesen*, 65; cited in Hoffmann-Krayer, 'Luzerner Akten', 81 n. 1; cf. also Hansen, *Quellen*, 586.

1486, Nürnberg: 2 women tried by municipal court for taking potentially magical pieces of clothing from people executed on wheel; released. L: Kunstmann, *Zauberwahn*, 33.

[1486, Tiersberg: See above, 1486, Diersberg.]

1486 or 1487, Altdorf: Trial for defamation before secular court; 4 or 5 women accused of witchcraft. L: Schweizer, 'Der Hexenprozess', 27f. (from MS).

1487, Cologne: Woman and daughter buried alive for sorcery. S: *Chroniken der deutschen Städte*, XIV, 913; Hansen, *Quellen*, 586 (not the same as cited material in *Chroniken der deutschen Städte*).

[1487, Rouvroy: Woman banished by secular court, possibly for sorcery. L: La Fons, 'Les sorcières', 441.]

1487, Zürich: Woman tried by municipal court for diabolism and sorcery (illness to animals and men, death to men) and curing. L: Hansen, *Quellen*, 586; Schweizer, 'Der Hexenprozess', 28 (from MS); Lea, *Materials*, I, 256.

[1487–8, Dauphiné: Ecclesiastical trial of Waldensians, accused *inter alia* of attending 'synagogues', though diabolical character of these assemblies is only vaguely suggested. S: Chevalier, *Mémoires historiques*, 69–72 nn.; Raynald, *Annales*, a.a. 1487, no. 25. L: Hansen, *Zauberwahn*, 412.]

1488, Anniviers: 2 men burned by secular court for witchcraft. L: Bertrand, 'Notes sur les procès', 179 n.

1488, Béarn (a): Woman tried for witchcraft by secular court; acquitted. S: Lespy, 'Les sorcières', 61.

1488, Béarn (b): Woman tried for witchcraft by secular court; acquitted. S: Lespy, 'Les sorcières', 61f.

1488, Metz: 31 women and 4 men tried by secular court for weather magic; 29 burned. S: Huguenin, *Chroniques*, 482 Hansen, *Quellen*, 586f. L: Hansen, *Zauberwahn*, 507f.; Lea, *Materials*, 256.

[1488–9, Cologne: Man threatened with ecclesiastical censures and fines for astrology and necromancy. S: Hansen, *Quellen*, 502–6. L: Hansen, *Zauberwahn*, 504.]

1489, Baden (Switzerland): Woman tried by secular authorities for weather magic. S: Segesser, *Eidgenössische Abschiede*, 323; reprinted in Hansen, *Quellen*, 587f.

1489, Béarn (a): Woman tried by secular court for witchcraft; acquitted. S: Lespy, 'Les sorcières', 62f.

1489, Béarn (b): Woman fined by secular court for witchcraft. S: Lespy, 'Les sorcières', 63f.

1489, Béarn (c): Woman fined by secular court for witchcraft. S: Lespy, 'Les sorcières', 64.

1489, Béarn (d): Woman tried by secular court for witchcraft; released on surety. S: Lespy, 'Les sorcières', 64.

1489, Béarn (e): Woman tried by secular court for witchcraft; released on surety. S: Lespy, 'Les sorcières', 64.

1489, Béarn (f): Woman tried by secular court for witchcraft; released on surety. S: Lespy, 'Les sorcières', 64.

1489, Lucerne: Woman tried by secular court for sorcery (illness to men and animals, death to animals). S: Hoffmann-Krayer, 'Luzerner Akten', 88–91; cited in Hansen, *Quellen*, 588.

1489, Nürnberg: Woman tried for sorcery, presumably by municipal court; exposed publicly wearing mitre with picture of devil, then banished. S: *Chroniken der deutschen Städte*, XI, 550; excerpt in Hansen, *Quellen*, 587. L: Lea, *Materials*, I, 256; Kunstmann, *Zauberwahn*, 34 (partly from MS).

1490, London: Woman tried by commissary for image magic. S: Hale, *Series of Precedents*, 20. L: Kittredge, *Witchcraft*, 85; Thomas, *Religion*, 455 n. 1.

1490, Lucerne (a): Woman taken to Lucerne as witch, and presumably tried by municipal court. S: Hoffmann-Krayer, 'Luzerner Akten', 40.

1490, Lucerne (b): Woman burned by secular court for weather-magic and diabolism. S: Hansen, *Quellen*, 588. L: Schneller, 'Hexenwesen', 352; Kasimir Pfyffer, *Geschichte der Stadt und des Kantons Luzern*, I (Lucerne, 1850), 240f.

1490, Lucerne (c): Woman tried by municipal court as witch and evil woman (*böss wib*). L: Schacher, *Hexenwesen*, 65 (from MS).

1490, Lucerne (d): 2 women burned by municipal court, presumably as witches. S: Hansen, *Quellen*, 588.

1490, Solothurn: Woman burned, probably by secular court, for weather magic and diabolism. L: Kocher, 'Regesten', 122.

1490, Vivarais: Woman burned by inquisitor for witchcraft (diabolism, killing animals). S: Abbé Garnodier, *Recherches archéologiques sur Saint-Romain-de-Lerp et ses environs* (2nd ed., Valence, 1860), 234 n. 1. L: Jules Baissac, *Les grands jours de la sorcellerie* (Paris, 1890), 340 n. 2 (continued from previous page); Régné, 'Sorcellerie en Vivarais', 482; cited in Hansen, *Quellen*, 506; Hansen, *Zauberwahn*, 503.

c. 1490, Solothurn: Woman drowned by secular court for sorcery (theft). S: Hansen, *Quellen*, 588. L: Kocher, 'Regesten', 122; Lea, *Materials*, I, 256.

1491 (at latest), vicinity of Boucoiran: At least 3 women tried (presumably by secular authorities) for witchcraft; at least 1 executed; case known only from reference in later proceedings. S: Bligny-Bondurand, 'Procédure contre une sorcière', 390, 396.

1491 (at latest), Hochkirchen: Woman burned, probably by secular court, for witchcraft; case known only from reference in later proceedings. S: Pauls, 'Zauberwesen und Hexenwahn', 237.

1491, Béarn: Woman tried for witchcraft by secular court; acquitted. S: Lespy, 'Les sorcières', 65.

1491, Bergheim-Erft: Woman tried by secular court for witchcraft. S: Pauls, 'Zauberwesen und Hexenwahn', 237f.; further material in Hansen, *Quellen*, 588f.

1491, Boucoiran: Martiale Espaze tried by secular court; witnesses accused her of sorcery (death to infants and animals) and immorality; under interrogation, confessed diabolism and sorcery (death to infants and animals, illness to men). S: Bligny-Bondurand, 'Procédure contre une sorcière'.

1491, Lucerne (a): Woman tried by municipal court as witch. L: Hansen, *Quellen*, 588.

1491, Lucerne (b): Woman tried by municipal court as witch. L: Hansen, *Quellen*, 588.

1491, Neuchâtel: Man burned by secular court for witchcraft. L: Chabloz, *Les sorcièrs*, 102 (from MS); cited in Hansen, *Quellen*, 588.

1491, Pforzheim: 2 women tried by municipal court as witches, one of them a midwife. L: J. G. F. Pflüger, *Geschichte der Stadt Pforzheim* (Pforzheim, 1861), 211 (from MS); cited in Hansen, *Quellen*, 590.

1491, Veringen: 1 person executed as witch. L: Midelfort, *Witch Hunting*, 201, from Rolf Burkarth, *Hexenprozesse in Hohenzollern (mit den 1803 dazuge-kommenen Gebieten)* (unpublished thesis, Pädagogische Hochschule, Reutlingen, 1965), 14.

1491, Zutphen: 3 women tried by municipal court for sorcery (weather magic, illness to animals); precautions taken to counteract devil's power before torture. S: Hansen, *Quellen*, 589f. L: Lea, *Materials*, I, 256.

1492, Béarn: Woman banished by secular court for witchcraft. S: Lespy, 'Les sorcières', 56f.

1492, Langendorf: Charge made that all but 2 women of area were witches; investigation made by secular authorities. L: Kocher, 'Regesten', 122.

1492, London: Trial for fraudulent love magic; client sentenced to public penance by ecclesiastical court, and man claiming to serve as agent for magician ordered by court to restore goods given in payment. S: Hale, *Series of Precedents*, 32f. L: Kittredge, *Witchcraft*, 61, 107.

1492, Metz: Woman released from municipal prison on visit of Maximilian I, after imprisonment over 4 years on charge of witchcraft. S: Huguenin, *Chroniques*, 587; Hansen, *Quellen*, 590.

1492–4, lands of count of Virneburg and archbishop of Trier: c. 30 women executed by secular authorities (including archbishop as secular lord) for sorcery (killing) and diabolism. S: Hansen, *Quellen*, 592–4. L: Grotefend, 'Hexen in Frankfurt', 73f.; Hansen, *Zauberwahn*, 508; Lea, *Materials*, I, 257.

1493, Béarn: Woman fined by secular court for witchcraft. S: Lespy, 'Les sorcières', 65–7.

1493, Constance: Woman tried by secular court for diabolism; allegedly killed by devil in jail. S: Hansen, *Quellen*, 592. L: Lea, *Materials*, I, 257.

1493, Fribourg: Woman burned by secular court for diabolism, sorcery (illness to men and animals, death to animals), and curing; reference made to numerous other executions in recent past. S: Hansen, *Quellen*, 590–2. L: Lea, *Materials*, I, 256.

1493, London: Woman tried by ecclesiastical court for weather magic, killing by incantation, divination, and other offenses. S: Hale, *Series of Precedents*, 36f. L: Kittredge, *Witchcraft*, 155, 474 n. 27; Thomas, *Religion*, 455 n. 1.

1493, Lucerne: Woman banished by municipal court for witchcraft. S: Excerpt in Hansen, *Quellen*, 592. L: Schacher, *Hexenwesen*, 65 (from MS).

1493, Zürich: Woman tried by secular court for diabolism and sorcery (weather magic, theft of milk). L: Hansen, *Quellen*, 592; Schweizer, 'Der Hexenprozess', 28f. (from MS).

1494, Coblenz: Woman tried by ecclesiastical and secular authorities for sorcery; released. L: Hansen, *Quellen*, 595 (from MS).

1494, Lucerne (a): Trial for defamation; people of Russwil charged 2 men of defaming them as harboring witches guilty of weather magic. S: Hansen, *Quellen*, 595.

1494, Lucerne (b): Woman burned by vogt of Baden for witchcraft: S: Paraphrase in Segesser, *Eidgenössische Abschiede*, 451; reprinted in Hansen, *Quellen*, 594.

1494, Zürich: Woman tried by secular court for witchcraft, magic, and riding on wolf. S: Paraphrase in Segesser, *Eidgenössische Abschiede*, 449; reprinted in Hansen, *Quellen*, 594. L: Schweizer, 'Der Hexenprozess', 29 (same case?).

1495, Béarn: Trial of unspecified number of persons by secular court for witchcraft. S: Lespy, 'Les sorcières', 67f.

1495, Constance: Woman burned by secular court for diabolism and weather magic. S: Hansen, *Quellen*, 595.

1495, Lucerne (a): Unspecified number of women tried by municipal court on other witches' charge of witchcraft. L: Hansen, *Quellen*, 595 (from MS).

1495, Lucerne (b): Unspecified number of women tried by municipal court on other witches' charge of witchcraft. L: Hansen, *Quellen*, 595 (from MS).

1495, Stein am Rhein: Woman imprisoned by secular court for witchcraft; later released. L: Hermann Tüchele, *Kirchengeschichte Schwabens*, II (Stuttgart, 1954), 307.

1496, Hildesheim: 2 men beheaded, presumably by secular court, for love magic. S: Hansen, *Quellen*, 595. L: Jacobs, 'Der Brocken', 793.

1496, London: 3 conspirators accused by Frenchman (their own agent) of attempt on lives of royal family and councilors through use of magical substances. S: Frederic Madden, 'Documents relating to Perkin Warbeck, with Remarks on his History', *Archaeologia*, XXVII (1838), 171–8, 205–9 (with commentary). L: Kittredge, *Witchcraft*, 50; Ewen, *Witchcraft and Demonianism*, 38.

[1496–7, Frankfurt: Man tried for astrology. L: Hansen, *Quellen*, 506 n. 1.]

[1497, Bavaria: Henry Institoris active against witches; not clear whether trials ensued. S: Hansen, *Quellen*, 506–10. L: Riezler, *Geschichte der Hexenprozesse*, 97–100; Hansen, *Zauberwahn*, 504.]

1497, London: Trial for defamation (obscurely worded, but implying theft by sorcery). S: Hale, *Series of Precedents*, 63.

[1497, Modena: Woman tried by ecclesiastical court for counter-sorcery. L:

Ferdinando Gabotto, 'Per la storia della coltura nel quattrocento', *Rassegna critica della letteratura italiana*, II (1897), 253.]

1497, Nancy: Woman tried by secular court for possession and witchcraft. S: Bournon, *Coupures*, 34. L: Foucault, *Les procès de sorcellerie*, 304.

1497, Oldenburg: Woman tried by municipal court for sorcery. S: Dietrich Kohl and Gustav Rüthning, eds., *Oldenburgisches Urkundenbuch*, I (Oldenburg, 1914), 216f. L: Herbert Schwarzwälder, 'Die Geschichte des Zauber- und Hexenglaubens in Bremen', *Bremisches Jahrbuch*, XLVI (1959), 189 n. 118.

1497, Vivarais: Woman executed for witchcraft by ecclesiastical court. Source and literature as above, 1490, Vivarais.

1498, diocese of Lausanne (a): Woman tried by ecclesiastical court for diabolism and sorcery (harm to men and animals); confessed upon confrontation with testimony from convicted witches. S: Archives Cantonales Vaudoises, MS Ac 29, fol. 349–62.

1498, diocese of Lausanne (b): Man tried by ecclesiastical court for witchcraft; witnesses accused him of sorcery (killing animals and child, poison attempt) and falling from sky; under interrogation, confessed diabolism. S: Archives Cantonales Vaudoises, MS Ac 29, fol. 365–87, 396f.; cf. *ibid.*, 405. L: Reymond, 'Cas de sorcellerie', 91–4.

1498, diocese of Lausanne (c): Woman tried by ecclesiastical court for diabolism and sorcery (killing children and animals). S: Archives Cantonales Vaudoises, MS Ac 29, fol. 399–409.

1498, diocese of Lausanne (d): Man tried by ecclesiastical court for sorcery (killing men and animals) and diabolism; confessed after torture. S: Archives Cantonales Vaudoises, MS Ac 29, fol. 415–34. L: Reymond, 'La sorcellerie', 11f.

[1498, Vienna: Woman executed by secular court for magic. L: J. E. Schlager, 'Die Zauberey die im Rechten verpotten seyn', *Wiener-Skizzen aus dem Mittelalter*, N.S. II (1842), 37f.; cited in Hansen, *Quellen*, 595.]

1499, Angermund: 2 women tried by secular court for sorcery (harm to animals). S: Pauls, 'Zauberwesen und Hexenwahn', 239f. (cf. *ibid.*, 211); cited in Hansen, *Quellen*, 596. L: Kessell, *Geschichte der Stadt Ratingen*, II, 167.

1499, 'Belynges Parva' (England): Woman tried by ecclesiastical court for sorcery (killing); allowed purgation. L: Jenkins, 'Cardinal Morton's Register', 71.

1499, Breslau: 2 women tried by municipal court for sorcery. L: Klose, *Darstellung*, 102; cited by Hansen, *Quellen*, 596.

1499, Lucerne: Woman tried by municipal court for sorcery (weather magic, poisoning, illness to men) and riding on wolf. S: Hoffmann-Krayer, 'Luzerner Akten', 91–5; cited in Hansen, *Quellen*, 596.

1499, Ratingen: Woman tried by secular court for sorcery. L: Kessell, *Geschichte der Stadt Ratingen*, II, 167; cited in Hansen, *Quellen*, 596.

1499, Rheinberg: Woman burned by secular court for sorcery and diabolism. S: Pauls, 'Zauberwesen und Hexenwahn', 238; cited in Hansen, *Quellen*, 596.

1499, 'Rushbrok' (England): Man tried by ecclesiastical court for pact with devil. L: Jenkins, 'Cardinal Morton's Register', 71.

1499, diocese of Winchester: Man tried by ecclesiastical court for invocation (?). L: Thomson, *Later Lollards*, 79 (from MS).

List of Abbreviated Titles

An extensive bibliography on witchcraft would duplicate those of Jeffrey Russell, in *Witchcraft in the Middle Ages*, and of H. C. Erik Midelfort, 'Recent Witch Hunting Research', *Papers of the Bibliographical Society of America*, LXII (1968), 373–420. The following list therefore gives only those works which have information on multiple witch trials from the period 1300–1500, and which have thus been cited in abbreviated form in the Calendar of Witch Trials.

Ammann, Hartmann, 'Der Innsbrucker Hexenprocess von 1485', *Zeitschrift des Ferdinandeums für Tirol und Vorarlberg*, ser. 3, XXXIV (1890), 1–87.

Anshelm, Valerius, *Die Berner-Chronik*, Bern, 1884.

Aubenas, Roger, *La sorcière et l'inquisiteur: Épisode de l'Inquisition en Provence, 1439* (Archives de Provence, I), Aix-en-Provence, 1945.

Bader, Guido, *Die Hexenprozesse in der Schweiz*, Affoltern a.A., 1945.

Baroja, Julio Caro, *The World of the Witches*, English ed., London, 1964.

Berchtold, Jean Nicolas Elisabeth, *Histoire du canton de Fribourg*, Fribourg, 1841–52.

Bernard, Paul P., 'Heresy in Fourteenth Century Austria', *Medievalia et Humanistica*, X (1956), 50–63.

Bertrand, J.-B., 'Notes sur les procès d'hérésie et de sorcellerie en Valais', *Annales valaisannes*, IV (1920), 151–94.

Bligny-Bondurand, Édouard, 'Procédure contre une sorcière de Boucoiran (Gard), 1491', *Bulletin philologique et historique*, 1907, 380–405.

Bonomo, Giuseppe, *Caccia alle streghe: La credenza nelle streghe dal secolo XIII al XIX, con particolare riferimento all'Italia*, Palermo, 1959.

Bournon, Jacques, *Chroniques, lois, moeurs et usages de la Lorraine, au moyen-âge*, ed. Jean Cayon, Nancy, 1838.

Brucker, Gene A., 'Sorcery in Early Renaissance Florence', *Studies in the Renaissance*, X (1963), 7–24.

Brucker, Gene A., ed., *The Society of Renaissance Florence*, New York, 1971.

Buff, Adolf, 'Verbrechen und Verbrecher zu Augsburg in der zweiten Hälfte des 14. Jahrhunderts', *Zeitschrift des Historischen Vereins für Schwaben und Neuburg*, IV (1878), 160–231.

Buxtorf-Falkeisen, Carl, *Baslerische Stadt- und Landgeschichten aus dem sechszehnten Jahrhundert*, Basel, 1863–8.

Calendar of the Patent Rolls Preserved in the Public Record Office, London, 1891– .

Cauzons, Thomas de, *La magie et la sorcellerie en France*, Paris, [1910–11 ?].

Chabloz, Fritz, *Les sorcières Neuchâteloises*, Neuchâtel, 1868.

Chevalier, Jules, *Mémoire historique sur les hérésies en Dauphiné avant le XVIe siècle*, Valence, 1890.

Chroniken der deutschen Städte, ed. Historische Kommission bei der Bayerischen Akademie der Wissenschaften, Leipzig, etc., 1862– .

Cohn, Norman, *Europe's Inner Demons: An Enquiry Inspired by the Great Witch-Hunt*, London, 1975.

Depositions and Other Ecclesiastical Proceedings from the Courts of Durham, Extending from 1311 to the Reign of Elizabeth (Publications of the Surtees Society, XXI), London, 1845.

Dodt, J. J., 'Aanteekeningen uit de besluiten des raads, genomen gedurende de eerste helfte der XV. eeuw', *Archief voor kerkelijke en wereldsche geschiedenissen, inzonderheid van Utrecht*, V (1846), 177–218.

DuCange, Charles du Fresne, sieur, ed., *Glossarium mediae et infimae latinitatis*, Niort, 1883–7.

Dumont, Charles Emmanuel, *Justice criminelle des duchés de Lorraine et de Bar*, Nancy, 1848.

Duplès-Agier, Henri, ed., *Registre criminelle du Châtelet de Paris du 6 septembre 1389 au 18 mai 1392*, Paris, 1861–4.

Eubel, Conrad, 'Vom Zaubereiunwesen anfangs des 14. Jahrhunderts (Mit urkundlichen Beilagen)', *Historisches Jahrbuch der Görres-Gesellschaft*, XVIII (1897), 608–31.

Ewen, Cecil l'Estrange, *Witch Hunting and Witch Trials*, London, 1929.

Ewen, Cecil l'Estrange, *Witchcraft and Demonianism*, London, 1933.

Floquet, Amable, *Histoire du parlement de Normandie*, Rouen, 1840–2.

Foucault, Maurice, *Les procès de sorcellerie dans l'ancienne France devant les jurisdictions séculières*, Paris, 1907.

Fredericq, Paul, ed., *Corpus documentorum inquisitionis haereticae pravitatis Neerlandicae*, Ghent and The Hague, 1889–1906.

Friedrich, J., 'La Vauderye (Valdesia): Ein Beitrag zur Geschichte der Valdesier', *Sitzungsberichte der philosophisch-philologischen und der historischen Classe der königlichen bayerischen Akademie der Wissenschaften zu Munchen*, 1898, I, 163–200.

Germain, A., ed., 'Inventaire inédit concernant les Archives de l'Inquisition de Carcassonne', *Mémoires de la Société Archéologique de Montpellier*, IV (1885), 287–308.

Grémaud, l'Abbé J., ed., *Documents relatifs à l'histoire du Vallais*, Lausanne, 1875–98.

Grotefend, (Stadtarchiv Dr.), 'Hexen in Frankfurt', *Mittheilungen des Vereins für Geschichte und Alterthumskunde in Frankfurt a.M.*, VI (1881), 70–8.

Guerrini, Paolo, ed., *Le cronache bresciane inedite dei sec. XV–XIX*, Brescia, 1922.

Hale, William Hale, *A Series of Precedents and Proceedings in Criminal Causes*, London, 1847.

Hansen, Joseph, *Zauberwahn, Inquisition und Hexenprozess im Mittelalter, und die Entstehung der grossen Hexenverfolgung* (Historische Bibliothek, XII), Munich, 1900.

Hansen, Joseph, ed., *Quellen und Untersuchungen zur Geschichte des Hexenwahns und der Hexenverfolgung im Mittelalter*, Bonn, 1901.

Hartlieb, Johann, *Buch aller verbotenen Kunst*, ed., Dora Ulm, Halle a.S., 1914.

Hoffmann-Krayer, E., 'Luzerner Akten zum Hexen- und Zauberwesen', *Schweizerisches Archiv für Volkskunde*, III (1899), 22–40, 81–122, 189–224, 291–329.

Huguenin, Jean François, ed., *Les Chroniques de la ville de Metz*, Metz, 1838.

Jacobs, Ed., 'Der Brocken und sein Gebiet', *Zeitschrift des Harz-Vereins für Geschichte und Alterthumskunde*, III (1870), 1–209, 755–898; IV (1871), 114–56, 291–322.

Jacquier, Nicholas, *Flagellum haereticorum fascinariorum*, Frankfurt, 1581.

Jenkins, Claude, 'Cardinal Morton's Register', *Tudor Studies presented by the Board of Studies in History in the University of London to Albert Frederick Pollard*, ed. R. W. Seton-Watson, London, 1924, pp. 26–74.

Kämpfen, Peter Jos., *Hexen und Hexenprozesse im Wallis*, Stans, 1867.

Kirchner, Anton, *Geschichte der Stadt Frankfurt am Main*, Frankfurt, 1807.

Kittredge, George Lyman, *Witchcraft in Old and New England*, Cambridge, Mass., 1929.

Klose, Samuel Benjamin, *Darstellung der inneren Verhältnisse der Stadt Breslau* (*Scriptores rerum Germanicarum*, ed. Gustav Adolf Stenzel, III), Breslau, 1847.

Knapp, Hermann, *Das alte Nürnberger Kriminalrecht*, Berlin, 1896.

Kocher, Ambros, 'Regesten zu den Solothurnischen Hexenprozessen', *Jahrbuch für Solothurnische Geschichte*, XVI (1943), 121–40.

Kunstmann, Hartmut H., *Zauberwahn und Hexenprozess in der Reichsstadt Nürnberg* (Schriftenreihe des Stadtarchivs Nürnberg, I), Nürnberg, 1970.

Kurze, Dietrich, 'Zur Ketzergeschichte der Mark Brandenburg und Pommerns, vornehmlich im 14. Jahrhundert: Luziferianer, Putzkeller und Waldenser', *Jahrbuch für die Geschichte Mittel- und Ostdeutschlands*, XVI/XVII (1968), 50–94.

La Fons, Alphonse de, baron de Mélicocq, 'Des sorcièrs aux XVme. et XVIme. siècles', *Mémoires de la Société Royale d'Émulation d'Abbeville*, 1841–3, pp. 435–48.

La Fons, Alphonse de, baron de Mélicocq, 'Les médecins et les chirurgiens de la ville de Lille au XVe et XVIe siècles', *Archives historiques et littéraires du Nord de la France et du Midi de la Belgique*, ser. 3, VI (1857), 197–221.

Lamothe-Langon, Étienne-Léon, baron de, *Histoire de l'Inquisition en France*, Paris, 1829.

Langlois, Charles Victor, 'L'affaire du cardinal Francesco Caetani (Avril 1316)', *Revue historique*, LXIII (1897), 56–71.

Lavanchy, J.-M., 'Sabbats ou synagogues sur les bords du Lac d'Annecy', *Mémoires et documents publiés par l'Académie Salésienne*, VIII (1885), 381–440. Also published separately.

Lea, Henry Charles, *A History of the Inquisition of the Middle Ages*, New York, 1887–8.

Lea, Henry Charles, *Materials toward a History of Witchcraft*, Philadelphia, 1939.

Lehugeur, Paul, *Histoire de Philippe le Long, roi de France, 1316–1322*, I, Paris, 1897. [No further volumes forthcoming.]

Lerner, Robert E., *The Heresy of the Free Spirit in the Later Middle Ages*, Berkeley, Los Angeles, and London, 1972.

Lespy, V., 'Les sorcières dans le Béarn', *Bulletin de la Société des Sciences, Lettres et Arts du Pau*, ser. 2, IV (1874–5), 28–86.

Martène, Edmond, and Ursin Durand, eds, *Veterum scriptorum et monumentorum historicorum, dogmaticorum, moralium, amplissima collectio*, Paris, 1724–33.

Martin, C. Trice, 'Clerical Life in the Fifteenth Century, as Illustrated by Proceedings of the Court of Chancery', *Archaeologia*, LX (ser. 2, X) (1907), 353–78.

Marx, Jean, *L'Inquisition en Dauphiné: Étude sur le développement et la répression de l'hérésie et de la sorcellerie du xive siècle au début du règne de François Ier*, Paris, 1914.

Menéndez y Pelayo, Marcelino, *Historia de los heterodoxos españoles* (Edición nacional de las obras completas de Menéndez Pelayo, XXXV–XLII), Santander, 1946–8.

Michel, Robert, 'Le procès de Matteo et de Galeazzo Visconti: L'accusation de sorcellerie et d'hérésie, Dante et l'affaire de l'envoûtement (1320)', *Mélanges d'archéologie et d'histoire*, XXIX (1909), 269–327.

Midelfort, H. C. Erik, *Witch Hunting in Southwestern Germany, 1562–1684: The Social and Intellectual Foundations*, Stanford, 1972.

Molhuijsen, P. C., 'Bijdrage tot de geschiedenis der heksenprocessen in Gelderland', *Bijdragen voor vaderlandsche geschiedenis en oudheidkunde*, N.S., I (1859), 194–209.

Muller, Samuel, ed., *De middeleeuwsche rechtsbronnen der stad Utrecht* (Werken der Vereeniging tot Uitgave der Bronnen van het Oude Vaterlandse Recht, ser. 1, III), The Hague, 1883–5.

Nider, Joannes, *Formicarius*, published in vol. I of Jacobus Sprenger and Henricus Institoris, *Malleus maleficarum*, Lyon, 1669, pp. 305–54.

Notestein, Wallace, *A History of Witchcraft in England*, Washington, D.C., 1911.

Ochsenbein, Gottlieb Friedrich, *Aus dem schweizerischen Volksleben des 15. Jahrhunderts: Der Inquisitionsprozess wider die Waldenser zu Freiburg i.U. im Jahre 1430*, Bern, 1881.

Paris, Paulin, ed., *Les grandes chroniques de France, selon que elles sont conservées en l'Eglise de Saint-Denis en France*, Paris, 1836–8.

Pauls, Emil, 'Zauberwesen und Hexenwahn am Niederrhein', *Beiträge zur Geschichte des Niederrheins: Jahrbuch des Düsseldorfer Geschichts-Vereins*, XIII (1898), 134–242.

Poullet, Edmond, *Histoire du droit pénal dans l'ancien duché de Brabant*, Brussels, 1867.

Raynaldus, Odoricus, *Annales ecclesiastici*, Lucca, 1747–56.

Recueil des historiens des Gaules et de la France, Paris, 1738–1904.

Régné, Jean, 'La sorcellerie en Vivarais et la répression inquisitoriale ou séculière du XVe au XVIIe siècle', *Mélanges d'histoire offerts à M. Charles Bémont*, Paris, 1913, pp. 481–508.

Reymond, Maxime, 'La sorcellerie au pays de Vaud au XVe siècle', *Schweizerisches Archiv für Volkskunde*, XII (1908), 1–14.

Reymond, Maxime, 'Cas de sorcellerie en pays fribourgeois au quinzième siècle', *Schweizerisches Archiv für Volkskunde*, XII (1909), 81–94.

Riezler, Sigmund von, *Geschichte der Hexenprozesse in Bayern, im Lichte der allgemeinen Entwicklung dargestellt*, Stuttgart, 1896.

Robbins, Rossell Hope, *The Encyclopedia of Witchcraft and Demonology*, New York, 1959.

Rose, Elliott, *A Razor for a Goat: A Discussion of Certain Problems in the History of Witchcraft and Diabolism*, Toronto, 1962.

Russell, Jeffrey Burton, *Witchcraft in the Middle Ages*, Ithaca and London, 1972.

Rymer, Thomas, ed., *Foedera, conventiones, literae, et cujuscunque generis acta publica*, 3rd ed., The Hague, 1739–45.

Sayles, G. O., ed., *Select Cases in the Court of King's Bench under Edward III*, V–VI (Publications of the Selden Society, LXXVI, LXXXII), London, 1958–65.

Schacher, Joseph, *Das Hexenwesen im Kanton Luzern, nach den Prozessen von Luzern und Sursee, 1400–1675*, Lucerne, 1947.

Scheltema, Jacobus, *Geschiedenis der heksenprocessen: Eene bijdrage tot den roem des vaderlands*, Haarlem, 1828.

Schiess, Emil, *Das Gerichtswesen und die Hexenprozesse in Appenzell*, Trogen, 1919.

Schneller, Joseph, 'Das Hexenwesen im sechszehnten Jahrhundert (Nach den Thürmbuchern Lucerns)', *Der Geschichtsfreund*, XXIII (1868), 351–70.

Schönach, L., 'Zur Geschichte des ältesten Hexenwesens in Tirol', *Forschungen und Mitteilungen zur Geschichte Tirols und Vorarlbergs*, I (1904), 62f.

Schultheiss, Werner, ed., *Die Acht-, Verbots-, und Fehdebücher Nürnbergs von 1285–1400* (Nürnberger Rechtsquellen, Lieferung 1/2), Nürnberg, 1959.

Schweizer, Paul, 'Der Hexenprozess und seine Anwendung in Zürich', *Zürcher Taschenbuch*, N.S., XXV (1902), 1–63.

Segesser, Anton Philipp, ed., *Die Eidgenössische Abschiede aus dem Zeitraum von 1478 bis 1499* (Amtliche Sammlung der älteren Eidgenössischen Abschiede, III, pt 1), Zürich, 1858.

Sprenger, Jacobus, and Henricus Institoris, *Malleus maleficarum*, Lyon, 1669; transl. Montague Summers, 2nd ed., London, 1948.

'Le streghe nella Leventina nel secolo XV', *Bollettino storico della Svizzera italiana*, VI (1884), 144f., 169–71, 233–35, 262f.; VII (1885), 61f., 82–4, 113–15, 146–9, 170f., 191–4.

Thomas, Keith, *Religion and the Decline of Magic*, London, 1971.

Thomson, John A. F., *The Later Lollards, 1414–1520*, London, 1965.

Thorndike, Lynn, *A History of Magic and Experimental Science*, New York and London, 1923–58.

Tobler, G., 'Zum Hexenwesen in Bern', *Schweizerisches Archiv für Volkskunde*, II (1898), 59f.; IV (1900), 236–8.

Trummer, Carl, *Vorträge über Tortur, Hexenverfolgungen, Vehmgerichte, und andere merkwürdige Erscheinungen in der Hamburgischen Rechtsgeschichte*, Hamburg, 1844–50.

Türler, Heinrich, 'Ueber Hexen- und Zauberwesen im Obersimmental im Mittelalter', *Blätter für bernische Geschichte, Kunst, und Altertumskunde*, III (1907), 79–86.

Vayra, A., 'Le streghe nel Canavese, con due processi inediti dell'Inquisizione 1474', *Curiosità e ricerche di storia subalpina*, I (1874), 82–132, 209–63, 654–721.

Verga, Ettore, 'Intorno a due inediti documenti di stregheria milanese del secolo

XIV.', *Rendiconti del Reale Istituto Lombardo si Scienze e Lettere*, ser. 2, XXXII (1899), 165–88.

Villette, P., 'La sorcellerie dans le nord de la France du milieu du XVeme siècle à la fin du XVIIeme siècle', *Mélanges de science religieuse*, XIII (1956), 39–62, 129–56.

Villette, P., 'La sorcellerie à Douai', *Mélanges de science religieuse*, XVIII (1961), 123–73.

Winterthur, Johann von, *Chronica Iohannis Vitodurani*, ed. Friedrich Baethgen (Monumenta Germaniae historica, Scriptores rerum Germanicarum, N.S., III), Berlin, 1924.

Wright, Thomas, ed., *A Contemporary Narrative of the Proceedings against Dame Alice Kyteler, prosecuted for sorcery in 1324 by Richard de Ledrede, Bishop of Ossory*, London, 1843.

Wright, Thomas, 'The Municipal Archives of Exeter', *Journal of the British Archaeological Association*, XVIII (1862), 306–17.

Notes

CHAPTER I   INTRODUCTION

1 Alan Macfarlane, *Witchcraft in Tudor and Stuart England* (London, 1970); Keith Thomas, *Religion and the Decline of Magic* (London, 1971), esp. 435–583.

2 The objection is that of H. C. Erik Midelfort, *Witch Hunting in Southwestern Germany, 1562–1684* (Stanford, 1972), 4.

3 1448, diocese of Lausanne (d): Archives Cantonales Vaudoises, MS Ac 29, fol. 56–68; see also Calendar of Trials.

4 The question whether Norse mythology (in the sagas, and especially in the eddas) derives from popular or learned tradition has long been disputed; see e.g. Georges Dumézil, *Gods of the Ancient Northmen* (English ed., Berkeley, Los Angeles and London, 1973), and Nils Lid, 'The Paganism of the Norsemen', in W. Edson Richmond, ed., *Studies in Folklore* (Bloomington, Ind., 1957), 230–51. The learned origin of medieval hagiography has been argued in František Graus, *Volk, Herrscher und Heiliger im Reich der Merowinger* (Prague, 1965), esp. 197–302, in opposition to scholars (such as C. Grant Loomis) who have emphasized the similarities between legends of the saints and modern folklore. For agrarian festivals, see George Caspar Homans, *English Villagers of the Thirteenth Century* (Cambridge, Mass., 1941), 353f.—though Homans deals more with the distinction between medieval and early modern sources than with that between learned and popular evidence. For related considerations see C. M. D. Crowder, 'Popular Culture in the Middle Ages', *Journal of Popular Culture*, IV (1971), 1071–82.

5 Rossell Hope Robbins, *Encyclopedia of Witchcraft and Demonology* (New York, 1959), 9; cf. 144.

6 Joseph Hansen, *Zauberwahn, Inquisition und Hexenprozess im Mittelalter* (Munich, 1900).

7 Jacob Grimm, *Teutonic Mythology*, III (English ed., London, 1883), 1031–1104.

8 Summers's main work is *The History of Witchcraft and Demonology* (London, 1926).

9 The most important of Murray's works is *The Witch-Cult in Western Europe* (Oxford, 1921); for a later exposition of her views, see *The God of the Witches* (London, 1931). Michael Harrison, *The Roots of Witchcraft* (London, 1973), expresses ideas derived from Murray. Carlo Ginzburg, *I Benandanti* (Turin, 1966), has attempted a partial rehabilitation of the thesis that witchcraft is a pagan survival.

10 Elliot Rose, *A Razor for a Goat* (Toronto, 1962).
11 Jules Michelet, *Satanism and Witchcraft* (English ed., New York, 1939), is the most accessible statement of the author's opinions. For a similar position, see Emmanuel LeRoy Ladurie, *Les paysans de Languedoc* (Paris, 1966), 407–13, translated in E. William Monter, ed., *European Witchcraft* (New York, 1969), 164–72.
12 Pennethorne Hughes, *Witchcraft* (2nd ed., Harmondsworth, 1965), esp. 84–6.
13 Jeffrey Burton Russell, *Witchcraft in the Middle Ages* (Ithaca and London, 1972).
14 Rose, *Razor*, 172f.
15 H. C. Erik Midelfort, 'Recent Witch Hunting Research, or Where Do We Go from Here?', *Papers of the Bibliographical Society of America*, LXII (1968), 375.
16 Hansen, *Zauberwahn*, 359.
17 On the influence of sermons and woodcuts, see Johan Huizinga, *The Waning of the Middle Ages* (paperback ed., Garden City, N.Y., 1954), 138.
18 1460, Soissons: Joseph Hansen, *Quellen und Untersuchungen zur Geschichte des Hexenwahns und der Hexenverfolgung im Mittelalter* (Bonn, 1901), 575.
19 See below, pp. 49f.
20 Hansen, *Zauberwahn*, 275–7, discusses the different conceptions of the pact in the Middle Ages.
21 Cf. Hansen, *Zauberwahn*, 171.
22 1390, Velay: Augustin Chassaing, *Spicilegium brivatense: Recueil de documents historiques relatifs au Brivadois et à l'Auvergne* (Paris, 1886), 441.
23 1449, Stade: *Chroniken der deutschen Städte*, XXX, 94.
24 E. E. Evans-Pritchard, 'Witchcraft (*mangu*) amongst the Azande', *Sudan Notes and Records*, XII (1929), 163–249; cf. also the same author's *Witchcraft, Oracles, and Magic among the Azande* (Oxford, 1937).
25 Cf. Macfarlane, *Witchcraft*, 3f., 310–12. Macfarlane adopts a modified version of Evans-Pritchard's definition; he speaks of witchcraft as involving an internal power within the witch, possibly implanted by the devil. In the records of the fourteenth and fifteenth centuries, however, there is seldom if ever any basis for determining whether internal powers or external acts and substances accomplished the magical results. Even when external means are mentioned, that is no guarantee that internal powers played no role; and when there is no mention of external means one cannot assume that internal forces were decisive. It is not clear what the basis is for Norman Cohn's statement, in *Europe's Inner Demons* (London, 1975), 147, that a distinction like Evans-Pritchard's was recognized in Europe; presumably Cohn has isolated literary references in mind.

CHAPTER II   CHRONOLOGICAL SURVEY

1 Here and elsewhere in this book, the designation 'France' will be used to apply to all French-speaking territories, and 'Germany' will apply to all German-speaking lands, with the one exception of Switzerland, which will be treated separately.

2 Joseph Hansen, *Zauberwahn, Inquisition und Hexenprozess im Mittelalter* (Munich, 1900), 355.

3 1306–14, France: See the literature cited in the Calendar of Trials.

4 1308–13, France: Abel Rigault, *Le procès de Guichard évêque de Troyes, 1308–1313* (Paris, 1896).

5 1315, France (a): See the literature cited in the Calendar of Trials.

6 1316, France; 1317, France; 1319, France; 1326, Toulouse; 1327, France; 1331, France (a); 1331, France (b). For details, consult the Calendar of Trials.

7 For the Avignonese papacy generally, cf. Guillaume Mollat, *The Popes at Avignon* (London, 1963). Hansen, *Zauberwahn*, 250–8, discusses John XXII's superstition and his involvement in witch trials. For an important document see Konrad Eubel, 'Vom Zaubereiunwesen anfangs des 14. Jahrhunderts', *Historisches Jahrbuch der Görres-Gesselschaft*, XVIII (1897), 627f. I have not been able to obtain an article by Esquieu, 'Le couteau magique de Jean XXII', *Bulletin de la Société des Études littéraires, scientifiques et artistiques du Lot*, XXV.

8 1317, Avignon: Edmond Albe, *Autour de Jean XXII: Hugues Géraud, évêque de Cahors: L'affaire des poisons et des envoûtements en 1317* (Cahors, 1904).

9 1319, Carcassonne: Barthélemy Hauréau, *Bernard Délicieux et l'Inquisition albigeoise, 1300–1320* (Paris, 1877), 194ff.

10 Joseph Hansen, *Quellen und Untersuchungen zur Geschichte des Hexenwahns und der Hexenverfolgung im Mittelalter* (Bonn, 1901), 2–6.

11 1320, Avignon.

12 1320–6, March of Ancona.

13 1327, France; 1331, France (a).

14 1314 or 1315, England: George Lyman Kittredge, *Witchcraft in Old and New England* (Cambridge, Mass., 1909), 51f.

15 1301–3, England.

16 1306–14, France.

17 1324, Kilkenny: Thomas Wright, ed., *A Contemporary Narrative of the Proceedings against Dame Alice Kyteler* (London, 1843).

18 Elliot Rose, *A Razor for a Goat* (Toronto, 1962), 65f., and Norman Cohn, *Europe's Inner Demons* (London, 1975), 198–204.

19 Cohn, in *Europe's Inner Demons*, esp. 164–73 and 180–97, discusses these trials in detail, and emphasizes the role of learned invocation (or what he calls 'ritual magic'). His emphasis is probably excessive: this kind of offense was dominant only during the first phase of prosecution, and even then it was by no means the sole allegation. Later trials may have been stimulated by these notable prototypes (as I suggest here), but the emphasis in the charges shifted. I also suspect that Cohn presents invocation as a phenomenon more standardized and systematized than it probably was.

20 1329, Carcassonne: Henry Charles Lea, *A History of the Inquisition of the Middle Ages*, III (New York, 1888), 657–9.

21 On the problem of antinomianism, see Walter L. Wakefield and Austin P. Evans, eds, *Heresies of the High Middle Ages* (New York and London, 1969), 666f. n. 13; Norman Cohn, *The Pursuit of the Millennium* (2nd ed.,

London and New York, 1970), esp. 148–86, 287–90; Jeffrey Burton Russell, *Witchcraft in the Middle Ages* (Ithaca and London, 1972), esp. 138–42; and in particular Robert E. Lerner, *The Heresy of the Free Spirit in the Later Middle Ages* (Berkeley, Los Angeles, and London, 1972).

22 See Lerner, *Free Spirit*, 25–34.

23 Eg., 1315, Krems; 1318, Avignon (b).

24 On the case c. 1340 at Novara, see Cohn, *Europe's Inner Demons*, 138–45.

25 Étienne-Léon de Lamothe-Langon, *Histoire de l'Inquisition en France* (Paris, 1829).

26 Hansen, *Quellen*, 449–53, 456, 500; Hansen cites Lamothe-Langon in numerous other instances without quotation.

27 Eg., Charles Edward Hopkins, *The Share of Thomas Aquinas in the Growth of the Witchcraft Delusion* (Philadelphia, 1940), 179; cf. H. C. Erik Midelfort, 'Recent Witch Hunting Research, or Where Do We Go from Here?', *Papers of the Bibliographical Society of America*, LXII (1968), 376.

28 Lamothe-Langon, *Histoire de l'Inquisition*, III, 226.

29 I wrote this passage before I read or knew about Norman Cohn's exposition of these forgeries in *Europe's Inner Demons*, 128–38. I have left my treatment as I wrote it originally, even though my conclusions are stated much more cautiously than Cohn's (perhaps too cautiously). The reader will note that Cohn's discussion of the matter is more extended than mine, but that in certain details I furnish further evidence. Cohn and I both based our discoveries in large part on the biographical data in Switzer's book of 1962 (below, n. 33), which explains the coincidence of our independently reaching the same conclusion.

30 Charles Molinier, in *L'Inquisition dans le Midi de la France au XIIIe et au XIVe siècle* (Paris, 1880), xvi–xxvii, discusses the history of southern French inquisitorial archives.

31 Jeffrey Russell, in *Witchcraft*, 328 n. 26, notes this anachronism, but explains it merely as an incidental error on the part of Lamothe-Langon. Cf. also the implausible reference to inquisitors delegated for 'the entire kingdom of France' but 'operative in Carcassonne', in Lamothe-Langon, III, 210.

32 Lamothe-Langon, *Histoire de l'Inquisition*, I, esp. xli.

33 For the following information see Richard Switzer, *Étienne-Léon de Lamothe-Langon et le roman populaire française de 1800 à 1830* (Paris, 1962), 34–71.

34 A. Germain, ed., 'Inventaire inédit concernant les Archives de l'Inquisition de Carcassonne', *Mémoires de la Société Archéologique de Montpellier*, IV (1855), 287–308.

35 Apart from the cases cited in the Calendar of Trials, there is a letter from Philip VI, dated 1334, forbidding the officials of southern France from disturbing inquisitorial efforts against idolaters, magicians, and heretics. See Hansen, *Zauberwahn*, 325 n. 1, and Henry Charles Lea, *Materials toward a History of Witchcraft*, I (Philadelphia, 1937), 230.

36 Inquisitorial procedure was even established in German towns at this time, and did not await the introduction of Roman law in the fifteenth century; cf. Alfons Vogt, 'Die Anfänge des Inquisitionsprozesses in Frankfurt am Main', *Zeitschrift der Savigny-Stiftung für Rechtsgeschichte*, Germanistische Abteilung, LXVIII (1951), 234–307.

37 On judicial procedures, cf. A. Esmein, *A History of Continental Criminal Procedure* (Boston, 1913).

38 1451, Strassburg: Hansen, *Quellen*, 556.

39 William M. Bowsky, ed., *The Black Death: A Turning Point in History?* (New York, 1971), gives a convenient compilation of essays, many dealing with the social effects of the plague.

40 Eg., H. R. Trevor-Roper, 'The European Witch-craze of the Sixteenth and Seventeenth Centuries', in *Religion, the Reformation and Social Change* (London, 1967), esp. 103f.

41 I intend to discuss this general topic in a different context at a later date.

42 1383, Olten: Conrad Justinger, *Die Berner-Chronik*, ed. Gottlieb Studer (Bern, 1871), 156; 1397, Appenzell: Emil Schiess, *Das Gerichtswesen und die Hexenprozesse in Appenzell* (Trogen, 1919), 93; 1398, Lucerne: Hansen, *Quellen*, 524; 1399, Basel: Carl Buxtorf-Falkeisen, *Baslerische Stadt- und Landgeschichten aus dem sechszehnten Jahrhundert*, IV (Basel, 1868), xii.

43 c. 1395–1405, Simmenthal: Joannes Nider, *Formicarius* (Lyon, 1669), 314–16; reprinted in Hansen, *Quellen*, 91–9.

44 L'Abbé J. Grémaud, ed., *Documents relatifs à l'histoire du Vallais*, VII (Lausanne, 1894), 549–51; Hansen, *Quellen*, 533–7.

45 Gene A. Brucker, 'Sorcery in Renaissance Florence', *Studies in the Renaissance*, X (1963), 13–16.

46 1384, Milan: Ettore Verga, 'Intorno a due inediti documenti di stregheria milanese del secolo XIV.', *Rendiconti del Reale Istituto Lombardo di Scienze e Lettere*, ser. 2, XXXII (1899), 166f.

47 The general topic of pagan survivals is both complex and broad; for an excellent discussion of the specific question of witchcraft as pagan survival, see Rose, *Razor*, esp. 131–3. I believe that Rose overestimates the role of pagan survivals in European witchcraft; yet for those trials that were based on remnants of paganism, Rose's comments are highly illuminating.

48 1390, Milan (a): Verga, 'Documenti', 167.

49 Hansen, *Zauberwahn*, 278–84; the connection between notions of heresy and ideas of witchcraft is a pervasive theme of Russell's *Witchcraft*.

50 Heinrich Denifle and Émile Chatelain, *Chartularium universitatis Parisiensis*, IV (Paris, 1897), 32–6; cf. Hansen, *Zauberwahn*, 283f.

51 The essential text is Alexander IV's *Quod super nonnullos*, section 4; this text was incorporated into canon law; see Emil Albert Friedberg, ed., *Corpus iuris canonici*, II (Leipzig, 1881), 1072.

52 Much of this literature is reprinted in Hansen, *Quellen*.

53 Cohn, in *Europe's Inner Demons*, 237f., denies that literary works brought about the shift, and demonstrates that the charges set forth in the trials of the early fifteenth century were more elaborate than those suggested in contemporary literature. Yet the essential amalgamation of sorcery and diabolism (discussed below, pp. 79–88) was contained in early works such as that of Nider; the intellectual suppositions that underlay the link between sorcery and diabolism had been formed and (more importantly) were being disseminated. The preoccupation of intellectuals with these notions surely fostered a cultural climate within which there could be widespread trials for diabolism.

54 Joannes Nider, *Formicarius*; standard ed. published along with Jacobus Sprenger and Henricus Institoris, *Malleus maleficarum* (Lyon, 1669), I, 305-54.

55 On the *Malleus* and its authors, see Hansen, *Quellen*, 360-408.

56 1453, Marmande: 'Exécution faite à Marmande de plusieurs femmes accusées de sorcellerie (1453)', *Bulletin de l'École des Chartes*, ser. 2, V (1848-9), 372-6; reprinted in Hansen, *Quellen*, 449-61.

57 1459-62, Arras and vicinity.

58 1459, Andermatt: Hansen, *Quellen*, 571-5.

59 1477, Villars-Chabod: J.-M. Lavanchy, 'Sabbats ou synagogues sur les bords du Lac d'Annecy', *Mémoires et documents publiés par l'Académie Salésienne*, VIII (1885), 424-40; reprinted in Hansen, *Quellen*, 487-99.

60 1493, Constance: Hansen, *Quellen*, 592.

CHAPTER III   DISTINCTION OF POPULAR AND LEARNED TRADITIONS

1 Elliot Rose, *A Razor for a Goat* (Toronto, 1962), 113.

2 It is in this sense that Jeffrey Russell, *Witchcraft in the Middle Ages* (Ithaca and London, 1972), 116, seems to use the phrase 'popular tradition.'

3 See below, pp. 9of.

4 1406, Lucerne; 1407, Basel; 1423, Nieder-Hauenstein; 1427, Zürich; 1433, Basel; 1448, diocese of Lausanne (b); 1448, diocese of Lausanne (d); 1454, Lucerne; 1464, diocese of Lausanne; c. 1480, Lucerne; 1481, Neuchâtel; 1486, Lucerne (a); 1489, Lucerne; 1498, diocese of Lausanne (b); 1499, Lucerne. For bibliographic information, see Calendar of Trials. The trial at Geneva in 1401 might be included, except that the charges brought forth by the witnesses do not even fit the definition of witchcraft here employed.

5 1451, Strassburg; 1458, Constance; 1485, Innsbruck.

6 1439, Draguignan; 1459, Avalon (note that in this trial tales of diabolism were related by secular officials, but not by the original witnesses); 1491, Boucoiran. I am excluding here the trial of Guichard of Troyes (1308-13) because the charges were patently influenced by political considerations; if included, however, this case would strengthen the argument set forth in this chapter. I am also omitting the trial of Alice Kyteler, for which the original depositions are lacking, although the narrative source tends to corroborate the present thesis; cf. Norman Cohn, *Europe's Inner Demons* (London, 1975), esp. 201.

7 Norman Cohn, in *Europe's Inner Demons*, 239-43, cites a few of these Swiss cases and recognizes their importance as evidence. There is no strict connection, though, between this type of evidence and the judicial procedures used in Switzerland, as Cohn suggests. Testimony of witnesses was taken in secular and ecclesiastical courts throughout Europe; it was sometimes spontaneous and sometimes solicited, but in either case yields valuable information.

8 1402, Lucerne; 1441, Bern (a and b); 1482, Bern (b); 1486 or 1487, Altdorf; 1494, Lucerne (a); 1494, Zürich.

9 1302, Exeter (a); 1435, Durham; 1452, Durham; 1470, England; 1476, London; 1497, London.

10 1448, Fürth.

11 See esp. Joannes Nider, *Formicarius* (Lyon, 1669), 314–16, 318–20, 329–31; reprinted with important notes in Joseph Hansen, *Quellen und Untersuchungen zur Geschichte des Hexenwahns* (Bonn, 1901), 91–9. There are various cases in which ecclesiastical and lay courts cooperated in interrogation, and in any event lay courts were bound by the Church to carry out capital sentences when obdurate or relapsed heretics—or witches—were released to them, in which process they would naturally learn the charges.

12 One of the earliest of these was Johann Hartlieb, *Buch aller verbotenen Kunst*, ed. Dora Ulm (Halle an der Saale, 1914), written in 1456. Not many such vernacular works survive; one may conjecture that there were originally more of them, but that they were less in demand than Latin works and thus less copied.

13 See A. Esmein, *A History of Continental Criminal Procedure* (Boston, 1913). A distinction is sometimes made between inquisitorial and denunciatory procedure, depending on whether public repute or an individual informant provides the basis for the charges; see Nicolaus Eymericus, *Directorium inquisitorum* (Rome, 1585), 443–8. For present purposes this distinction is not crucial, and the term 'inquisitorial procedure' is used to cover both types.

14 Eg., 1401, Geneva: Hansen, *Quellen*, 524–6.

15 An excellent example of such a general inquisition for witchcraft is 1485, Innsbruck: Hartmann Ammann, 'Der Innsbrucker Hexenprocess von 1485', *Zeitschrift des Ferdinandeums für Tirol und Vorarlberg*, ser. 3, XXXIV (1890), 1–87.

16 See below, pp. 34f. and 69–71.

17 1454, Lucerne: E. Hoffmann-Krayer, 'Luzerner Akten zum Hexen- und Zauberwesen', *Schweizerisches Archiv für Volkskunde*, III (1899), 33–9.

18 c. 1480, Lucerne: *ibid.*, 81–3.

19 1464, diocese of Lausanne: Archives Cantonales Vaudoises, MS Ac 29, fol. 160–86; summarized in Maxime Reymond, 'Cas de sorcellerie en pays fribourgeois au quinzième siècle', *Schweizerisches Archiv für Volkskunde*, XIII (1909), 87–90.

20 1498, diocese of Lausanne (b): Archives Cantonales Vaudoises, MS Ac 29, fol. 365–87; Reymond, 'Cas de sorcellerie', 91–4.

21 1491, Boucoiran: Édouard Bligny-Bondurand, 'Procédure contre une sorcière de Boucoiran (Gard), 1491', *Bulletin philologique et historique*, 1907, 380–405.

22 1481, Neuchâtel: Fritz Chabloz, *Les sorcières Neuchâteloises* (Neuchâtel, 1868), 51–4.

23 1407, Basel: Carl Buxtorf-Falkeisen, *Baslerische Stadt- und Landgeschichten aus dem sechszehnten Jahrhundert*, IV (Basel, 1868), 1–25.

24 1439, Draguignan: Roger Aubenas, *La sorcière et l'inquisiteur* (Aix-en-Provence, 1956).

25 1485, Innsbruck: Ammann, 'Der Innsbrucker Hexenprocess'.

26 *Ibid.*, 10.

27 *Ibid.*, 15.

28 *Ibid.*, 20.

29 *Ibid.*, 46.
30 *Ibid.*, 48.
31 *Ibid.*, 49.
32 *Ibid.*, 61.
33 1435, Durham: *Depositions and Other Ecclesiastical Proceedings from the Courts of Durham* (London, 1845), 27.
34 1448, Fürth: Werner Sprung, 'Der Eberhardshof und der Muggenhof', *Mitteilungen des Vereins für Geschichte der Stadt Nürnberg*, L (1960), 66.
35 See for example Lucy Mair, *Witchcraft* (London, 1969), 36–42.
36 The only trials for explicit diabolism in the entire British Isles seem to be those of 1301–3 in England and 1324 in Kilkenny (see Calendar of Trials), though invocation appears to have been more common, and sometimes involved a pact with the devil.
37 These statistics are based only on those cases in which the original court records were available for determination of language. Cases in which information comes from chronicles or correspondence are not included.
38 1335, Carcassonne: Étienne-Léon de Lamothe-Langon, *Histoire de l'Inquisition en France*, III (Paris, 1829), 226–30.
39 See Hansen, *Quellen*, 38f.
40 Russell, *Witchcraft*, 77f.; H. C. Erik Midelfort, *Witch Hunting in Southwestern Germany, 1562–1684* (Stanford, 1972), 15–17.
41 See esp. John T. McNeill, 'Folk Paganism in the Penitentials', *Journal of Religion*, XIII (1933), 450–66.
42 Two works on this topic are Herbert Achterberg, *Interpretatio christiana: Verkleidete Glaubensgestalten der Germanen auf deutschem Boden* (Leipzig, 1930), and Rudolf Schomerus, *Die Religion der Nordgermanen im Spiegel christlicher Darstellung* (Borna, 1936).
43 Essentially the same point is made in George Lyman Kittredge, *Witchcraft in Old and New England* (Cambridge, Mass., 1929), 244f.; cf. Rose, *Razor*, 107f.
44 Ernst Alfred Philippson states in his *Germanisches Heidentum bei den Angelsachsen* (Leipzig, 1929), 'Die erhaltenen Gesetze gegen abergläubischen Zauber sind ausserordentlich zahlreich, nicht nur weil die betreffenden Verbote immer wiederholt werden—sie entsprechen dem Bedürfnis' (p. 210). This judgment would be difficult to substantiate. It is no doubt true that certain elements of pagan culture persisted, but it would be hazardous to use the penitentials as evidence for the survival of any specific custom or belief, without auxiliary evidence.
45 Jan de Vries, in *Contributions to the Study of Othin, especially in his Relation to Agricultural Practices in Modern Popular Lore* (Helsinki, 1931), as in other of his writings, makes the important point that even when pagan notions and practices survive past the conversion to Christianity they do not necessarily persist in their original form, and that modern folklore is thus not a valid source of information for pagan notions. Modern lore about the 'wild hunt' thus does not count as evidence for the survival of the ideas cited in the canon *Episcopi*, despite their similarity.
46 On vilification of Waldensians see Dietrich Kurze, 'Zur Ketzergeschichte der Mark Brandenburg und Pommerns vornehmlich im 14. Jahrhundert',

Jahrbuch für die Geschichte Mittel- und Ostdeutschlands, XVI/XVII (1968), 50–94.

47 Eg., 1387–8, vicinity of Turin and Pinarolo: Girolamo Amati, 'Processus contra Valdenses in Lombardia superiori, anno 1387', *Archivio storico italiano*, ser. 3, I, pt 2 (1864), 3–52; II, pt 1 (1865), 3–61.

48 Eg., c. 1450, Savoy or vicinity: Hansen, *Quellen*, 122.

49 In addition to the trials cited above (pp. 21f.), cf. 1450/7, diocese of Brixen. The subjects in this instance were Italian-speaking women. Their confessions seem partly stereotyped; Nicholas of Cusa, the judge, was clearly familiar with demonological literature, and made reference to the work of Johannes Nider. But genuine survivals from paganism may have formed the basis for the charges. Particularly intriguing is the reference to a 'domina Abunda' who was led about in a cart. This is conceivably a survival of the early Germanic practice narrated in Tacitus, *Germania*, 40, and elsewhere.

50 Jean Marx, *L'Inquisition en Dauphiné* (Paris, 1914), 31.

51 Cited in Mair, *Witchcraft*, 170f.

52 Eg., Margaret Alice Murray, *The Witch-Cult in Western Europe* (Oxford, 1921), 279f. See most recently Michael J. Harner, 'The Role of Hallucinogenic Plants in European Witchcraft', in Michael J. Harner, ed., *Hallucinogens and Shamanism* (London, 1973), 125–50; cf. also the works cited in Cohn, *Europe's Inner Demons*, 288 n. 38.

53 In the following trials the unguent was applied to sticks or other implements: 1428, Valais; c. 1450, Lucerne (a); c. 1450, Savoy or vicinity; c. 1460, Lyonnais; 1475, Bressuire; 1477, Villars-Chabod; 1477, diocese of Lausanne (b); 1482, diocese of Lausanne; 1498, diocese of Lausanne (a, c, and d). The application of the ointment in the trial of 1492–4, lands of count of Virneburg and archbishop of Trier, is unspecified. One witch, tried 1461 in the diocese of Lausanne (b), is supposed to have rubbed the unguent directly on to his body. Likewise, Alfonso of Tostado at least gives the impression that it was thus employed (Hansen, *Quellen*, 109 n. 1). Perhaps the best evidence for bodily application of a hallucinogenic ointment is the second-hand story in Nider, *Formicarius*, ii, c. 41, and even here the relevant words read merely 'applicatisque verbis maleficis et unguento.'

54 See for example Norman Cohn, *The Pursuit of the Millennium* (2nd ed., London, 1970), 150.

55 For one classic instance, see the comments on Marguerite Porete in Robert E. Lerner, *The Heresy of the Free Spirit in the Later Middle Ages* (Berkeley, Los Angeles, and London, 1972), esp. 68–78, 200–8.

56 See below, pp. 75–8.

CHAPTER IV THE CONTENT OF POPULAR TRADITION

1 For general treatments of this subject, see Johan Huizinga, *The Waning of the Middle Ages* (paperback ed., Garden City, N.Y., 1954), 151–225; Otto Clemen, *Die Volksfrömmigkeit des ausgehenden Mittelalters* (Dresden and Leipzig, 1937); Willy Andreas, *Deutschland vor der Reformation* (6th ed., Berlin, 1972), 133–201; A. G. Dickins, *The English Reformation* (London,

1964), 1–21; and Keith Thomas, *Religion and the Decline of Magic* (London, 1971), 25–50.

2 See below, p. 76.

3 Apart from the cases cited below, cf. 1390, Velay; 1407, Basel; 1492–4, lands of count of Virneburg and archbishop of Trier; 1498, diocese of Lausanne (b); 1499, Lucerne.

4 Hartmann Ammann, 'Der Innsbrucker Hexenprocess von 1485', *Zeitschrift des Ferdinandeums für Tirol und Vorarlberg*, ser. 3, XXXIV (1890), 39.

5 See Clyde Pharr, 'The Interdiction of Magic in Roman Law', *Transactions of the American Philological Association*, LXIII (1932), 272–4; also Joseph Hansen, *Zauberwahn, Inquisition und Hexenprozess im Mittelalter* (Munich, 1900), 54–6, 75f.

6 1308, Paris; 1399 or 1400, Berlin; c. 1436, Osnabrück; 1446, Berlin; 1471, Nürnberg (judging from the wording of the secondary report); 1477, Hildesheim; 1499, Lucerne.

7 1420, Appenzell: Emil Schiess, *Das Gerichtswesen und die Hexenprozesse in Appenzell* (Trogen, 1919), 93.

8 1460, diocese of Soissons: Alphonse de La Fons, 'Des sorcièrs aux XVme. et XVIme. siècles', *Mémoires de la Société Royale d'Émulation d'Abbeville*, 1841–3, pp. 437f.

9 On the question of toad poison, see Margaret Murray, *The Divine King* (London, 1954), 40. The article Murray cites is Edwin S. Faust, 'Ueber Bufonin und Bufotalin, die wirksamen Bestandtheile des Krötenhautdrüsensecretes', *Archiv für experimentelle Pathologie und Pharmakologie*, XLVII (1902), 278–310. Faust gives $C_{34}H_{46}O_{10}$ as a chemical formula for toad poison.

10 Apart from the cases cited below, cf. 1331, Southwark; 1371, Salurn.

11 James George Frazer, *The Golden Bough: A Study in Magic and Religion*, I (3rd ed., London, 1917), 55–174.

12 Ernst Alfred Philippson, *Germanisches Heidentum bei den Angelsachsen* (Leipzig, 1929), 222f.

13 A. J. Robertson, ed., *Anglo-Saxon Charters* (Cambridge, 1939), xxxvii.

14 Philippson, *Germanisches Heidentum*, 223.

15 1315, France (a); 1331, Southwark; 1347, Mende.

16 F. B. Jevons, 'Graeco-Italian Magic', in Arthur J. Evans, *et al.*, *Anthropology and the Classics: Six Lectures Delivered before the University of Oxford*, ed. R. R. Marett (Oxford, 1908), 93–120.

17 1490, London: William Hale Hale, *A Series of Precedents and Proceedings in Criminal Causes* (London, 1847), 20.

18 Between 1480 and 1515, St David's: C. Trice Martin, 'Clerical Life in the Fifteenth Century, as Illustrated by Proceedings of the Court of Chancery', *Archaeologia*, LX (1907), 374–6.

19 1384, Florence: Gene A. Brucker, 'Sorcery in Early Renaissance Florence', *Studies in the Renaissance*, X (1963), 15.

20 La Fons, 'Des sorcièrs', 439 n. 4.

21 Ammann, 'Der Innsbrucker Hexenprocess', 18; cf. also 1475, Bressuire.

22 Ammann, 'Der Innsbrucker Hexenprocess', 53f.

23 Between 1480 and 1515, Southwark: Martin, 'Clerical Life', 373f.

24 1371, Salurn: Hartmann Ammann, 'Ein Mordversuch durch Zauberei im Jahre 1371', *Mitteilungen des österreichischen Instituts für Geschichtsforschung*, X (1889), 137.

25 1320, Avignon: Robert Michel, 'Le procès de Matteo et de Galeazzo Visconti, *Mélanges d'archéologie et d'histoire*, XXIX (1909), 269–327.

26 Thomas Wright, ed., *A Contemporary Narrative of the Proceedings against Dame Alice Kyteler* (London, 1843), xxiii–xxix (see also Calendar of Trials).

27 1308–13, France; 1315, France; 1326, Toulouse; 1327, France; 1331, France (b).

28 1317, Avignon: Edmond Albe, *Autour de Jean XXII: Hugues Géraud, évêque de Cahors* (Cahors, 1904) (see also Calendar of Trials). Baptism and other rituals were common in trials that involved clerics; in one case (1319, Paris) a priest insisted that the image had to be anointed three times for the desired effect; cf. 1317, Paris.

29 1392, France; 1401, France; 1465, Péronne; 1470, England.

30 Ammann, 'Der Innsbrucker Hexenprocess'.

31 *Ibid.*, 16.

32 *Ibid.*, 20.

33 *Ibid.*, 45f. Cf. Jacobus Sprenger and Henricus Institoris, *Malleus maleficarum* (Lyon, 1669), 148f. (Summers ed., 137f.)

34 Ammann, 'Der Innsbrucker Hexenprocess', 50; cf. 54, 56.

35 *Ibid.*, 59–63.

36 1428, Todi: Candida Peruzzi, 'Un processo di stregoneria a Todi nel '400', *Lares: Organo della Società di Etnografia Italiana-Roma*, XXI (1955), fasc. I–II, 12.

37 c. 1480, Lucerne; 1485, Innsbruck.

38 1427, Zürich; 1432–43, England; c. 1475, Heidelberg; 1485, Innsbruck.

39 c. 1475, Heidelberg; 1485, Innsbruck.

40 1446, Berlin; 1485, Innsbruck.

41 1485, Innsbruck.

42 1325, Coventry; 1428, Todi; 1485, Innsbruck.

43 Édouard Bligny-Bondurand, 'Une sorcière de Boucoiran (Gard), 1491', *Bulletin philologique et historique*, 1907, pp. 380–405.

44 'Exécution faite à Marmande de plusieurs femmes accusées de sorcellerie (1453)', *Bulletin de l'École des Chartes*, ser. 2, V (1848–9), 372–6; reprinted in Joseph Hansen, *Quellen und Untersuchungen zur Geschichte des Hexenwahns und der Hexenverfolgung im Mittelalter* (Bonn, 1901), 449–61.

45 1397, Appenzell; 1420, Appenzell; 1427, Appenzell; 1455, Torcy; 1462, Zürich (a); c. 1480, Lucerne; 1489, Lucerne; 1491, Boucoiran; 1491, Zutphen; 1498, diocese of Lausanne (b); 1499, Angermund.

46 1427, Appenzell: Schiess, *Das Gerichtswesen*, 93f.

47 Ammann, 'Der Innsbrucker Hexenprocess', 45f.

48 1414, Basel; 1448, diocese of Lausanne (a); c. 1453, Regensburg; 1498, diocese of Lausanne (a).

49 1480, Brescia (a); Paolo Guerrini, ed., *Le cronache bresciane inedite dei sec. XV–XIX* (Brescia, 1922), 183–5.

50 1390, Velay: Augustin Chassaing, ed., *Spicilegium brivatense* (Paris, 1886), 442.

51 1428, Todi: Peruzzi, 'Un processo di stregoneria', 13.
52 Robert Redfield, *The Folk Culture of Yucatan* (Chicago, 1941), 335f.
53 See David Herlihy, 'The Tuscan Town in the Quattrocento: A Demographic Profile', *Medievalia et Humanistica*, N.S., I (1970), 81–109, esp. 93f., and 'Mapping Households in Medieval Italy', *Catholic Historical Review*, LVIII (1972), esp. 10–15; there is further relevant information in Herlihy's *Medieval and Renaissance Pistoia: The Social History of an Italian Town, 1200–1430* (New Haven and London, 1967), 83f.
54 1379, Augsburg; 1380, Paris; 1384, Florence; 1385, Augsburg; 1421, Kempten; 1446, Durham; 1446, Gouda; 1448, Fürth; c. 1450, Lucerne (b); 1452, Durham; 1454, Ferrara; 1456, Breslau; 1473, Aargau; 1474, Nürnberg; 1481, London; 1496, Hildesheim.
55 Philippson, *Germanisches Heidentum*, 211.
56 1375, Reggio; 1406, Nürnberg; 1474, Nürnberg.
57 1404, Florence.
58 1428, Todi.
59 1428, Todi.
60 1376, England; 1428, Todi.
61 1375, Reggio; 1428, Todi.
62 1448, diocese of Lausanne (b); 1463, Lucerne (a and b).
63 1465, Lucerne. Although the purpose of the sorcery is not stated explicitly, it can be conjectured with reasonable confidence. Cf. the story in Sprenger and Institoris, *Malleus maleficarum*, 50f. (Summers ed., 51), about the woman who bewitched a succession of abbots by feeding them her own excrement, thus causing them to fall in love with her.
64 1372, Metz; 1408, Lorraine; 1441, London; 1450, Reimerswael.
65 1408, Lorraine: Jacques Bournon, *Chroniques, lois, moeurs et usages de la Lorraine, au moyen-âge*, ed. Jean Cayon (Nancy, 1838), 23.
66 1427, Florence: Brucker, 'Sorcery', 16f.
67 1428, Todi: Peruzzi, 'Un processo di stregoneria', 10.
68 1375, Reggio: Aldo Cerlini, 'Una strega reggiana e il suo processo', *Studi storici*, XV (1906), 64–6f.
69 1317, France: Hansen, *Zauberwahn*, 357.
70 Chassaing, *Spicilegium*, 442.
71 1461, Putten: Hansen, *Quellen*, 576.
72 1463, Lucerne (a and b): E. Hoffmann-Krayer, 'Luzerner Akten zum Hexen- und Zauberwesen', *Schweizerisches Archiv für Volkskunde*, III (1899), 22f.; cf. 1499, Lucerne (*ibid.*, 93).
73 1375, Florence: Brucker, 'Sorcery', 9f.
74 1428, Todi: Peruzzi, 'Un processo di stregoneria', 9f.
75 *Ibid.*, 10f.
76 1472 (at latest), Tournai: Paul Fredericq, ed., *Corpus documentorum inquisitionis haereticae pravitatis Neerlandicae* (Ghent and The Hague, 1889–1906), I, 428f.
77 1376, England: *Chronicon Angliae . . . auctore monacho quodam Sancti Albani*, ed. Edward Maunde Thompson (London, 1874), 97–100.
78 1404, Florence: Brucker, 'Sorcery', 10f.
79 1428, Todi: Peruzzi, 'Un processo di stregoneria', 9, 12.

80 1485, Innsbruck: Ammann, 'Der Innsbrucker Hexenprocess', 10.

81 1428, Todi: Peruzzi, 'Un processo di stregoneria', 10f.

82 1375, Reggio: Cerlini, 'Una strega reggiana', 67.

83 *Ibid.*, 67: 'Et ad hoc ut maiorem amorem in ea poneret, docuit eam vituperium infrascriptum, videlicet quod dum dictus suus maritus esset in actum iacendi cum ea, ipsa mulier poneret manum ad vuluam, deinde poneret od [*sic* in Cerlini] os suum, et dictum suum maritum oscularetur dictis suis labiis pudibondis; et tunc ipse maritus suus in amore ipsius exarderet.'

84 1394, Florence: Brucker, 'Sorcery', 10.

85 1428, Todi: Peruzzi, 'Un processo di stregoneria', 11.

86 1435, Durham; 1485, Innsbruck. Cf. also the undated case in Jean Berchtold, *Histoire du canton de Fribourg*, I (Fribourg, 1841), 238, in which one marshal rendered another sterile (impotent?).

87 Brucker, 'Sorcery', 10f.

88 Sprenger and Institoris, *Malleus maleficarum*, 130 (Summers ed., 121).

89 Ammann, 'Der Innsbrucker Hexenprocess', 86.

90 W. Gordon East, *The Geography behind History* (2nd ed., London, 1965), 52–5.

91 1326, Agen; 1383, Olten; 1409, Pisa; 1441, Bern (b); 1451, Strassburg; 1453, Constance; 1456, Cologne; 1458, Constance; 1473, Bern; c. 1480, Lucerne; 1482, Lucerne (e); 1485, Innsbruck; 1486, Lucerne (a); 1488, Metz; 1489, Baden; 1489, Lucerne; 1491, Zutphen; 1493, London; 1494, Lucerne (a); 1499, Lucerne; cf. also the obscure reference in 1407, Basel.

92 See below, pp. 98–101.

93 Thomas, *Religion*, 560.

94 Philippson, *Germanisches Heidentum*, 210.

95 Wilfrid Bonser, 'Survivals of Paganism in Anglo-Saxon England', *Transactions of the Birmingham Archaeological Society*, LVI (1932), 64.

96 c. 1480, Lucerne: Hoffmann-Krayer, 'Luzerner Akten', 81–6.

97 1486, Lucerne (a): Hoffmann-Krayer, 'Luzerner Akten', 87f.

98 1441, Bern (b); Heinrich Türler, 'Ueber Hexen- und Zauberwesen im Obersimmental im Mittelalter', *Blätter für bernische Geschichte, Kunst, und Altertumskunde*, III (1907), 80.

99 1488, Metz: Hansen, *Quellen*, 587; cf. Thomas, *Religion*, 31f. and elsewhere.

100 1383, Olten; Conrad Justinger, *Die Berner-Chronik*, ed. Gottlieb Studer (Bern, 1871), 156.

101 c. 1480, Lucerne: Hoffmann-Krayer, 'Luzerner Akten', 81f.

102 1302, Exeter (a); 1424, Zwickau; 1482, Appenzell.

103 1482, Breslau: Samuel Benjamin Klose, *Darstellung der inneren Verhältnisse der Stadt Breslau* (Breslau, 1847), 101.

104 1458, Gnechwitz: *ibid.*, 101. Cf. also the obscure case of 1497, London.

105 1401, Paderborn; 1406, Berlin.

106 Hansen, *Quellen*, 42.

107 Eg., Hansen, *Quellen*, 210, 261.

108 Jacob Grimm, *Teutonic Mythology*, III (London, 1883), 1072.

109 1458, Constance; 1477, Nürnberg; 1485, Innsbruck; 1491, Zutphen.

110 1454, Lucerne; c. 1480, Lucerne.
111 1449, Stade; 1483, Cologne; 1485, Innsbruck.
112 1315, France (a).
113 1497, Oldenburg: Dietrich Kohl and Gustav Rüthning, eds, *Oldenburgisches Urkundenbuch*, I (Oldenburg, 1914), 216f.
114 1481, Breslau: Klose, *Darstellung*, 101.
115 Peter Browe, 'Die Eucharistie als Zaubermittel im Mittelalter', *Archiv für Kulturgeschichte*, XX (1930), 134–54.
116 c. 1322, Ehingen; 1482, Hamburg; 1482, Lucerne (c).
117 1423, Berlin.
118 1444, Nürnberg.
119 See above, p. 49.
120 1375, Reggio: Cerlini, 'Una strega reggiana', 67.
121 1428, Todi.
122 1384, Florence: Brucker, 'Sorcery', 13–16.
123 Cf. 1493, London, for a possible exception.
124 Jevons, 'Graeco-Italian Magic', discusses defixion at some length.
125 Grimm, *Teutonic Mythology*, III, 1223–49.
126 Wilfrid Bonser, 'The Dissimilarity of Ancient Irish Magic from that of the Anglo-Saxons', *Folklore*, XXXVII (1926), 286–8.
127 On the druids, see Nora K. Chadwick, *The Druids* (Cardiff, 1966), and Stuart Piggott, *The Druids* (London, 1968).
128 E. E. Evans-Pritchard, 'The Morphology and Function of Magic: A Comparative Study of Trobriand and Zande Rituals and Spells', *American Anthropologist*, XXXI (1929), 619–41.
129 Pharr, 'Interdiction of Magic', esp. 275–80.
130 Konrad Jarausch, 'Der Zauber in den Isländersagas', *Zeitschrift für Volkskunde*, N.S. I (1929–30), 244.
131 Walter Baetke, *Die Religion der Germanen in Quellenzeugnissen* (Frankfurt, 1938), 142.
132 Robert Redfield, *Peasant Society and Culture* (Chicago, 1956), 70.
133 See below, pp. 96f.
134 Thomas, *Religion*, 502–12.
135 1388, London; 1404, Florence; c. 1350, Brünn; 1371, Southwark; 1376, England.
136 1317, Avignon: Albe, *Autour de Jean XXII*.
137 Wright, *Contemporary Narrative*, xxiii–xxix.
138 1404, Florence: Brucker, 'Sorcery', 10f. Cf. 1331, Southwark; 1384, Florence; 1486, Diersburg (relevant information not in Hansen's reprinting).
139 E. E. Evans-Pritchard, *Witchcraft, Oracles, and Magic among the Azande* (Oxford, 1937), 475–8.
140 1477, Lucerne: Hoffmann-Krayer, 'Luzerner Akten', 24.
141 1439, Draguignan: Roger Aubenas, *La sorcière et l'inquisiteur* (Aix-en-Provence, 1956).
142 1472 (at latest), Tournai: Fredericq, *Corpus documentorum*, I, 439.
143 1410, Carcassonne: Hansen, *Quellen*, 454f.
144 1412, Florence: Brucker, 'Sorcery', 11f.

145 1337, Hatfield: Cecil l'Estrange Ewen, *Witchcraft and Demonianism* (London, 1933), 33f.
146 1465, Norfolk: Augustus Jessopp, *Random Roaming and Other Papers* (2nd ed., London, 1894), 109–12.
147 1323, Château-Landon.
148 1499, Lucerne: Hoffmann-Krayer, 'Luzerner Akten', 91–5.
149 1494, Zürich.
150 1433, Basel: Carl Buxtorf-Falkeisen, *Baslerische Stadt- und Landgeschichten aus dem sechszehnten Jahrhundert*, IV (Basel, 1868), xiii.
151 See above, p. 32.
152 1459, Andermatt: Hansen, *Quellen*, 571–5.

CHAPTER V   THE IMPOSITION OF LEARNED NOTIONS

1 1428, Todi: Candida Peruzzi, 'Un processo di stregoneria a Todi nel '400', *Lares: Organo della Società di Etnografia Italiana-Roma*, XXI (1955), fasc. I–II, 1–17.
2 1456, Cologne: Joseph Hansen, *Quellen und Untersuchungen zur Geschichte des Hexenwahns und der Hexenverfolgung im Mittelalter* (Bonn, 1901), 566–569.
3 See esp. Wolfgang Ziegler, *Möglichkeiten der Kritik am Hexen- und Zauberwesen im ausgehenden Mittelalter: Zeitgenössische Stimmen und ihre soziale Zugehörigkeit* (Cologne and Vienna, 1973).
4 For one exception, cf. 1455, Andermatt: Hansen, *Quellen*, 571–5.
5 See below, pp. 98–101.
6 Keith Thomas, *Religion and the Decline of Magic* (London, 1971), esp. 560.
7 Seven occurrences in the diocese of Lausanne: 1438, 1448 (a and d), 1461 (b), 1464, 1477 (b), and 1498 (d); also 1447, Büren; c. 1450, Lucerne (a); c. 1450, Lucerne (b); 1457, Fribourg; 1457–9, Faido; 1459, Andermatt; 1466 and 1467, Biel; 1484, Ravensburg; 1490, Lucerne (b); 1490, Solothurn; 1493, Zürich; 1495, Constance.
8 1438, La Tour du Pin; c. 1450, Savoy or vicinity; 1452, Provins; 1456, Metz; c. 1460, Lyonnais; 1462, Chamonix; 1481, Metz.
9 c. 1450, Savoy or vicinity: Hansen, *Quellen*, 120.
10 1459, Andermatt; 1466, Biel.
11 c. 1450, Savoy orvic inity: Hansen, *Quellen*, 120.
12 1453, Marmande;14 91, Boucoiran.
13 Infanticide occurred most frequently in the diocese of Lausanne: 1448 (d), 1458, 1461 (a and b), 1464, 1477 (b), 1479, 1480 (b), 1482, 1498 (c).
14 c. 1450, Lucerne (b); 1459, Andermatt; 1467, Biel.
15 There are exceptions: 1329, Carcassonne; 1383, Siena; c. 1450, Lucerne (b); 1467, Biel; 1480, Brescia (a).
16 Jacobus Sprenger and Henricus Institoris, *Malleus maleficarum* (Lyon, 1669), esp. 47–62, 126–31, 181–8 (Summers ed., 48–61, 117–22, 167–75).
17 Cf. Joseph Hansen, *Zauberwahn, Inquisition und Hexenprozess im Mittelalter* (Munich, 1900), 88–95.
18 The notion of image magic for harm occurs in 1417, Chambéry; c. 1460,

Lyonnais. That of harm through contact with magical substances arises 1459, Andermatt; 1475, Bressuire.

19 1477, Villars-Chabod: J.-M. Lavanchy, 'Sabbats ou synagogues sur les bords du Lac d'Annecy', *Mémoires et documents publiés par l'Académie Salésienne*, VIII (1885), 424–40; reprinted in Hansen, *Quellen*, 487–99.

20 1479, diocese of Lausanne: Archives Cantonales Vaudoises, MS Ac 29, fol. 269.

21 1448, diocese of Lausanne (a), fol. 10: the devil gave the subject an unguent, saying, '"tange dictum Johannem de Mossel de hujusmodi unguento per testiculos, et videbis quid faciet." Et tunc dictus Jaquetus secrete in quadam nube existens ad dictum Johannem [*Jaquetum* in MS] ivit et cum manu dextra testiculos per retro tetigit. Et incontinenti dictus Johannes incepit ire per dictam vineam, et redire huic et inde, et non poterat durare.'

22 Édouard Bligny-Bondurand, 'Procédure contre une sorcière de Boucoiran (Gard), 1491', *Bulletin philologique et historique*, 1907, pp. 384, 386.

23 1483 or 1484, diocese of Lausanne, fol. 338: 'Dixit quod idem magister suus sibi et suis complicibus precipiebat quod facerent multa mala. Interrogatus que mala, dixit nocere hominibus, animalibus, etc. Tamen dixit se nichil fecisse nec umquam alicui nocuisse.' This testimony is repeated fol. 339.

24 1461, diocese of Lausanne (b), fol. 143.

25 Eg., Hansen, *Quellen*, 119f., 141, 295; Henry Charles Lea, *Materials toward a History of Witchcraft* (Philadelphia, 1939), 274.

26 H. R. Trevor-Roper, *Religion, the Reformation and Social Change* (London, 1967), 123, 132, 184. Cf. also Thomas, *Religion*, 255, 268.

27 Hansen, *Quellen*, 104.

28 Joannes Nider, *Formicarius* (Lyon, 1669), 320; reprinted in Hansen, *Quellen*, 96.

29 For a similar sacrifice, reported 1436, cf. 1428–47, Dauphiné.

30 Sprenger and Institoris, *Malleus maleficarum*, 156 (Summers ed., 145).

31 Thomas Aquinas, 'Expositio in librum beati Job', c. 1, lect. 3, in *Opera omnia*, XIV (Parma, 1863), 8; cf. Hansen, *Quellen*, 95 n. 1.

32 Lea, *Materials*, 459.

33 Eg., Hansen, *Quellen*, 142.

34 *Ibid.*, 120.

35 *Ibid.*, 350.

36 Lea, *Materials*, 460f.; cf. *ibid.*, 267f.

37 *Ibid.*, 460f.

38 *Ibid.*, 460f.

39 *Loc. cit.*: 'daemon enim ipsos decipit maleficos'.

40 Hansen, *Quellen*, 260.

41 *Ibid.*, 287.

42 Sprenger and Institoris, *Malleus maleficarum*, 17 (Summers ed., 20); Hansen, *Quellen*, 230; 104.

43 *Ibid.*, 210.

44 Hansen, *Quellen*, 165f.

45 *Ibid.*, 193.

46 In anthropological investigations one finds reference to acts of spirits (ancestral or otherwise) and to acts of witches, but these two notions are

seldom joined, with spirits and witches acting in conjunction. For the most part, witches are viewed as having a special substance within themselves responsible for their powers, and sorcerers are seen as making use of the intrinsic properties of certain materials, such as herbs. Hence, neither need the services of spirits. See, in general, Lucy Mair, *Witchcraft* (London, 1969). John Beattie, 'Sorcery in Bunyoro', in John Middleton and E. H. Winter, eds, *Witchcraft and Sorcery in East Africa* (London, 1963), 37, distinguishes two broad types of sorcery: 'First there are those techniques which involve the use of "medicines", that is, of material substances of some kind; and secondly, there are those which utilize spirit agents. One reason why the two categories are not mutually exclusive is that Nyoro culture tends to "spiritualize" entities which are conceived as specially powerful and dangerous.' But the second form of sorcery is apparently a fairly recent development, and it is 'especially in this century under the spread of Western influence' that 'the range of spiritual beings which can affect and "possess" people has enormously increased' (p. 40).

47 Lea, *Materials*, 464.
48 Sprenger and Institoris, *Malleus maleficarum*, 52, 61, 86f. (Summers ed., 52, 60, 82).
49 *Ibid.*, 139 (Summers ed., 129).
50 *Ibid.*, 131 (Summers ed., 122); Lea, *Materials*, 317.
51 On the *ignis sacer*, cf. H. E. J. Cowdrey, 'The Peace and the Truce of God in the Eleventh Century', *Past and Present*, no. 46 (Feb. 1970), 42–67.
52 Lea, *Materials*, 452.
53 Sprenger and Institoris, *Malleus maleficarum*, 146 (Summers ed., 135).
54 *Ibid.*, 158f. (Summers ed., 146).
55 *Ibid.*, 5 (Summers ed., 6); the idea recurs throughout the book.
56 Hansen, *Quellen*, 80.
57 Hansen, *Zauberwahn*, 171.
58 Nicholas Jacquier, *Flagellum haereticorum fascinariorum* (Frankfurt, 1581), 42.
59 Lea, *Materials*, 459.
60 Hansen, *Quellen*, 287.
61 *Ibid.*, 68.
62 *Ibid.*, 72.
63 Lea, *Materials*, 459, 467f.
64 Hansen, *Quellen*, 293.
65 1477, Villars-Chabod: Lavanchy, 'Sabbats ou synagogues', 424–40.
66 1461, diocese of Lausanne (b): Archives Cantonales Vaudoises, MS Ac 29, fol. 150.
67 1461, diocese of Lausanne (a and b).
68 Herbert Grundmann, 'Ketzerverhöre des Spätmittelalters als quellen-kritisches Problem', *Deutsches Archiv für Erforschung des Mittelalters*, XXI (1965), 564–6.
69 H. C. Lea, *A History of the Inquisition of the Middle Ages*, I (New York, 1887), 422.
70 Sprenger and Institoris, *Malleus maleficarum*, 250 (Summers ed., 231).
71 1459–62, Arras and vicinity.

72 1461, diocese of Lausanne (b).

73 1438, diocese of Lausanne; 1448, diocese of Lausanne (c).

74 1487, Zürich: Hansen, *Quellen*, 586; Paul Schweizer, 'Der Hexenprozess und seine Anwendung in Zürich', *Zürcher Taschenbuch*, N.S. XXV (1902), 28.

75 Eg., 1458, diocese of Lausanne.

76 Cf. Antoine Dondaine, 'Le manuel de l'inquisiteur (1230–1330)', *Archivum fratrum praedicatorum*, XVII (1947), 85–194.

77 C. Calvert and A. W. Gruner, *A Hangman's Diary* (London, 1928), 17f.

78 Hansen, *Quellen*, 553 n. 2.

79 Peter Jos. Kämpfen, *Hexen und Hexenprozesse im Wallis* (Stans, 1867), 49.

80 Grundmann, 'Ketzerverhöre des Spätmittelalters'.

81 Eg., 1477 (b), fol. 232 and 236; 1479, fol. 265 and 267; 1498 (d), fol. 428.

82 See above, p. 4.

83 1477 (a), fol. 213.

84 1498 (a), fol. 352f.

85 1498 (d), fol. 418, 421f.

86 1448 (d), fol. 58. A brief passage from the trial of Joan of Arc (1431, Rouen) might be interpreted in similar fashion: asked about people who went out with fairies, Joan knew only that the excursions occurred on Thursday, and added that she thought of such activity as *sortilegium* (*sorcerie*); cf. *Procès de condamnation de Jeanne d'Arc*, ed. Pierre Tisset, I (Paris, 1960), 178. But it is not clear from the context whether by *sortiligium* she meant diabolism or merely magic and superstition, nor is it apparent that this folklore had any practical relevance for her (see above, pp. 39f.).

87 See above, pp. 39f.

88 There is clearly a need for work on popular witch beliefs during the later centuries. H. C. Erik Midelfort, however, has called my attention to a forthcoming study by Robert Muchembled on witchcraft in northern France in the sixteenth and seventeenth centuries, in which the findings of the present study are largely corroborated. If Muchembled's findings are typical for the sixteenth and seventeenth centuries, diabolism was not a popular concern even in this later period.

CHAPTER VI   THE SOCIAL CONTEXT OF WITCH TRIALS

1 H. R. Trevor-Roper, *Religion, the Reformation and Social Change* (London, 1967), 105–8. Jeffrey Russell, in *Witchcraft in the Middle Ages* (Ithaca and London, 1972), 200, argues the reverse hypothesis, that witchcraft 'spread with heresy *into* the mountains.' This notion, however, seems gratuitous.

2 See above, pp. 16–18.

3 The major exceptions are 1459, Andermatt; and 1485, Innsbruck. In addition, there were trials for sorcery (not diabolism) in Appenzell, which, though not highly urbanized, lay on the border of mountain terrain.

4 See for example the place names given throughout Alan Macfarlane, *Witchcraft in Tudor and Stuart England* (London, 1970).

5 See esp. David Herlihy, 'Mapping Households in Medieval Italy', *Catholic Historical Review*, LVIII (1972), 1–24.

6 Keith Thomas, *Religion and the Decline of Magic* (London, 1971), 562f.
7 Robert Redfield, *The Folk Culture of Yucatan* (Chicago, 1941), 326–37. The use of these particular data from Redfield does not, of course, necessarily involve acceptance of Redfield's broader theories.
8 Lucy Mair, *Witchcraft* (London, 1969), 160–79, discusses treatment of witchcraft in societies that have been subject to social transformation. See also Max Marwick, ed., *Witchcraft and Sorcery* (Harmondsworth, 1970), 164–98.
9 William M. Bowsky, ed., *The Black Death: A Turning Point in History?* (New York, 1971). For the example of Florence, see Millard Meiss, *Painting in Florence and Siena after the Black Death* (Princeton, N.J., 1951), 69, and works there cited.
10 See above, pp. 18f.
11 Carl Buxtorf-Falkeisen, *Baslerische Stadt- und Landgeschichten aus dem sechszehnten Jahrhundert*, IV (Basel, 1868), 1–25.
12 Eg., 1428–47, Dauphiné; 1439, Neuchâtel.
13 Édouard Bligny-Bondurand, 'Procédure contre une sorcière de Boucoiran (Gard), 1491', *Bulletin philologique et historique*, 1907, esp. 381.
14 Hartmann Ammann, 'Der Innsbrucker Hexenprocess von 1485', *Zeitschrift des Ferdinandeums für Tirol und Vorarlberg*, ser. 3, XXXIV (1890), 66.
15 c. 1350, Brünn: Joseph Hansen, *Quellen und Untersuchungen zur Geschichte des Hexenwahns und der Hexenverfolgung im Mittelalter* (Bonn, 1901), 518.
16 1390, Paris; 1390–1, Paris; 1456, Breslau; 1485, Innsbruck.
17 Thomas, *Religion*, 526–34.
18 Also 1446, Douai; 1454, Lucerne.
19 1481, Breslau: Samuel Benjamin Klose, *Darstellung der inneren Verhältnisse der Stadt Breslau* (Breslau, 1847), 101.
20 1485, Innsbruck: Ammann, 'Der Innsbrucker Hexenprocess', 16, 46.
21 1472 (at latest), Tournai: Paul Fredericq, ed., *Corpus documentorum inquisitionis haereticae pravitatis Neerlandicae*, I (Ghent and The Hague, 1889), 428f.
22 Aldo Cerlini, 'Una strega reggiana e il suo processo', *Studi storici*, XV (1906), 59–68.
23 Candida Peruzzi, 'Un processo di stregoneria a Todi nel '400', *Lares: Organo della Società di Etnografia Italiana-Roma*, XXI (1955), fasc. 1–11, 1–17.
24 Paolo Guerrini, ed., *Le cronache bresciane inedite dei sec. XV–XIX* (Brescia, 1922), 183–5.
25 Augustin Chassaing, ed., *Spicilegium brivatense* (Paris, 1886), 438–46.
26 Conrad Justinger, *Die Berner-Chronik*, ed. Gottlieb Studer (Bern, 1871), 156.
27 1384, Florence: Gene A. Brucker, 'Sorcery in Early Renaissance Florence', *Studies in the Renaissance*, X (1963), 13–16.
28 Between 1480 and 1515, St David's: C. Trice Martin, 'Clerical Life in the Fifteenth Century', *Archaeologia*, LX (1907), 374–6.
29 1460, diocese of Soissons: Alphonse de La Fons, 'Des sorcièrs aux XVme. et XVIme. siècles', *Mémoires de la Société Royale d'Émulation d'Abbeville*, 1841–3, pp. 437f.

30 1454, Lucerne: E. Hoffmann-Krayer, 'Luzerner Akten zum Hexen- und Zauberwahn', *Schweizerisches Archiv für Volkskunde*, III (1899), 33–9.

31 *Ibid.*, 81–6.

32 For one treatment of this question, cf. Philip Mayer, 'Witches', in Max Marwick, ed., *Witchcraft and Sorcery*, 53–60.

33 This pattern applies specifically in the case of sporadic prosecution. Entirely distinct factors underlay the mass prosecutions that occurred in early modern Continental Europe, and sometimes also in England and New England. For studies of large-scale hunts, see H. C. Erik Midelfort, *Witch Hunting in Southwestern Germany, 1562–1684* (Stanford, 1972), 85–192, and Paul Boyer and Stephen Nissenbaum, *Salem Possessed* (Cambridge, Mass., 1974).

34 La Fons, 'Des sorcièrs', 439f.

35 1454, Lucerne: Hoffmann-Krayer, 'Luzerner Akten', 33f.

36 1464, diocese of Lausanne: Archives Cantonales Vaudoises, MS Ac 29, fol. 160–78.

37 c. 1480, Lucerne: Hoffmann-Krayer: 'Luzerner Akten', 81–6.

38 1428, Todi: Peruzzi, 'Un processo di stregoneria' 12.

39 Peter Jos. Kämpfen, *Hexen und Hexenprozesse im Wallis* (Stans, 1867), 50.

40 Hoffmann-Krayer, 'Luzerner Akten', 88–91.

41 Eg., Mair, *Witchcraft*, 171. For examples from the sixteenth and seventeenth centuries, see Thomas, *Religion*, 509.

42 Ammann, 'Innsbrucker Hexenprocess', 45f., 53, 56f.; cf. also 24, 50.

43 Henri Duplès-Agier, ed., *Registre criminelle du Châtelet de Paris du 6 septembre 1389 au 18 mai 1392* (Paris, 1861–4), I, 327–62; II, 280–343; excerpts in Hansen, *Quellen*, 518–23.

44 1441, Dauphiné; 1491, Boucoiran.

45 1499, Lucerne: Hoffmann-Krayer, 'Luzerner Akten', 91–5.

46 1491, Boucoiran: Bligny-Bondurand, 'Procédure contre une sorcière'.

47 Eg., 1457, Breslau.

Addenda

For most of the following additional information I am indebted to E. William Monter.

1434, Besançon: Woman executed by archiepiscopal court for invocation and diabolism. S: 'Un procès de sorcellerie à Besançon en 1434', *Archives historiques, artistiques et littéraires*, I (1889–90), 69.

1446, Saint-Martin: Woman tried by secular court for sorcery (bodily harm, manipulation of affections). L: Forthcoming work by Robert Muchembled on witchcraft in northern France. NB: contains depositions of witnesses.

1465, Grünberg: 2 women tried by secular court for sorcery (bodily harm). S: Fritz Byloff, ed., *Volkskundliches aus Strafprozessen der osterreichischen Alpenländer* (Berlin and Leipzig, 1929), 7f.

1481, Montbéliard: 2 women and girl banished by inquisitor for witchcraft. S: Bibliothèque Municipale de Besançon, Coll. Duvernoy, No. 61, fol. 32–33^v.

1488, Montbéliard: Execution of unspecified number of witches, by ecclesiastical court. S: MS cited in preceding entry.

1493, Wolfsberg: 3 women tried by secular court for sorcery (image magic, bodily harm) and repudiation of faith. S: Byloff, *Volkskundliches* (as above), 12f.

For a new edition of the record of 1438, Todi, with English translation, see Domenico Mammoli, *The Record of the Trial and Condemnation of a Witch, Matteuccia di Francesco, at Todi, 20 March 1428* (Rome, 1972).

Index